Becoming a Cosmopolitan

Becoming a Cosmopolitan

What It Means to Be a Human Being
in the New Millennium

Jason D. Hill

ROWMAN & LITTLEFIELD PUBLISHERS, INC.
Lanham • Boulder • New York • Oxford

ROWMAN & LITTLEFIELD PUBLISHERS, INC.

Published in the United States of America
by Rowman & Littlefield Publishers, Inc.
4720 Boston Way, Lanham, Maryland 20706
http://www.rowmanlittlefield.com

12 Hid's Copse Road
Cumnor Hill, Oxford OX2 9JJ, England

British Library Cataloguing in Publication Information Available

Library of Congress Cataloging-in-Publication Data

Hill, Jason D., 1965–
    Becoming a cosmopolitan : what it means to be a human being in the new
millennium / Jason D. Hill.
        p.   cm.
    Includes bibliographical references and index.
    ISBN 0-8476-9754-1 (cloth)
    1. Self (Philosophy).   2. Ethics.   3. Internationalism.   I. Title
BD438.5H55   2000
170—dc21   99-046258
                                                                         CIP

Printed in the United States of America

⊗ ™
    The paper used in this publication meets the minimum requirements of
American National Standard for Information Sciences—Permanence of Paper for
Printed Library Materials, ANSI/NISO Z39.48–1992.

To my mother, Diane Hill,
and my grandmother Ivy Polack
for making the journey to America possible

CONTENTS

PREFACE

I write from the perspective of an immigrant who identifies himself as a moral cosmopolitan; an immigrant from Jamaica; an immigrant who is regarded as black under the racial classificatory schemes of the United States of America. I remain convinced that a cosmopolitan world is the best world for someone such as myself.

A world that naturalizes whiteness has to maintain racial categories as natural dividers. Such a world is not a morally healthy world for persons of color, nor is it a morally healthy world for whites. The United States is not a cosmopolitan society. There are those who would say that the United States is not a tribal society.

It is.

So long as heads still turn when a black man walks arm-in-arm with a white woman; so long as anyone with a shred of African ancestry in her background is classified as black despite her literal skin color (which could be brown or white); so long as we have a racial convention in America that acknowledges that a white woman is capable of giving birth to a black child or a white child but denies that a black woman—any black woman—can give birth to a white child; so long as we are inclined to impute moral value and worth to people on the basis of morally irrelevant features such as their so-called race or ethnic and national background—then we are living in a highly tribalistic society. What saves America from full-fledged tribal wars is that our culture's rampant tribalism is buffered by a set of constitutional principles. Though our civic and social lives are organized around ethnic and racial lines, we are partially protected by political principles that, at least theoretically, recognize the humanity and rights of all persons regardless of their tribal background. The single thread of the political saves us from destruction. But we continue to harbor illusions about ourselves and about those different from us whom we label as Other. The thrust of my writing is international. I do not mean to suggest that any discussion should be centered solely around social problems in America. The hideous outbreaks of tribal war in Yugoslavia, much of Europe, and Africa are all factored into discussions of the perniciousness of tribalism.

This book is written out of a profound love for humankind, a love I can no more explain than I can my love for certain types of music and genres of literature. I have made a covenant with the new millennium, and ultimately with God, to increase that love as much as I can and to embrace moral becoming as a way, not of finding out my essence, but of cultivating an essence through my contacts and intercourse with my fellow human beings. To make a covenant is to make a promise that one regards as sacred and binding. When I look into my soul, I see a spirit that I have allowed to be tarnished and sullied by the stories and myths generated by a culture incapable of understanding itself. Moral cosmopolitanism is an elitism of the soul, but it is an elitism to which all are invited. The equation of cosmopolitanism with jet planes and world travelers will cease, because those journeys and experiences do not radically alter one's soul nor transform the moral consciousness one needs to navigate within the world. To make a covenant means that one keeps looking forward, that one embraces the greatest expression of freedom, because the covenant points the way to the highest form of self-realization possible. One makes the covenant with the morality of cosmopolitanism, not against the pressure of apocalyptic reverberations on the order of "We are running out of time," but because there is a wisdom that falls upon us from time to time. History repeats itself over and over again, and some of us know that those repeating patterns are not inevitable. Some of us still believe in moral progress, and our covenant is motivated by less dramatic pressures. Quietly, we simply feel that it's about time we damn well morally grow up.

ACKNOWLEDGMENTS

The writing of this book has been a long journey. In a way it seems as if my entire life has been a preparation for the ethos and spirit that I have tried to capture in it. There have been numerous persons without whose help I might not have been able to complete this book.

William McBride provided expert editorship and conceptual clarification as well as a general enthusiasm for my project at all times. Calvin Schrag was open to my project from my third week as a first-year graduate years ago when in his class on postmodernism I decided to write a paper on moral becoming. Leonard Harris has been wonderful in helping me maintain my soldier ethos, especially when I felt weakened by the challenges of teaching and writing. His insistence on getting this book out as quickly as possible motivated me considerably.

I would also like to thank Purdue's philosophy department in general for providing me with a congenial work environment. My thanks to Pam Connelly for helping me with many details of the manuscript and also for her warmth and humanity. Lisa Goolsby saved me form computer crashes and mayhem by retyping my entire manuscript a few weeks before my deadline.

The Department of Philosophical Studies at Southern Illinois University lightened my teaching load considerably, enabling me to finish this book far sooner than I had anticipated. My thanks to then chair John Danley for all his warmth, support, and enthusiasm for my project and for making me feel like a welcome member of the department. Bill Hamrick has saved me from many computer problems associated with writing this book.

I am grateful to the Society for the Humanities at Cornell University for awarding me a fellowship on the strength of my manuscript and for providing office space in which to complete the book. Many thanks to my editor at Rowman & Littlefield, Maureen MacGrogan, for her enthusiasm for this book, and to Cheryl Hoffman, my copyeditor, for a first-rate job.

I have benefited from the support of friends who have been there for me from the moment I conceived of this book right to the very end: Daphne Rolle, Ramon Girvan, Albert Judge, Kevin Abel, and T. Nevada Powe, whom I also thank for his brilliant mind.

Thanks to my beloved family: my brother Philip, for his generous heart and his commitment to supporting all things that make his big brother happy; my grandmother Ivy Polack for her unconditional love, prayers, indomitable spirit, and devotion to the lives of her loved ones; my mother, Diane Hill, the most courageous woman I know, for all the sacrifices she made to keep alive the vision of my life I so desperately needed—it was worth it; my sister-in-law, Donna Hill, for her support; and my father, Philip Hill Sr., for his love during the early years and his unfailing belief in my ability as a writer. Thomas Sims provided four years of love and support and was there to mend my spirit when it needed mending. Finally, my gratitude to my secret sharer and kindred spirit, Fred Neuhouser, for all the technical support, love, and, above all, for the future.

INTRODUCTION

The new millennium has opened against the backdrop of continued racial, ethnic, and nationalistic tensions, or escalating tribalism.

In this book I defend a radical new way of combating these maladies. This volume lays the groundwork for a new morality as well as a new view of the self. It calls for the outright moral rejection of all forms of racial, ethnic, and national tribalism, which it labels as psychic infantilism, and instead proposes a new moral identity that engenders moral maturity of persons. This new identity reflects a model for the new millennium person, which I refer to as *moral cosmopolitanism*.

Humanity in this new era needs to be renegotiated, updated, and made heroic. Our humanity has failed us because we have not inscribed in our collective moral consciousness the stoic and arduous task of ridding our souls of the one feature that has been responsible for the major carnage, butchery, and horrific devastation in humankind: tribalism. The time has come for the maturation of our collective soul. This book urges our moral human evolution further than it has ever been. It is the first volume of a trilogy outlining a comprehensive cosmopolitan system. Other volumes will address the issues of cosmopolitan aesthetics, sexuality, education, and politics.

As a Jamaican immigrant who arrived in this country at the age of twenty, I found myself faced with questions like: What sort of world would I most want to live in? And what sort of moral character would be necessary for such a world to be possible? These questions were motivated by specific observations I made about American society in general and, more specifically, about the models on which contemporary ideals of the self are based. The contemporary self is to a large extent mired within racial and ethnic paradigms that define it exclusively in such terms. That is, the self is seen mainly as an ethnic and/or racial construct. This view of the self is predicated on several assumptions that philosophical reflection shows to be problematic. Included among them is the assumption that racial and ethnic concepts of the self are stable, objective, and closed. Such views are also predicated on a further assumption: that this sort of self is static and nonevolving. The problem with this model is that the self always has to define itself in such a way that certain involvements and associations in the world must be judged out of order; that is, contact with others becomes regulated by a set of clearly understood cultural and ethnic markers. To behave in a certain way, or to adopt the lifestyles of others, is to become culturally or ethnically or racially inauthentic. Ethnic and racial particularism demands that one treat others as if they were radically different from oneself, but in ways that are morally irrelevant. That is, we take the markers of race and ethnicity as if they were constitutive and permanent features of one's humanity and as if such markers held moral value.

The philosopher Edmund Husserl notes that in its historical situation humankind, or what he terms the closed community (race/nation), has always lived inside the paradigm of some attitude whose life expression always has a normative orientation. These attitudes become glorified and ontologized as attitudes. They often function as standards by which truth is judged. Sometimes they are treated as truths. Ultimately they serve as paradigmatic markers that relegate others to their appropriate stations in the social arena. Part of what Husserl has described here is what he calls the Natural Attitude. Tribal mentality, with its obsession with categorization and labels, names us all authoritatively and dares us to construct identities and self-images outside the sociofactual paradigm it invokes with a metaphysical authority that is hard to resist.

But why ought conventional notions of the self predicated on ethnic and racial models be seen as the only real ones? Moral imagination and various works in developmental psychology enable us to realize that the self is always either potentially or actually in a process of *becoming* and thus open to revision and reconfiguration. Morality sometimes demands that we give up old selves and commit ourselves to the goal of fashioning new moral identities. This is often accomplished by inviting the other in, letting go of the seriousness of one's identity, and allowing oneself to be remade by taking the other into oneself. If one can come to see that ethnic and racial identities are bequeathed and hence unchosen and that these identities have morally questionable features built into them (racism, ethnocentrism, and national chauvinism); if one can accept the fluidity of the self and its capacity for self-reinterpretation, then one recognizes self-ownership as a viable option. What then do moral philosophy and psychology have to say about how identities are formed and how individuals can acquire the resources to develop alternative identities to the ones they were given by their societies? What is the antidote to the problems identified? That is, what is the best moral identity one can have, and what would such an identity look like? This book examines, as a viable alternative to the racial/ethnic identities inherited by contemporary selves, the possibility of a cosmopolitan identity. Moral cosmopolitanism above all is a fight for a new moral self, a nontribal self. Its instantiation as such is the moral antithesis of tribalism. It defeats by example. The new humanity in the new millennium is recognized in a person whose inner being is not buried beneath the narcissism and myopia of tribalism. The new millennium man or woman is someone who desires a new moral self and, like a willed work of art, consciously constructs his or her moral self according to the system that is capable of uniting all humankind: moral cosmopolitanism. Because much of who we are has been passively accepted and unconsciously crafted, we have really lost the ability to radically transform our lives and our selves. The self stands as the greatest mystery because from the beginning of our conscious moral lives, the implicit message we have received is that the self is an impenetrable mystery. But to take ownership of our lives requires that we debunk the shibboleths and sundry pseudofoundations of those proffering their theories of authentic selfhood. Since the self is a compound of several value inheritances, we are very much canvases on which every unqualified dipper and dabbler is permitted to make his mark, his imperious signature. We are the walking canvases of other people's ideas, values, and—sadly—antiprinciples and prejudices. It is with the moral vision of a new and freely chosen ideal that the new millennium self must be chosen and morally re-created.

Identities that are predicated on static notions of the self are identities that people cannot change in any meaningful way. If much of our identity is conferred on us, and if the raw material of that identity is primarily ethnic,[1] the challenge that begins to emerge is: How can individuals be equipped to change their given identities to ones that are both voluntarily chosen and morally acceptable? This book locates the specious assumptions underlying conventional notions of the self that are primarily predicated on false notions of race and ethnicity. This book demonstrates that categories of identity are fluid and nonstable and are open not just to conceptual scrutiny but also to moral revision. A life of radical becoming, then—one that works toward acquiring a cosmopolitan identity—is the life and identity defended in this project. Moral becoming and radical self–re-creation are prerequisites for the emergence of a cosmopolitan ethos. The moral cosmopolitan cannot emerge ex nihilo. Her cosmopolitan identity emerges after moral becoming is embraced as a principled way of living in the world. The self's becoming, as I articulate it, can be a way of throwing off the past, a past constituted on the principle of containment. Becoming is seen as an ideal with a definite telos in mind: to become a cosmopolitan. The process I examine, therefore, is an ordered, goal-directed moral becoming. To create the self, to resocialize the self as a way of broadening nontribal contact, one has to undo the spirit of seriousness that attaches to one's sociocultural inheritance. A self that is open to becoming already invites the cosmopolitanism of spirit that signals authentic liberation from the shackles of the ontologized rules, attitudes, and categories that define ethnicity and race.

Becoming is radical freedom, an opening up of oneself to all forms of human culture that are accessible to the identity of human beings in the world. Becoming and self-creation are forms of moral transcendence leading to a psychological reorientation and resocialization of the self inspired by the question: Can I have autonomy if the fundamental aspects of my identity imposed on me by the community are not open to modification but instead resisted by the same social forces that construct those identities?

For the cosmopolitan, for me the immigrant and foreigner, and perhaps for all those who wish to construct a new moral self, the challenge is: What happens when becoming places one in a state inimical to the norms and codes of the community? I argue that the insistence of binding an individual to specific forms of identity and the environment in which such an identity is affirmed, validated, and allowed expression is irrational. Whether it is the family that tries to bind its offspring to the image of parental hopes and aspirations, or the ethnic or racial community that demands that one's identity and thinking align themselves with the schemata of the group, such bondage retards the individual's capacity to evolve and become. It hinges on the premise that he or she is embalmed, static, and nonevolving—that twenty years from now his or her values and orientation will be in sync with those of the community. I argue that to embrace becoming and to prepare oneself for a radical cosmopolitan ethos, one must find creative ways of undermining notions of ethnic, racial, and national particularism.

This book explores several options an agent en route to becoming a radical cosmopolitan may pursue when avenues to meaningful human interactions are denied because of the threat of ethnic inauthenticity. Chief among these options is *the right to forget where one came from.* Common sense informs us of the difficulty of ridding ourselves of our historicity. Yet the past that has formed the "this" that we are need not be antagonistic to the "that" of our becoming. It is the extent of our fixation on particular genres of self and the absolutizing of these identities that make it difficult to overcome history and personal culture. The need to selectively forget is a moral imperative that is also an invitation to those whose standpoints are naturalized, or taken to be the norm. Hence, in the racial dynamic of America the need to forget is also offered as a moral invitation to whites. What does it mean to forget that one is white? What does it really mean to be white? What does it mean to cease acting like one is white? If we accept that whiteness is not an ethnic identity but a social badge of privilege, a badge that ceases to be socially functional in the absence of distinct Others (blacks, Latinos, Chicanos, Asians) whose formal identities in America are defined by whites; and if we ask what being white in America would mean if there were no "one-drop rule" to identify black people, we might see a world in which whiteness was absent (though not people whose skin color is white, a category that would include a number of people now classified as black) and in which identity transformation was seen as a natural part of the process of an evolving humanity.

Moral forgetting is a way of bracketing one's past, along with the often tyrannical, outdated, or perhaps just bland schemata and value systems bequeathed to one, value systems that are antithetical to the constantly modified states of being one is immersed in when one embraces becoming as a career. Forgetting is applicable to the individual who invents himself on the basis of what I shall refer to as an ordered moral becoming, that is, a becoming inspired by the ideal and ideated self spawned by one's moral imagination.

Forgetting is part of the psychological machinery that equips the would-be cosmopolitan to eventually create and then practice a cosmopolitan ethos. Selves in need of moral resocialization need to forget. Agents feel the need to rid themselves of the psychological, conceptual, and emotional baggage they inherit from an overdetermined and oppressive community. The weight of the community becomes too much to bear, and the cosmopolitan in the making must shrug it off, exorcise it from his or her psyche. Unlearning the past, throwing off the tyranny of false legacies, is a new way of infusing the world with an assemblage of that which is truly one's own. To create a new moral self is to create a self that is willing to undo the old self in many respects. It entails creating a self that is an affront to the values of the former self. This book adopts the position that moral evolution and nontribal contacts with others are blunted by the prejudices, expectations, and frames of reference we carry from our own world. It is important to note, however, that forgetting is not meant to invite moral amnesia or the dismissal of trauma. Selective moral forgetting must be accompanied by a criterion of forgetting. This study explores the politics of forgetting. I submit that before a cosmopolitan ethos can be practiced, the self has to be thoroughly socialized and morally re-created. We have both the moral and ontological license to create a new self. The self must be divested of its old accouterments, the tired, outworn, and false labels it has worn. *We must learn to forget where we came from* in order to write in our hearts the new paeans of moral evolution and therefore liberation. My prevailing mantra is: Until we reach a cosmopolitan universe, we are not yet fully human. And there is a lot that interferes with our capacity to become fully human, but our proclivity for tribalism, which some might argue is an innate tendency, is the major factor. Our tendency to embrace racial/ethnic and national tribalism as something good is a severe form of idolatry that is born of a deep narcissism that needs to see oneself as special because of one's particular racial, ethnic, or national identity. We frown upon homosexuality but accept *homoraciality* and *homoethnicity* as natural features of the human world. We have weaned ourselves from our mothers' breasts, but we have substituted for the breast the name of the tribe, the race, the ethnos, and the *Volk*. The prolonged nursing sanctioned by the state and conventional morality has prevented us from achieving the grandeur, moral heroism, and cleanliness of spirit that are our natural birthright. We are petty, parochial little creatures who deify our tribe because it is ours. Five-year-olds behave the same way towards their mothers. To give up the neurotic fixation with our tribes is going to be called a sacrifice, but such a sacrifice must be made to show what is possible for humankind: heroic transcendence of the social contingencies that lead us astray from the moral path. The moral cosmopolitan is a transcendent hero whose spirit elevates itself above the routine and soul-killing shackles of ethnic/racial and national squabbles and glorification and, yes, even his historicity. The moral cosmopolitan above all is a soldier fighting forces in the world and primarily within himself. He celebrates the continuous desire to overcome himself while celebrating what he has yet to become. Current glorification of self-acceptance and unconditional love breeds a complacency that offers persons little incentive to rise above their rottenness. The moral cosmopolitan recognizes that he struggles to overcome forces over which he may have little control. He knows that the mores, values, neuroses, and prejudices with which he has been inculcated since childhood arrest the moral development of humankind. But he struggles. His hallowed anthem: *Remember we remake the world by individually remaking the images of our own selves.*

Wherein lies the value of the cosmopolitan's soldier ethos? The dilemma that the enlightened moral cosmopolitan will face wherever he battles racial and ethnic tribalism is the central one faced by any individual who does not take race and ethnicity as metaphysical or ontological issues: He will be seen as a freak because he refuses to acknowledge as binding the arbitrary and nonobjective categorizations of race. He must remember, however, that when a culture suffers from an idiotic present in which a pathological and diseased frame of reference is the standard paradigm, it is the healthy individual who is seen as the freak, the one who is distorted, simply because he is trying to recover a universal human ethic.

I am not and never have been interested in relating to human beings as ethnicities, races, or national constructs. I am profoundly in love with this world of mine. I see a person who does not speak the same language as I do, whose ethnic and national origins are different from mine. I look in her eyes. A smile appears on her face, and I too smile because any gesture of the beautiful in the human is infectious. I smile. And I am at peace, and all bewildering thoughts about how it is possible that people can feel love only for their "own kind" dissipate. We share a smile and I know that we share a humanity.

I write in order to become the person I would like to be. I write to aspire to become what I am not yet. I write to redefine myself according to the highest standards of that which I espouse; and what I espouse is moral cosmopolitanism.

Cosmopolitans are individuals who, against their origins, choose a transnational identity "situated at the crossing of boundaries."[2] Cosmopolitans are destroyers of parochial markers. Identifying with the world as home and with human beings qua human beings, they reject the rigid and provincial designators of race and national identity that subvert becoming and confine the self to a degenerate existential ghetto. Cosmopolitanism combats provincialism, parochialism, ethnic and racial particularism, and the narrowness of identity and vision concomitant with them. It hails the finding of common ground in a shared human identity. It recognizes that human identity is made and lived: it is not a "natural" feature of the world. Moreover, the cosmopolitan identity is a weaned identity. I follow Freud's lead in characterizing ethnic and racial fixations as forms of psychic infantilism. That is, the individual transfers the infantile need for protection onto a sublimated parent: the tribe at large. Unlike the childlike creatures of their surroundings who cling to ethnic, national, and racial identities the way a neurotic forty-year-old clings to his mother's skirt, moral cosmopolitans have no preference for their "own kind." They see contingencies, shortcomings, and the grandeur of their subcultures as derivatives of larger and more complex matrices: the world at large. Moral cosmopolitans, as a moral necessity, make a monumental leap beyond their roots. They must not only repudiate the worst of their traditions and those of others but also demonstrate that their leap beyond their own origins is a maturation of the soul with important moral, political, and spiritual consequences. Like those who leave their homes to wed, moral cosmopolitans achieve a maturity of soul by wedding themselves to the world at large. They rid themselves, not of the desire for personal preferences and for some identification with their points of origin, but of the neurotic need to be determined by their national, ethnic, or racial identities. For cosmopolitans mere ethnic kinship brings about an angst, an existential yearning and hunger spawned by the gnawing question, *Is this all there really is?* For them the familiarity and security reinforced by cultural kinship establishes boredom.

Moral cosmopolitans are out to detribalize the world. Hybridization is a moral goal because it destabilizes zones of purity and privilege. Cosmopolitanism entreats one to reach for a self beyond what one is now. Moral cosmopolitans are creatures constituted in part by culture. Agreed. But the cosmopolitan who embraces moral becoming and forgetting realizes also that we are projects in process. We are not finished products.[3] Cosmopolitanism represents a decency of the human spirit. For some it could well be an attempt to recover heroic individualism in modern life. It does, in my estimation, represent a world in which the fullest realization of human agency is possible. In a real sense those marked as Others stand outside the world. Legal or illegal, they are aliens in the human community when that community is defined by those whose identities are normalized and naturalized features of the world. Cosmopolitanism is the attempt to get rid of a world in which Others are truly noncitizens. Above all, moral cosmopolitanism stands as a definite philosophy of, and for, the future. I write as a moral intellectual who writes not for his time but for the future. That I may never see the universe I long for is a possibility I shall have to live with. That I am able to articulate its moral architectural design is in itself a form of the universe that will one day be fully realizable.

There are those, undoubtedly, who will argue that my viewpoint is naïve, unrealistic. and impractical. Morality is, however, a very demanding enterprise. Its function is not to mirror what we necessarily desire on the spur of the moment. Unlike friends, whom we sometimes choose as clones of ourselves, morality cannot reproduce for us the images we wish to create to assuage the fears and insecurities of modern life. Moral living is an act of faith: We leap and know that we will be radically redefined by a process whose endpoint we cannot conceptually fathom but whose instructional guidance is necessary for our very survival. No moral system can entreat its students to aspire to the best and highest form of living if it does not demand much of them. Psychological realism does not demand that we water down our moral systems so that they fit the conception of human nature in fashion at the moment. The moral self cannot be twisted like putty to fit the mutating perversions of a modern culture that beguiles its inhabitants with cosmetic appearances of their souls and inculcates in them the idea that their essence is to be found in their tribal identities. Psychological realism demands that any moral system assume a set of basic attributes about the human person that can be practiced because it is humanly possible. Moral cosmopolitanism, then, is concerned not so much with the conception of self persons find themselves valorizing but instead with the future self, the *not-yet self,* the self that ought to exist. Morality above all is the journey of moral becoming and moral retransformation. Like Christianity and all other great religions, moral cosmopolitanism may be regarded as an expansionist doctrine that appeals to the sense of common humanity in all of us. There is nothing of the "we are the chosen" element to it, there is no appeal to the intrinsic value or worth of any culture because it is someone's culture. Quite the contrary. We know that cultures can be oppressive and evil. We know that cultures can interfere with the moral evolution of human souls. There is an argument, then, to be made about the moral virtue of cultural annihilations. In this book I make and defend that argument. Some cultures, on moral cosmopolitan grounds, ought to be annihilated. I do not mean that persons in cultures are to be obliterated. Rather, the codified set of practices and norms and the overall ethos of certain cultures are to be gotten rid of. Moral cosmopolitanism, if it is to be a serious moral force and not mere sentiment, cannot pay unconscionable lip service to the equal value of all cultures. If it is to function as a morality, then it has to assume basic social moral goods that are indispensable for the survival of each person. If cultures are in violation of such requirements, then they must be reckoned with.

1

CREATING THE SELF:

THE SELF IN MORAL BECOMING

THE METAPHYSICS OF BECOMING AND THE BURDEN
OF OVERDETERMINED IDENTITIES

At the start of our journey stands the necessity of a self in becoming. It is a self that is capable of a set of truly innovative feats and features. It faces the future and its myriad possibilities with eagerness, trepidation, reverence, and irreverence. This self recognizes that its constituency in the world is determined long before it is born. From the moment of conception it exists as a predetermined entity already constituted in a world of which it is not yet fully a member. The mother thinks it is a boy. A name has been fixed for him, Brian. He inherits a last name, Padria. The name Padria, he is told sternly from about the age of four, means perseverance, success, and stamina. "Your great-grandmother and great-grandfather embodied these qualities. It is because of them that we are in America. Those qualities are what got us all here. Don't ever forget it. And don't ever forget to live up to everything that that name has come to mean in this family. And don't forget where you came from, either."

The type of children he will play with has been established. The type of woman his mother already envisions as his ideal (without a doubt, she comforts herself, it will be someone from his ethnic and socioeconomic background) is communicated to him in subtle ways early on. That he may one day grow up and decide to marry a man has not even crossed his mother's mind. Such a possibility is simply not a part of her world. She knows of no homosexuals and has never met any. Her son's decision to marry a man will be interpreted as his desire not to belong to her world nor participate in the current structures and arrangements of her society. His decision is an offensive blow. It is a form of disengagement from the tribal decorum and values of his local environment.

The individual when he emerges as a child will be thrust into an ideology that constitutes him as defined with specific features.[1] His environment will furnish the resources and tools he needs to make sense of his world. Indeed, the way he initially sees the world and his fellow human beings, his views on sex and sexual relations, his sense of his place in the world, and his judgments about others based on features that are either valued or devalued by the ethos of his society will all be influenced greatly by his culture's worldview. This schema of interpretations and attitudes takes on the aura of authenticity and natural fact. The individual will find himself a secondhand consumer of ready-made values. In essence, he experiences the world as a series of finished buildings made by others.[2]

If he is born with skin as pasty as the dough his grandmother uses to make dumplings but has an iota of African ancestry in his background and has either the misfortune or the good fortune of being born in North America, he is, and will always be, a black man in his country of birth. He is overdetermined by this racial ascription. He is black before he is anything else. If he continues to live in America, he will, to the extent that he becomes self-respecting and autonomous, have to find ways to combat this overdetermination.

At the age of eighteen he takes his first trip abroad and goes to Barbados in the West Indies. There he will be treated as a white or a "high-brown" man and accorded the deference and respect enjoyed by aristocrats. His offhand announcement to one of his hosts that he is a black man is viewed suspiciously. Is he neurotic and crazy? he hears one of them whisper. Back in America he realizes that it is his own country that suffers a deep pathology by attempting to universalize its prejudices and moral stains.

He knows that only a very small part of his knowledge originates within his personal experience. Most of it is socially derived, as Alfred Schutz writes,

handed down to me by my friends, my parents, my teachers, and the teachers of my teachers. I am taught not only how to define the environment (that is, the typical features of the relative natural aspect of the world prevailing in the in-group as the unquestioned but always questionable sum total of things taken for granted until further notice), but also how typical constructs have to be formed in accordance with the system of relevances accepted from the anonymous unified point of view of the in-group.[3]

He will be constantly faced with the task of self-interpretation. Living in the world I have just described, he will be forced to interpret his life, and it will be his responsibility to create a life based on the interpretation he renders. José Ortega y Gasset writes that the inheritance of mores, values, and descriptions actually frees one from the effort of creation. This inheritance seduces one into inertia. He who receives an idea from his forebears "tends to save himself the effort of rethinking it and recreating it within himself."[4] Ortega defines a generation as an integrated manner of existence or a fashion of living that fixes itself indelibly on the individual. This fixation might form a permanence on the identity index of the individual. Ortega writes that "among certain savage peoples the members of each coeval group are recognized by their tattooing. *The fashion in epidermal design which was in vogue when they were adolescents has remained encrusted in their beings.*"[5]

An important ingredient in becoming a new type of human being in the context of becoming a moral cosmopolitan is the capacity to create a self that one consciously authors; that is, a self that has the capacity to scrutinize its attributes and, when appropriate, to reject those attributes it finds objectionable on specific moral grounds. The racial and ethnic tribal self, I believe, is a self whose particular ascriptive identity needs serious moral revision. Moral revision is needed because the self spawned by tribal predications generationally and institutionally promotes the idea of seeing persons first and foremost as racial and ethnic constructs—attributes that are morally neutral but that attempt to locate the moral status of human beings. Such predications mandate the categorization of persons into racial/ethnic entities with the tribal ascriptions they have been accorded serving as criteria of moral worth and value. Such predications, to the extent that they are granted some form of legalistic sanction, are inescapable and, to those on the lowest stratum of the moral-worth index, absolutely oppressive. Persons in other words are overdetermined. A person whose self is in becoming will combat his overdeterminedness partly by seeing his life as an ongoing process. As Owen Flanagan writes, the human project is truly one of self-creation, of making ourselves into as many as we can of the different kinds of beings we can possibly be.[6]

In the face of such a universe anyone committed to rewriting the self may be daunted at the prospect of self-creation. It is a wonder that Brian, realizing his encapsulation within a massive sociohistorical cultural context, does not reverse into the birth canal to snuggle timidly back into his mother's womb. If he had known the enormity of the task ahead of him, perhaps he would have found a way to do that. The task of dealing with a world that is constantly shaping him in this way and that way is a lifelong career.

The set of skills that will be needed to change from an entity possessing the identity of a biological life form to a rich and robust self are not yet in his possession. He will have to go through several stages to become a self with an autonomous identity he feels to be uniquely his own, or, to borrow Doris Lessing's captivating phrase, that which is *"continuing to burn"* behind the various roles he will play.[7] The self in becoming that I am constructing is not one that sees itself atomically. Seeing oneself atomically involves a failure to acknowledge that others made me the person that I am and that others contribute to making me the person I aspire to be. As a self in becoming I see myself democratically; that is, I see myself as a self conditioned by, and expressed through, participatory decision making built on dialogue and contextual thinking.[8] I also express values such as autonomy, openness, a rights-based society, liberty, tolerance, and reasonableness. I deny neither my historicity, sociality, or communality nor the way my encapsulation in a cultural milieu has shaped and civilized me. The task is in balancing the degree to which others determine me and in determining in the end whose narrative counts more, theirs or mine. My narrative is developed in tandem with communities and with the aid of autonomy-competency skills and critical reflection. But the major challenge is determining how I shall deal with the canonized spirit that cements the Natural Attitude and thus circumscribes my own becoming.

So exactly what do we have? What do we start out with that enables us to begin the journey toward self-creation? What propels us outward despite the pull of the tribe to remain encased within its categories? What propels us, I submit, is the capacity to become. This capacity is as basic and elemental to the human condition as is the capacity to speak, to engage in a moral life, and to love.

John Dewey's theory of the self sets the stage for this most elemental notion of becoming. That is, becoming is posited as inevitable. It is, Dewey tells us, impossible for the self to stand still. Becoming is an inescapable feature of life. We are condemned to a life of becoming whether we choose to acknowledge it or not. The notion of becoming is not predicated on some normative ethical precept that one hopes the individual will adopt. It is a constitutive feature of the human condition. According to Dewey, "it is becoming, and becoming for the better or the worse. It is in the quality of becoming that virtue resides. We set up this and that end to be reached, but the end is growth itself."[9]

Primitive becoming can be acknowledged as a growth principle that individuals as biological organisms have. It is not something that teleologically propels us toward a codified and concrete end. It is incumbent upon us not to simply ignore this feature but to organize and express it in a meaningful manner that will permit us to construct and articulate meaning and purpose in our lives. The job of overcoming alienation and making sense of the process of living is laced with chance. The responsibility, however, belongs to us.[10]

Dewey's concept of the self captures what I deem to be an important feature of the rewriting self or the self that is committed to *moral re-creation:* a sense of incompleteness. From the start, there is no fixed and already constituted self. The self is an ongoing process. Diana Meyers notes, too, that the authentic self "is a moving target—one that skitters away as soon as it is pinned down."[11] Activity, movement, and becoming constitute the essential attributes of a human self. Dewey's formulation of the activity of becoming may be read as a metaphysics of becoming. The most primitive and elemental conception of this capacity that produces unregulated activity within the individual allows us to view it as a catalyst, a well-developed involuntary movement. But what starts as a primitive growth impulse develops, like the other capacities we possess, into a more sophisticated and robust disposition that we can subject to our will and manipulate in the service of life plans and so on.

In Dewey's metaphysics of becoming, the propulsion that first expresses itself in the expulsion of the fetus from the uterus into the world is properly a feature of the individual. This propulsive proclivity may be embraced and developed, or it may be denied, resulting in arrested self-development. We have the freedom, Dewey and a host of liberal theorists tell us, to create and re-create ourselves. But what does it mean to possess such a freedom? The answer is to realize that there exist multiple modalities within the individual. The development of these modalities is not only an antidote to stasis but also a way of embellishing and reconstituting a self in the making. This we may call one form of freedom. The self that we find ourselves in possession of at any moment need not be the self that we are saddled with for life. The attributes that form the primary substance of a moral self—the values and beliefs that determine the kinds of commitments and worldview held—may be, and in a great many cases ought to be, radically changed.

At the moment that becoming becomes a project of the rewriting self, two discoveries will pave the way for greater freedom for self-creation. The first is that social reality, while it carries a metaphysical aura, is not supported by any unshakable maxim or law of absolute determinacy. The second is that the world is incomplete because it lacks me—it lacks my narrative of myself, my narrative of the world. I have not yet painted the portrait of how I am in the world. The gestures, the tone of voice, the accent, the inflections, and the idiosyncrasies—they tell of a style of dealing with the world to purchase a life needed by its bearer. I have yet to show you or tell you the particular way in which I hate in this world and the way I defile others with my bitterness and anger, the way I seduce them with my capacity to hand them an image of themselves they are most in need of in the midst of what they perceive to be a dead planet. I have yet to portray the way I love in small doses and then at times in great bursts. My love for the world and for humanity can only be hinted at. The complexities and the ambiguities fall outside the either/or paradigms of our modern culture. I have yet to yet to spin my web with the material stuff of my life. I have yet to invest the world with what I feel is an original assemblage of myself. The self committed to moral re-creation is inspired by the first lines of

Rousseau's *Confessions:* "I am made unlike anyone I have ever met; I will venture to even say that I am like no one in the whole world. I may be no better, but at least I am different."[12]

This world in which I live and interact is still in the making, and I have a part in its creation; we all do as individuals. Dewey views any change that results from active interaction and participation with the community as an aspect of a universal process in which all things undergo change and development through their transactions with one another. Every new relation or connection carries with it possibilities of change and development.[13] The realization that the world is still being made is a crucial insight for the individual who is molding a self. It means that there is no necessary validation of any one dominant standardized category that one can appeal to with respect to the construction of any particular mode of being. Such an appeal cannot take precedence over one's experiences, for it is the experiences that shape the social world of meaning and thus the individual who is simultaneously creating a world of meaning and a world of self. The world stands incomplete before me, the agent who modifies it while it simultaneously subjects me to modification. And so a question that could be asked of myself when I turn eighty-three is: Am I any more Caribbean than I am American after having lived in America for forty years? I have forgotten somewhere along the way that I also lived for ten years in Budapest and nine in Cairo. I did not really forget. It's just that with age and repeated experiences, the demarcations of one's life that take on such importance in youth seem to blend so inconspicuously into the events of one's life as one grows older. My life seems like one continuous dream, the sort Socrates described in the *Apology.* But it is not just a dream. As a self in becoming or as an aspirant intent on embracing becoming as a moral imperative, I am moved by a maniacal will, by a vision of a heightened form of existence and again by a surge of movement, of restlessness, of a desire to create my self over and over. Because I am a self in becoming, my ruling emotions are dissatisfaction and a gnawing sense of incompleteness. The self in becoming is an eclectic, honorable thief in relation to ideas, to the world, and to its socialization. All must be put in the service of this hunger for completion. Appropriation, when governed by scrupulous means, becomes a moral imperative; failure to appropriate means complacency, stagnation, and eventual burial under the musty debris of the Natural Attitude, dated labels, and the weight of cultural traditions that are two sizes too small for the enormity of a hungry and ever expanding soul. The self in becoming faces the world it has inherited with a yawn and a sigh: *Is this all there is?*[14]

The person whose self is in becoming knows that everything before him is vital to his quest for becoming and actualization. He takes seriously Dewey's caveat that one can never divest oneself totally of the habits, values, and schema of the world of one's assimilated culture.[15] Past, present, and future events are all valid in determining his notion of selfhood. His world of multiple experiences has proven wrong those who have sought to make his birth and socialization as a Caribbean child some binding and constitutive aspect of his "humanness."

For Dewey, to be a human being means to learn to develop, through the give-and-take of communication, an effective sense of being an individually distinct member of a community. It entails a continuation and conversion of what he termed the organic powers into human resources and values. He writes: "This translation is never finished. The old Adam, the unregenerate element in human nature persists."[16] Self-modification through encounters with others is an ongoing task that furthers the principle of becoming and the constitution of the self and equips the individual with multiple skills that enhance his agency as a member of his community. This self exercises its dynamic reconstitutive and creative powers by encounters with others, even with those who are radically different. Becoming is the feature that allows one to be redefined through these encounters.

Dewey distinguishes between the old static and habitual self and the dynamic self. The old habitual self is encapsulated within the matrices of an unchanging frame of reference and thus assumes a standpoint of completion. It treats new conditions and new demands as hostile and foreign. Self-contradiction and denial become its regulative principles. The old, or "completed," self is the presentation made to the world; it is *the* standard of evaluation. It is closed off from future influences and appropriations. We note, for example, the way rigid identification with our ethnic, racial, and national identities may affect the way we see the world. Each of these designations has peculiar norms, practices, creeds, and ethical mandates. They regulate the way we see the world. Those who are white are socialized in varying degrees to see their whiteness as normal and as the standard of normative evaluations. Nonwhites who are under the cultural jurisdiction of whites are just not as socially endowed with the same degree of humanity. Nonwhites who are in positions of power do the same to nonwhites from whom they are tribally differentiated. Those who are subjugated feel they are much more than they have been labeled. Their capacities for feeling and being in the world cannot be gauged adequately by any of those labels. We are much more than that. These rigid encapsulations lead to feelings of closure and blockage. We feel incomplete; we are more than such states. There is a hunger in us. The growing self, however, expands as it meets new demands, aligning it with new life forces and heterogeneous models. It "welcomes untried situations."[17] Dewey does not view this tension as simply a psychological truism or some difficulty that one is mildly encouraged to transcend; rather, virtue and profound moral agency actually consist in the will to follow the command to go beyond what one has been and is now. This is especially the case if the self is identified with the body of desires, affections, and habits that have been potent in the past. He notes further: "Indeed, we may say that the good person is precisely the one who is most conscious of the alternative, and is the most concerned to find openings for the newly forming or growing self. No matter how good he is he becomes 'bad' as soon as he fails to respond to growth."[18]

Self-creation and the conditions that give rise to a created self carry moral responsibility. One must respond to growth or one becomes bad. A philosophical stage for self-liberation is set. It is now possible to address at least minimally some of the concerns we voiced at the start of our project. Let us take the question of authenticity. The individual who is a member of multiple social worlds and whose ethnic identity may be drawn from a host of transnational models may take note that intrinsically she is not wired to any one identity state. There are multiple layers of "otherness" within her. In other words, she has the capacity to develop other identities and an even greater capacity for moral development. There are sufficient spaces in her psychological and moral makeup to accommodate a compound of several identities. In the same way that she is equipped to learn and then conceptually function in any human language, she is also equipped to have her identities shaped or radically altered by the center from which such identities spring: human culture.

One could argue that persons could possibly feel a sense of uneasiness in attempting to sift though a host of possible identities. What roles do continuity and cohesion play in cementing a stable sense of self? To arrive at a robust, healthy state of self, one indeed has to participate in a deep, interactive relation with other beings, an interaction that has the capacity to bring out states one has previously never recognized. My position against the ways in which racial and ethnic tribal identities are cemented so early on in an individual's moral development is that the fluidity and capacity for growth and modification that are allowed in other areas of persons' lives (self-sufficiency and decision making, for example) are not seen as viable regarding their ethnoracial and national identities. Born and socialized as X type of ethnic person for the first five years of your life, you are somehow seen as essentially *that* type of person for the rest of your life. Even to entertain altering that identity earns you the label *inauthentic*.

Continuity, however, is part of growth. Previous complexes of organization and response are brought along into the new situations. Not only is the growth principle Dewey spoke of being activated, but also the very notion of being implies this interaction with others.[19] Changes in the self that result from interactions with the environment are for Dewey "an aspect of universal process in which all things undergo change and development through their countless transactions with one another. Every new relation or connection carries with it new possibilities of development."[20] It is only through engagement with varied processes of life that the self confronts a world of meaningful and relevant beings. The world one has experienced becomes an integral part of the self that acts and is acted upon in further experiences. What had seemed remote and alien becomes a home.[21] This is of crucial importance. Our theme at large, the development of a moral cosmopolitan identity, operates against the backdrop of a normative predication: what it means to be a new type of human being in the future. The racial/ethnic or robust tribal self limits the kinds of influences so-called foreigners or radical others can have on one's sacrosanct identity. Your tribal identity takes on the stature of a deity. You hold it as something that is tied to your deepest sense of who you are. But the deepest sense of who you think you are may not be the best type of thing to be. The tribal self, because of its glorification of the tribe, is used as a standard to judge unfairly the moral worth of others unlike you and to denigrate their lives. It cannot be used as a true measure of moral worth because the attributes it uses as a standard of value (racial/ethnic/national) are morally neutral and specify nothing about a person's moral consciousness. This type of self uses its tribal superiority perhaps to occupy three-quarters of a territory and slaughter one-third of the population that does not have the honor of having the most valued trait in the world: being of its own kind. If you realize the truth about the tribal self, then you have the moral responsibility to repudiate such a self and cast it away. Since the majority of humankind's slaughter stems from tribal impulses, then you have a moral responsibility to ensure that persons are not seen first and foremost as ethnic and racial creatures. You carry forward this task in the name of the potential evolution in human moral consciousness. The task is enormous. It may take centuries to accomplish. But the moral reeducation that is required to liberate persons from destructive tribal impulses must begin today. Radical and authentic interaction with those classified as radically Other means that you let them in and experience them fully. A type of humility is required. A radical "race change" and "ethnic change" are not out of order. In fact, they may be necessary.

SELF-CREATION, MULTIPLE IDENTITIES, AND AUTHENTICITY

How is all of this relevant to the question of tribal authenticity? In the first place, many people seem to need to see themselves as culturally authentic, which is accomplished largely by appealing to racial/ethnic predications of the self.

In some intuitive way, many individuals recognize that their "humanness" falls outside any one identity state; yet many of them fasten on to some particular model that they believe best captures their "authentic self." In the process many of them fail to recognize competing identity options. The virtue of tribal authenticity is such an entrenched "social good" in our society that our efforts to establish ourselves as authentic according to specific tribal criteria escape rigorous moral scrutiny. We take it as a given and question its legitimacy only when we suspect abuse, never stopping for a moment to ponder the possibility that a specious principle that is defended in the first place is bound to lead to abuses over and over again. The principle itself (the value of displayed tribal authenticity) is a precondition and justification for the very abuses that are then condemned.

Liberal theorist Jack Crittenden argues convincingly that the notion of a fixed and unproblematic identity is not necessary to make sense of the membership world because many modern children are born not into a total community but into a network of subcultures. Out of this amalgam the child constructs a coherent worldview by aggregating rather than integrating perspectives. A network may include the shared conceptions of the society at large, such as its languages, mores, laws, history, and even competing worldviews. Crittenden writes:

> One parent might be a Roman Catholic, from a neighborhood that is ethnically homogeneous and from a family that continues to speak only Italian at family gatherings. The other parent might be Jewish, from a family that is both orthodox and Zionist. This child may be close to her parents but closest to a Zen Buddhist brother who lives with her and her family. For reasons of convenience and enrichment, the family may live in a neighborhood that is predominantly Chinese. The child may go to the best day-care facility run by Chinese who seek to raise community-minded children and who propagate the tenets of Confucianism. This child will absorb no fewer than four different value systems and will learn the rules and roles for governing each. Yet just as children up to a certain age can learn as many as eight languages without confusion, so they can absorb competing, even contradictory, world-views, because they do not need to integrate them. When self-reflection begins, conflicts and tensions arise.[22]

Theorists and radical culturalists who argue that children need a monolithic cultural environment to develop a healthy ethnic or cultural identity are wrong. I agree with Crittenden that psychologically the child can learn to assimilate a variegated set of cultural options. Maladjustment seems to be the result either of the social stigma attached to such options or of the enormous societal pressure to conform to clearly demarcated cultural paradigms that make political designations of ethnicity, race, and sociocultural backgrounds less problematic. When one considers the ways in which cultural goods are allocated on the basis of such designations, one sees clearly that the pathology lies not so much in the failure of individuals to conform to some alleged inherent psychological need for rigid cultural affiliation as in the arbitrary sociopolitical machinations and forms of exploitation that decree a fixed set of criteria for determining cultural membership and the pervasive societal ethos that prizes tribal membership as a social good in the first place.

I argue that authenticity is to be determined privately, against the backdrop of our vision of our lives, our life plans, and the clearly articulated responsibilities for which we are morally accountable. The self in moral becoming ought to be provided with the intellectual skills that will enable it to realize that the set of so-called cultural criteria (appeals to traditions, traditional values, labels, mores, customs, and categories of race and ethnicity, among others) that aim to evaluate its authenticity is linked to a bloated and false ontology that would impose its lies on others. This set of criteria decrees a genre of self that one is expected to wear for the world. And so we accept this externally handed self at the price of our own critical health. This external self acting as a tribal self, along with the social ontological weight that it carries, prevents the emergence of a contrary self. The weight of the prescribed self, whether it is self-induced or societally endorsed, militates against becoming. The given is taken as the ultimate standard. There is, therefore, no future for the self and ultimately no power it can exercise; it lacks creative agency. This is the crushing weight under which contemporary racially predicated selves struggle for survival.

For Dewey such a fixation on a static genre of self based on a particular kind of environment would clearly be negative. There is no inert and static relation between self and those things confronting it. A static standpoint is the posture of a self that convinces itself of its developmental completion, including its moral completion. This self refuses any type of modification, amplification, or meaningful metamorphosis in the face of unfamiliar experiences. A relation grounded in interaction, a "vital commerce" with other human beings, leads to a "complete inter-penetration of the self and the world of objects and events."[23]

The discussion so far depicts aspects of tensions experienced by members of multiple communities. Our communal engagements and socialization play a role in the particular identities we cull from the racial/ethnic tribes to which we belong. Dewey's theory supports the idea that there is nothing ontologically binding in my status as a West Indian or Caribbean man, nothing so intrinsic to my status as a human being that I could not, through experience with another culture, immerse myself in it and, through a metamorphosis wrought from such experience, construct a new, rich, and thriving identity. There is, so to speak, a new me, one that stands as an affront to the images codified and made sacred by the culture at large. I become in essence an offense at large. More than that, however, is the possibility that I stand responsible for helping to shape the ethos of my society and my milieu in the same way that it assumes the task of shaping me. There is no need to adopt a passive stance toward the so-called sanctity of one's culture. Culture and its values should no more be treated as givens and nonmodifiable than should character traits.

Such a new identity is possible because the portrait of self I hold is not so binding that it negates other meaningful modes of experience that result in change. I remain as functional a human being as any of my West Indian fellows who may choose to remain bonded to a limited portrait of self and therefore cut themselves off from cultural affinity with other groups. Not only am I not any less of a human being for having entertained an expanded portrait of self and concomitant identity states, I would say that I have not lost anything fundamental to my human status. In fact, I may have acquired new characteristics that enrich me far more than any I could have realized in my native environment. Too much emphasis is placed on the apparent intrinsic value of cultural or ethnic authenticity, a value I think is quite spurious and dubious in today's truly multicultural and therefore *multivalue* world. Paul Gilroy has demonstrated in *The Black Atlantic: Modernity and Double Consciousness* that after the African diaspora, which ultimately changed Western civilization, and after the opening of international borders to immigrants of various hues, it makes little sense to speak of rigid authenticity of cultures within a Western context. It is obvious that "Western culture," once exclusively a set of well-demarcated European customs, traditions, and value paradigms, is no longer delineable. Immigration, slavery, and colonialism changed its epidermal and morphological landscape as well as its inner coloration. Colonialism and border openings have obviously transformed the West. Syncretism, hybridization, and authentic multiculturalism are the norm. Members of the diaspora and voluntary immigrants have taken up the Western mantle and transformed it. They have properly appropriated it and infused it with their own experiences, traditions, and values in ways that would make Shakespeare, Descartes, and Homer wonder whether they were on a different planet. The so-called Americanization of the world via jet planes and Hollywood manifests itself in several forms: from gyrating Korean street kids showing off hip-hop moves to South American Indians decked out in shabby Adidas shorts and Nike tennis shoes. It is true that those features may be cosmetic and that they pale beside the extant customs of the respective cultures. Nevertheless, it is no longer simply a question of the West versus other cultures. The Western landscape is being transformed by the foreigners who are being brought into its reaches.

If syncretism and hybridization are the master paradigms, then it becomes useless to speak of authenticity vis-à-vis cultures. Such designations seem superficial in a polyvalent universe. Black rhythm and blues music is as indebted to Brazilian polyrhythms as Frank Sinatra and Nashville country music are to the

soul-searching strains of Billie Holiday. A true spirit of becoming and cosmopolitanism will place the cloak of authenticity where it properly belongs: the
personal sphere of the individual's life.

One of the virtues of embracing becoming is that the attendant autonomous
self that may emerge permits one to challenge the false roots of these deified
and reified attitudes, norms, and values that are treated with metaphysical reverence. The precursor to this autonomy can be found in *critical distancing*.
Charles Taylor points out that John Locke's theory both generates and reflects
an ideal of independence and self-responsibility, or a notion of reason as free
from established custom and locally dominant authority.[24] Distancing allows
us to stand back from our existing state and ourselves. We are thus permitted
the possibility of remaking ourselves more rationally and advantageously. This
is said to be what liberalism stands for. Taylor writes: "We are creatures of ultimately contingent connections: we have formed certain habits. But we can
break from them and re-form them. . . . [R]adical disengagement opens the
prospect of self-remaking."[25] This license permits us to take a radical stance of
disengagement toward our selves and the society around us. This Enlightenment ideal of what Taylor calls the "punctual" self is indeed a moral license for
autonomy, a license that allows us to scrutinize our traditions and habits. Radical communitarians, of course, will insist on the difficulty of achieving this and
will question the morality of those members of a community who wish to distance themselves from their moral starting points, or locations of origin.

But part of the agenda of the self in becoming and of the moral cosmopolitan as I envision him or her is to recognize creative ways of reconciling individualism not with community but with sociality in general. By "sociality" is
meant the large general spheres in which human social intercourse and civic life
take place.[26] I want to put this affirmative version of individualism in the service of the moral cosmopolitan. The affirmative individualism of the moral cosmopolitan, as distinct from the nihilistic individualism of the adolescent rebel-
without-a-cause, presupposes a wide geopolitical landscape of sociality as the
playing field. The metaphor of the playing field is not accidental. A playing
field presupposes a spirit of gamesmanship in which play—lest it degrade to
barbaric and chaotic primordial expression—must operate within open-ended
rules and regulations. The playing field, as a metaphor for the world, is open.
It invites onto its terrain those with an ethos and spirit of humanity extended
to strangers. But the players know that the term "stranger" is a misnomer,
because we are all strangers to ourselves. That is, the self as possibility, the self
in its deepest mode, is only vaguely intuited. The invitation to let others in is
a mature moral gesture: its telos is a reconstitution of the self. In the smallest
and most trivial encounter with another, one has the option of modifying one's
self, reconstituting it, and opening it up. The player's playing field is not

provincial. Its ethos is an assault against the communalists and culturalists who would seek to forever swath the individual in the musty cloak of traditional tribal identity. Even those playing fields or territories that are literally foreclosed to the self in becoming are accorded status in that immigrant friendly universe via an appeal to the basic principles of democratic humanism that expresses itself through discourse, textual exchanges, and an ethos that encourages one to cast a suspicious and critical eye on the descriptive schemata and false names one has been ordered to wear at the price of one's own growth and self-generated modifications. In the absence of firm orders, some accept out of habit the schemata of the world they have inherited. They become fixated on a specific genre of self, and the prospect of wandering outside the parameters of this genre is daunting, uncomfortable, and just plain boring. Dewey writes:

> Every living self causes acts and is itself caused in return by what it does. All voluntary action is a remaking of self, since it creates new desires, instigates to new modes of endeavor, brings to light new conditions which institute new ends. Our personal identity is found in the thread of continuous development which binds together these changes.[27]

The image of the thread is important; it is a metaphor that lends itself nicely to a plethora of inspirational options the self in becoming can employ. The thread forms the basis of the web of narratives the individual must both spin and earn with her life. The thread must weave itself beyond the contours of the tribe, the clan, and the nation. To the extent that individuals are literally precluded from this, in spirit and desire there must be a yearning for foreign contact, for experience with the other on as many levels as possible. If sociality, as opposed to mere community, is the playing field and the lived space within which one operates and dreams and makes life plans, then the authenticity longed for (as far as the self in becoming is concerned) is gauged by how much one has allowed one's voluntary associations to truly affect one's moral and value sensibilities. Are fundamental changes and a remaking of the self taking place? Has this change brought about a real reevaluation of one's ends, one's value judgments? Has one learned to experience and truly listen to the stories of others? World travelers trying to pass as cosmopolitans, emerging from their tour buses clutching Gucci suitcases, are best advised to call themselves what they are: tourists or world travelers. The reconstitution of the self in becoming is not a mere aesthetic indulgence. It is a moral way of life.

So far we have been discussing the self in becoming and its attributes. But one may ask: By what means are persons able to perform the complex feats necessary for authentic self-creation? How are they able to bracket their own historicity? What enables them to discriminate among the narratives that have been thrust on them, and how are they able to assess critically the very values, categories, ascriptions, and mores that they are intent on transcending? These questions are important. I have described a somewhat peripatetic self in the process of accomplishing a great many things. The first piece of psychomoral machinery that equips the self to operate and maneuver in the world with the dexterity required is *autonomy*. Some semblance of autonomy competency is presupposed by the very existence and efficacy of this self in moral becoming or *moral re-creation* that is simultaneously creating new moral communities and being created by them. I take autonomy to be a social good that is absolutely essential for any dignified life and certainly a psychological prerequisite for the moral development and maturity of the self in becoming.

What is known as the communitarian self is reflective of contemporary tribal selves in very crucial ways that I explicate later. In this section, however, I will examine a particular version of this type of self as outlined by political theorist and communitarian defender Michael Sandel. The communitarian self cannot become anything over and beyond the moral strictures and ethos of its community. I highlight this type of self not only because it stands in sharp distinction to the portrait of the moral cosmopolitan self I am drawing but also because it is a means of defending the need for autonomy competency. The communitarian self is so robustly formed by its community that it has little way of distancing itself from some of the community's basic ends and values. In chapter 6 I show why communitarians, especially those of the strongest kind, find such an option highly offensive.

THE COMMUNITARIAN SELF

Sandel's cognitive self is constituted by its ends, which are given prior to it. These ends are the values, roles, mores, norms, traditions, and customs of the community into which the self is born. It is the compilation of its community's ends, which constitute its very identity. It finds itself an involuntary member of certain institutions that it is required to cherish and respect.

The challenge for this type of self is to distinguish itself from its environment. Each person is a conception of the good evinced by its community. As a result of social experience, the self is full of ends. It is "radically situated" and adopts ends that it already contains, that is, ends endorsed by the community as proper for it to embrace. The self here has to discover its ends rather than choose them. How does the radically situated self differentiate itself from its ends? Sandel tells us that the self reflects on itself and inquires into its constituent nature, "discerning its laws and imperatives, and acknowledging its purposes as its own."[28] Reflective thinking, he states, is the criterion required for a sense of identity. The self in reflexivity turns its lights upon itself and reflects upon itself as an agent. Relevant questions to be faced by this self are: Who am I? and How am I to discern in this clutter of possible ends what is me from what is mine?[29] Too much is essential to the identity of the self because all sorts of competing claims, goods, and ends vie indiscriminately for identity status. The bounds of self are possibilities instead of fixtures. Reflexivity, Sandel notes, is a distancing faculty that issues in a certain type of detachment and allows the self to constitute an identity based on the knowledge of the self. This knowledge allows the self to constitute an identity based on given ends in which it finds itself ensconced. He says that the distancing notion

> succeeds by restoring the shrunken space between self and ends. In reflexivity, the self turns its light inward upon itself, making the self its own object of inquiry and reflection. When I am able to reflect on my obsession, able to pick it out and make it an object of my reflection, I thereby establish a certain space between it and me, and so diminish its hold. It becomes more an attribute and less a constituent of my identity and so dissolves from an obsession to a mere desire.[30]

Sandel regards his project as one of repairing the agency of his subject that has been disempowered because it is undifferentiated from its ends. Repair is to be found in its cognitive sense. Self-knowledge at this stage is based upon a relationship between the self and its pre-given ends.

Sandel's view that the self can somehow turn "its light inward upon itself, making the self its own object of inquiry and reflection" is problematic. If the self has not had the opportunity to distinguish itself from itself (that is, from its community's ends, roles, values and norms, etc.) then what "objective" criteria are being used to locate knowledge of the self independent from the literal raw materials that comprise it? If as a Jamaican I have been socialized to despise and morally repudiate homosexuals, if the denigration of their humanity has been an essential part of that ethnic identity, and if the communitarian ideal defines me essentially by those values of my community, and if, further, I am dissuaded from using value standards outside my community as a way of correcting or repudiating those values I might find specious, then how on earth am I going to be able to (a) legitimately cull a self separate and apart from the one culturally handed to me; and (b) inculcate my community with a set of "alien" and nontraditional values that, while attempting to address some of its pernicious moral objectives, would nevertheless jeopardize its authenticity and constitutiveness?

Sandel states that the self becomes its own object of inquiry. If the self, however, is constituted by its ends/roles provided by its community, then this reads like the self qua ends reflecting on other ends. Is the self that is reflecting on itself constituted by goods and ends that are more integral or essential than the other goods and ends that are potentially constitutive of its identity?

Self-knowledge and critical reflective skills will come about by the self's experimenting and involving itself with a multiplicity of ends, roles, and values. In this way it can construct a hierarchy of preferences and dislikes, separate temporary desires from more lasting ones, and thereby provide itself with a basis for building a life plan and formulating values based on knowledge of its own responses to these competing ends and goods. Since there is no fixed boundary to the self at this stage, it has no internal, "impervious-to-the-world" realm to which to appeal.

Self-knowledge for the self on a quest to become a different type of moral creature requires further what I would call *normative moral knowledge*. That is, it involves going beyond what one is to that which one ought to be. What is it that determines the criteria for constructing the means necessary for getting to this end? The type of moral person one would like to become is a person with specific traits. Some of these traits will not be accidental and irrelevant to the type of particular identity one holds. So, for example, if one wishes eventually to become a moral cosmopolitan, one cannot hold to the principles of a cultural nationalist or a racial tribalist. The specific nature of the person one wishes to become—that is, the attributes that are constitutive of the identity of one's moral ideal—will determine the normative moral knowledge one needs. If one is attempting to get from North America to Mexico by car, one ought to discover the necessary route. The route will be determined by the end itself— Mexico. The route will not be the same if one chooses a different end—say, Montreal.

With all of this in mind, I question the extent to which Sandel can legitimately accord any real epistemological privilege to the self in the process of discerning its preferences by somehow reflecting upon itself. If the self is constitutive of its ends, then in order to set up a system of preferences—a value hierarchy, so to speak—it is autonomy competency that the self needs and lacks in a robust sense. The communitarian self lacks this quality in any robust sense of the term that makes moral agency possible because the communitarian self cannot improve upon itself by repudiating its roles, its ends, and the value systems of the community, since to do this in a radical way would be to obliterate its own identity according to the communitarian criteria of self-identity. Such a self would be conceptually out of order, since it is the roles, ends, and values of its community that constitute its actual identity.

Sandel's distancing criterion may provide the groundwork for what will eventually resemble an autonomous self. It is an autonomous self in the weak sense, because, as I have argued, real autonomy has to include the type of freedom and ownership of one's life that allows the self to radically distance itself from the internalized value imperatives and edicts of its community, repudiate them, and proceed to discover new ones outside its designated community. Communitarianism cannot endorse such a strategy. I emphatically believe that failure to equip persons with such an option not only denies them the chance to modify their moral characters when they are in desperate need of modification but also makes them complicitous in the oppressive and sometimes morally repugnant values and traditions of their own communities.

The Sandelian communitarian self would like to see itself as able to critically assess its responses and relationships to the multiple goods and ends in which it has been involved and therefore develop a critical and detached endpoint by which to judge future goods and ends. Philosopher Diana Meyers maintains that critical reflection needs an individual standpoint marked by endorsed preferences. If we take the distancing and detached feature of Sandel's self far enough, this is the hoped-for result. The distance between the self and competing ends is the position that enables the self to judge: I respond this way to good X and this way to ends Y. This is, of course, the type of reflection and awareness in which the self must be involved in order to exercise self-governance and self-control, two features Meyers finds lacking in Sandel's radically situated self. Sandel's communitarian self is able to exercise some modicum of self-governance and -control by ascertaining what it really wants to do and by acting accordingly. Deciding what it wants to do arises from being able to distinguish preferences and wants and being able to assess its relationship to pregiven ends.

What I want to emphasize here is that this skill alone is limited. The communitarian self portrayed by Sandel is equipped with minimal autonomy skills: self-discovery that comes about by the self analyzing itself in relation to various goods and ends, and self-understanding as a by-product of self-discovery. I maintain that the line of demarcation, or critical distance, is not only a corollary of the autonomous individual but also a prerequisite for a life of becoming and the achievement of a cosmopolitan identity. Sandel's distancing feature can partially equip the self to adopt the detached stance only within the confines of its own community. It can judge and evaluate the multiple roles and ends of the community in which it is situated according to whatever competing options the community itself might endorse. But what would it mean for a self to say in effect, "My community is offensive to me. Its values and its principles, and the roles it has carved out for me are unacceptable. In fact, I do not wish to be a part of this community. I reject the limited conception of self and of moral agency that it has foisted on me. I reject the narrowness of it. I hold a moral vision of my life that cannot find expression within the limited confines of this community. I am compelled to disown the self I find myself in possession of. I am inspired to create a new type of self, a new type of human being.

The traits and attributes that this type of human being ought to have are not endorsed or even imagined by this community of mine. I have to leave. My community and its values and traditions are backward, primitive, and as far as I am concerned do not contribute to sound moral agency"?

Indeed, what would it mean for a self to utter such a thing? That is too much to answer right here at this moment. There is a trait or a capacity that the self must possess before it can even begin to seriously entertain such lofty aspirations. Autonomy competency is the machinery that will equip it to deal with and finally escape its radical situatedness.

AUTONOMY

Autonomy is an indispensable social good without which one is a depraved automaton at the mercy of any commissar or hegemonic metanarrative enunciated by the vanguards of culture, the creators of values, norms, and social goods. I follow Jack Crittenden's analysis of the liberal, whom he describes as a person who wants no encumbrances, including uncritical reliance on other persons, in choosing values, beliefs, ends, and attachments. Such a self resembles a transcendent chooser.[31] The autonomous liberal self for Crittenden is constituted by both individual autonomy and constitutive relationships—an independent self and other persons. Such an individual is a compound individual. The theory of compound individuality argues that the self, as it integrates the prior levels on which it existed, becomes a compound of those levels. At the autonomous level, the self can also be a compound in different ways. Selfhood is characterized by both autonomy and constitutive relationships. Agency becomes constituted not by communal attachments but by dyadic relationships, or relationships with a few particular others. The mutuality forged in these relationships makes one's self-definition relational, interactive, and intersubjective. The relationship is both internal, in that one's life story cannot be told or understood without that of the other, and external, in that one's life is expressed by, but not derived from, the relationship. The relationship creates a mutual life as the partners coregulate their identities.[32] Compound individuality can arise only out of the confrontation of the self with diverse ways of life and competing conceptions of the good.[33]

The primary question facing Sandel's communitarian self and all selves with aspirations of agency, whether they are chained on southern plantations or living in bourgeois affluence, is: Can we be autonomous selves and also be thickly constituted and bound by our clan, tribe, social customs, or community? Autonomy requires us to be separate from such ties, and it may require us to be self-sufficient.

Crittenden's depiction of the liberal self as a transcendent chooser is uncontroversial and a general given. Sandel himself characterizes the liberal self as a self that is antecedently given; that is, its selfhood exists prior to its ends and roles, which means that it has a revisability clause that enables it to detach itself from the value imperatives and moral judgments of its community. This type of self has the capacity to distance itself from its community and judge for itself which among the competing candidates for conceptions of the good it finds favorable. The obvious question, then, is, why do I simply not elect the liberal self as the ideal candidate for the self in moral becoming? The answer to this is clarified in chapter 6. I am reluctant to endorse the liberal self as the ideal candidate for the self in moral becoming because I remain unconvinced that this type of self has the resources to divest itself of its tribal makeup. It is for this reason that I look to the cosmopolitan self as the embodiment of the ideal of the self in moral becoming.

The autonomous person must be able to navigate successfully among the range of choices and options with which he or she is faced. The process of autonomy involves not only rationality "but also self-reflectivity, for to choose autonomously one must have some critical distance from the range offered."[34] Crittenden is, therefore, aware like Sandel of the importance of distancing oneself from one's core environment to decide independently what is right and appropriate for one. Crittenden, however, develops these skills more robustly than does Sandel. The communitarian self, while not wholly uncritical in its attempts to choose its ends, is too radically situated and enjoys too little critical space between itself, its ends, and its environment. It therefore lacks robust self-reflectivity. This self exists at the level Crittenden would call the membership level. That is, as a self it is the group, its norms, and *nomoi*.[35] The autonomous self will have to have distanced itself to some degree from the conventions of its social environment and the influences of the persons surrounding it. Its actions express principles and policies that it has ratified by a process of critical reflection.[36] Self-reflectivity reinforces and provides that critical distance. Crittenden writes: "Whereas at the membership level the limits of choice, however rational, were set by the norms and nomos of the group, at the autonomous level the norms and nomos themselves are self-imposed, adopted as a set of standards arrived at through critical reflection."[37] Crittenden is careful to point out that autonomy does not mandate that one's values or laws be created ex nihilo. They come as modified versions of those of the group. Like one's identity they are combined into a form that is properly one's own. The individual is no longer constituted by the group. Rather, she is constituted by those insights and principles by which she governs her life and makes her choices.[38] As I have argued before, moral evolution will at some time require that one repudiate the tenets and other value accouterments of one's community and seek inspiration from myriad (at times) unrelated communities, moral exemplars outside one's community, and one's own creative capacities—that is, from one's moral imagination.

A prerequisite for developing autonomy competence in persons is an acceptance of the idea that the values and customs, norms and mores of any community are not inherently sacrosanct and immune from radical moral scrutiny. And further, a culture that subjects its members to oppressive value systems and attributes—that is, value systems that undermine their dignity, prevent them from forming their own healthy conceptions of the good, and foster an atmosphere in which they denigrate the lives of those different from themselves—might properly earn the moral indictment of those outside and inside the community who have subjected its values and traditions to critical rational and moral scrutiny. This indictment might give us good reason to do what is in our power as moral agents to obliterate such cultures. This is not an advocacy of terminating the life of persons in such cultures; only the practices, values, and norms by which persons live a particular type of life should be destroyed.

To make persons autonomous requires that their encapsulation in any community that is the result of an accident of birth, chance, or the decision of those who brought them into the world be recognized for the contingent phenomenon that it is. If persons realize that, given a different set of circumstances, they could have been born in an entirely different culture with its set of peculiar norms and without an attendant loss to their humanity, then they may realize that they might be radically different persons but still valid and worthy human beings nevertheless. Legitimate autonomy requires, therefore, a particular moral attitudinal stance toward that which the subject is reacting to. On the one hand we must take seriously our socialization and the values and norms of our culture. On the other hand we must divest them of all seriousness in the negative sense by reconstituting them with our critical engagement and by treating them as open-ended systems. Such a stance is important because of our multiple experiences in our own communities and the myriad ways in which our communities exploit us. If, as the communitarians say, our moral starting points originate in our communities, and if we are constituted by the roles and values and ends of our communities, then we must have legitimate methods of dealing with the ways they actually confer moral identities on us and the ways they exploit us. This point is highlighted by Marilyn Friedman, who expresses a feminist concern with the communitarian emphasis on privileging those involuntary associations within the community from which the major thrust of our identities is culled. The major challenge faced by such a self is this: Where will it get its language of resistance?[39]

For Crittenden the autonomous person is rational, but he is also differential.

That is, he is separate from, or independent of, his cultural matrix and is able to reflect on it. Crittenden argues:

> The critical distance or independence comes from the emergence of the basic structure of formal operational thought. The person can now take the roles of others who are not in his sodality; he can scrutinize the sodality's worldview from the perspective of one outside it. He can now control or regulate the rules and roles, principles and practices, governing his life, something he could not do when identified by those rules and roles.[40]

Autonomy on this model is independence from the need to follow the norms and rules of one's social milieu. Role identity is replaced by autonomous ego identity. Autonomy demands that one be able to venture behind the lines of all particular roles and norms. One must be able to present oneself believably in any situation as an individual who can "satisfy the requirements of consistency even in the face of incompatible role expectations." This acting subject Jürgen Habermas calls "context free," which means that at the autonomous level the agent has the ability to construct new identities in conflict situations. He is no longer a compilation of specific roles. Crittenden writes:

> The actor is now free of any context, of any kind of traditional—what Habermas calls "imposed"—norms and can now distinguish and operate according to principles that generate norms. Not only can the person distinguish the general from the particular, the symbolic from the concrete, but also now he can make such generalizations himself.[41]

The autonomous individual who is free from the potential constitutiveness of the given ends and roles of his milieu can remove himself from the social matrix that helped to shape him. This, I maintain, is what a radically situated communitarian self is unable to accomplish. He is too closely intertwined within the social matrix of his origin. Diana Meyers argues that people cannot be autonomous unless they assert some sort of control over their socialization. It is this capacity to exert control over its socialization that the communitarian self needs. Such a self runs the risk of being a dumping ground or a repository of its culture's traditions and norms. To revise one's socialization in a radical manner is to jeopardize the sanctity of the community whose responsibility it is to spawn the values and principles by which one is socialized. To the extent that the self appropriates these values and exercises them, it becomes a moral automaton incapable of flexing its critical muscles to discern what it genuinely values and what it does not. Contemporary communitarian tribal selves are faced with this dilemma. Socialized as racial entities, they respond with surprise when they discover that the racial criteria that are part of their individual self-identities are not universal and do not describe anything metaphysically central to their biological makeup. It is precisely the reluctance to radically question such criteria and the hostility often expressed toward those who entice them to do so that lead me to conclude that in this realm of their lives persons are lacking in autonomy and overflowing with illusions. To imbue such criteria with moral weight and to use them as reliable gauges of the worth of persons is not only to lack autonomy but also to be complicitous in a morally specious value enterprise.

Meyers draws two important distinctions regarding autonomous self-direction. These distinctions will magnify the portrait of the self in moral becoming as I continue to construct it. They are *autonomous episodic self-direction* and *autonomous programmatic self-direction.*

Autonomous episodic self-direction occurs when a person confronts a situation head-on and asks specific questions about it on the order of, "What can I do with respect to it?" One then executes the decision this deliberation may yield.[42]

Autonomous programmatic self-direction has a broad sweep. Instead of posing the question, "What do I really want to do now?" it asks, "How do I really want to live my life?" Meyers argues that in order to answer this question, people must consider what qualities they want to have, what sorts of interpersonal relationships they want to be involved in, what talents they want to develop, and what goals they want to achieve.[43]

While autonomous episodic self-direction certifies the autonomy of several spontaneous actions, programmatically autonomous people have autonomous life plans. A life plan is a comprehensive projection of intent, a conception of what a person wants to do in life. It includes at least one activity that a person consciously wants to pursue. A life plan couples an ordering of assorted concerns and objectives with some notion of how to initiate progress toward fulfilling some of them and detailed schemes for ensuring the successful realization of others. Life plans are unfolding programs that are always subject to revision. Under scrutiny some aims may be abandoned, others adopted; life plans are dynamic. By introducing some degree of order into people's lives, life plans enable people to want more and to satisfy a greater number of their desires than random satisfaction-seeking possibly could.[44] Life plans force one to ask oneself what it is that one really wants. Since they undergo frequent revisions, they also support the vitality and openness to life's possibilities that are characteristic of autonomy. A successful life plan presupposes the possession of autonomy competency, that is, the set of skills that enables the individual to choose those values endorsed by his moral consciousness. This is where he will actually need the distancing feature that Sandel writes of; this is the line of demarcation that will legitimize his autonomy skills. Let us flesh this out with an existential situation. Sandel's radically situated self seems fairly representative of humans as they are situated in the Western industrialized empirical world. That is, each person to a large degree finds him- or herself ensconced in a multiplicity of worlds: a particular religion (to some extent this holds for the majority of people); a socio-economic class, and a racial and ethnic category, to name just a few. Now, one could argue that such ends are equally constitutive of an individual's identity. That is, one could reasonably assert that religious background is no more crucially constitutive of "identity" than, say, ethnic identity. It is experience and immersion in these multiple identities (Sandel's pre-given ends) and the concomitant preferences and evaluations that emerge that will determine how you will choose to fashion your "basic identity," that is, the sense in which you feel that affiliation with any of the potential identity states constitutes a version of who you feel you really are. "My Jewishness is really me," or "My middle-class status is more of a representation of who I feel I really am as opposed to my racial identity." It is quite plausible to interpret this as the juncture from which certain criteria used in future critical reflection will be drawn. However such criteria are not merely existing social norms. They are now harvested from a storehouse of value criteria that were initially drawn from the social arena but now exist independently of it.

Simonetta, for example, is an Italian Catholic. Most people in her community who engage in critical reflection rely on norms and mores drawn from their social background. Simonetta, like most people, is initially identified with other equally constitutive ends or attributes. That is, she is female, she was born in America, she is of middle-class background, and so on. Simonetta, in experiencing a host of ends, realizes that she prefers some to others. In time she identifies with being American more than being Italian, and she realizes that this identification puts her at odds with some of the social values that are part of her Italian identity. She begins to question her Italian Catholic heritage in ways that put her at odds with some of the features crucial for her designation as an Italian American. Over time she develops an independent set of preferences and tastes that she uses to assess her position as a member of multiple communities who also has other identities.

Simonetta, by distancing herself from myriad constitutive ends, is allowed to assess herself as she evolves in relation to the ends she is both participating in and distancing herself from. She should not be limited to prevailing social norms, nor should she be abandoned to socialization. Social norms are measured against her developing list of value preferences. These values partially form her sense of integrity and expanding moral identity. Ideally this occurs because of a growing independent self that emerges as she grows in autonomy competency and involves herself in a multiplicity of ends and life-world experiences.

This involvement will, it must be stressed, take her outside the bounds of her immediate community. She cannot exist as a closed system, as a creature untouched by, and impervious to, the larger competing communities with varied value systems, ways of life, worldviews, and conceptions of the good.

Part of what Sandel fails to address adequately is precisely the cultural resources needed for the achievement of this distancing mechanism as well as the set of cultural goods that individuals will need if they are to critique the particularities and roles imposed upon them by their communities. If, following Sandel's model of the radically situated self, we are constitutive of our roles and the values and the norms of our communities, then exactly how is the distancing technique that he has prefigured within his theory supposed to work? Exactly where would one's language of resistance, which serves as the conceptual base of one's moral consciousness, come from? Consider the case of the tightly encapsulated member of an extremely conservative religious community that has no contact with the outside world and that forces its females to marry at the age of fifteen and produce at least three children. Such an individual, if not privy to a set of cultural goods with which to combat the culture's questionable practices, roles, and ends, is left trapped within an oppressive matrix. Because communities confer moral identities on their members, we need a theory of community, of communities' interrelationships, and of their structures of power and dominance. This would, Friedman argues, allow us to assess the claims made upon us by communities by way of their traditions and customs.[45]

Equipped, however, with the requisite autonomy competency skills, the self in moral becoming might just be in a position to make use of a dialectics of participation and distanciation. Distanciation provides the critical space for us to stand back and question, examine, and criticize and also discover the multiplicity of forces that constitute our background world and situatedness. This space wrought by distanciation will aid our discernment of what is happening in the moment and the developments that formed us and played upon us of which we were unaware because of our intense participation with such forces. Yet our engagements with these forms and forces were important, for they forged the very conditions and practices that formed and played upon ourselves and others.[46]

Participation without distanciation paves the way for an excessive rule of tradition and custom, the rule of the obvious and the taken-for-granted. Distanciation without participation leads to abstract solipsism devoid of the contextual and interactive play of varied life forms, experiences with others, and competing value systems. Clearly an element of denying the forces that constitute one's identity as a social and historical being would be involved. As a logical entailment, one would also be denying one's own self-evolution.

The dialectics of participation and distanciation, along with autonomy competency, creates a space that can see the evolution of some form of healthy autonomy and moral individualism. It holds great potential for the individual to determine himself as an autonomous being who is capable of developing into a moral agent independent of the practices and standards of his community. The space can also lead him to recognize how he has become a moral being and permit him to contemplate his future relationships with the community. Do I continue to participate but with the critical bent, or do I engage in further distanciation? In fact, do I opt for another community, one that is more affirming to the now autonomous life plan I have carved for myself but that is not likely to be affirmed in the stifling and culturally bankrupt environment in which I exist? Do I forget where I came from and look toward the future and another, more liberating community?

Such questions are not just flights of fancy of a dreamy self. They are the legitimate concerns of the individual in moral becoming who, while realizing the sociohistorical significance of his situatedness within a community and the sense of self of which he feels himself in possession, simultaneously realizes that the base rootedness of his existence is not the equivalent of an immutable metaphysical substance. It is at best a first draft of what he might be and can be.

Such questions would be culturally out of order for the tribal self that I regard as a variation of a particular communitarian ideal. Communitarian advocates grant a special metaphysical privilege to the self's discovered and involuntary membership communities. Friedman notes: "Not voluntary but 'discovered' relationships and communities are what Sandel takes to define subjective identity for those who are bound by a 'sense of community.'[47] It is to the communities to which we are involuntarily bound that Sandel accords metaphysical pride of place in the constitution of subjectivity. What are important are not simply the 'associations' in which people 'cooperate' but the 'communities' in which people 'participate.'" The latter depict a commonly shared life consisting more in attachments people find than in relationships they have voluntarily entered.[48]

Free of this enslavement, our autonomous individual is wedded to a sociality but not community. He is now free, like a solitary snake, to seek new territories. There he may expand his omnivorous identity, there he will infuse it with his own peculiar vision, moral sensibilities, and commitments. Belonging to everyone but to no one in particular, he puts his self and his identity in the service of the world. Further becoming is his goal. Raising his head above the plains of the community, he catches sight of the larger world ahead and charts a course straight ahead.

2

THE EXISTENTIALIST SELF:

RADICALLY FREE AND REBELLIOUS

Life transcends the inert state of things by human causality, by means of an agent who wishes to make events happen. This will to action can also take a personal form, an act of self-creation, or a transformation that we want in spite of reality. Insofar as we are desirous of surpassing our present condition, we may apply creativity to the self. Consequently, the greatest and the most intimate of the many selves that each of us bears within is the self that each one wants to be, the self of our ambition.

— Paul Ilie, *Unamuno: An Existentialist View of the Self*

Existentialism and existential phenomenology in some form or other have always been concerned primarily with the individual and individualism in general. Because existentialism places such great emphasis on action, as we see in Jean-Paul Sartre, José Ortega y Gasset, Miguel de Unamuno, and other spiritual progenitors of this philosophic tradition, all of whom believe that any meaningful notion of the self can only be appealed to through a self that acts, I think that more than any other philosophy existentialism may be described as a rich and profound instance of applied philosophy.

Walter Kohan writes that the first thing philosophy does or should do is to develop the imagination. Rather than accept impositions, philosophers should imagine other forms. They should create the different and propose the dissimilar while widening the realm of possibility and rebelling against the one-dimensional character of established reality.[1] Although not written from an existentialist point of view, his article captures well the ethos and spirit of existentialism and presents what that philosophy is primarily about: expanded possibilities and consciousness and an expansive conception of selfhood coupled with a life of action.

I will further amplify the portrait of this self in creative becoming by appealing to two key features of existentialism. The first has to do with the existentialist account of the self as essentially natureless. The second pertains to the indeterminacy, malleability, and ambiguity of the social world we inhabit. I will borrow terminologies and concepts for practical use in ways that many of the thinkers who first used them might not have approved. For example, while I do not take all of Sartre's notion of the for-itself as a fully proper approach to understanding the self, I will find within its ontological DNA very useful applications to be put in the service of the self that I am attempting to construct. At times, therefore, I will use it in personal terms as opposed to treating it as an ontological entity. It is one of many useful tools to be appropriated by any self that may be intrigued by an existentialist schema for the world. The following characterization of Alain Locke's approach to philosophy by Leonard Harris is a good summary of the approach I have taken to the philosophers discussed in this chapter and the overall stylistic and methodological thrust of my work. Harris notes: "Locke studied the pragmatists of America and value theorists of Europe but was not conceptually confined to their worlds of philosophic debate; rather, he referenced their philosophies as a conduit for the expression of his own views."[2]

EXISTENTIAL ONTOLOGY.

"Existence precedes essence."[3] So writes Jean-Paul Sartre, invoking perhaps the most important statement within existentialist ontology. The unpacking of that simple statement will reveal all that we take to be fundamentally radical and somewhat "metaphysically" blasphemous about existentialism, not just in terms of traditional Western metaphysics, but also in its stance toward the idea of God itself.

Predicated on the conviction that there is no God to conceive of a human nature to metaphysically stamp humans either with an image of their own or with some predelineated concept of a species kind, the idea that existence precedes essence points to the status of beings who exist without an essence already defined. Their existence is a given, it is a fact of the world. But it is first only that. Human reality is not wired with any meaning, with any pre-given intentions, desires, states, or dispositions that mark persons off as essentially specific types of creatures. Just what is meant by saying that existence precedes essence? Sartre writes:

> It means that, first of all, man exists, turns up, appears on the scene, and, only afterwards, defines himself. If man, as the existentialist conceives him, is indefinable, it is because at first he is nothing. Only afterward will he be something, and he himself will have made what he will be. Thus, there is no human nature, since there is no God to conceive it. Not only is man what he conceives himself to be, but he is also only what he wills himself to be after this thrust toward existence.
>
> Man is nothing else but what he makes of himself. Such is the first principle of existentialism.[4]

Existence has priority over essence because existence "is the very paste of things." This also means that existence is prior to meaning since essence designates the fundamental meaning in things. Existence precedes essence both in humankind and in nature.[5]

At the root of existentialist ontology is the inescapable fact of human subjectivity as the basic creative and instigative force in human reality. Any features of the world that we fixate on, identify with, and seek to wrest meaning from are only human inventions. From the very beginning, Sartre notes, the individual is a plan that is aware of itself rather than a patch of moss or a piece of garbage. Nothing exists prior to this plan. There is nothing in heaven; individuals will be what they have planned to be.[6]

The Spanish existentialist philosopher José Ortega y Gasset writes that persons have to make their own existence at every single moment. They are given the abstract possibility of existing but not the reality. Of the individual, Ortega writes: "This he has to conquer hour after hour. Man must earn his life, not only economically but metaphysically."[7] Persons begin by being something that has no corporeal or spiritual reality. The individual is a project, something that is not yet but aspires to be.[8]

Similarly, Miguel de Unamuno holds to the theme that human life is something that must be metaphysically earned. Like Ortega, he distrusts the impositions and curtailments that society forces on the individual. Our existence is achieved by means of a search for authenticity that we accomplish by our own investigations, experiences, and discoveries. Human existence is a process of "becoming."[9] In the process of living, the self unfolds continually. It reveals itself in different phases and at progressive moments in time.[10] Unamuno is thought never to have believed in a real and constant self of the kind that was always there objectively and that one could always see if only circumstances did not get in the way.[11] He refrains from delineating any form of self-realization. Instead he stresses the self that we are and the self that we choose to become. As the future merges into the present, we always abandon one self to become another. We each bear within us a number of possible men, a multiplicity of destinies.[12] Unamuno, like Ortega, arrogates to humans the responsibility of creating selves that they seek after their own conception of being. We are not primarily reactionary selves; selves are not constructed against the edifice of a rejected model (although often this is part of the process). Rather, thrown into a world that needs our input to be made and maintained, we are forced to realize a vision of the self we want and must be.

Ortega and Sartre both ground the constitutionality of humanness within a paradigmatic ontology of indeterminacy and contingency. Already we can see the sort of effrontery that they bring to bear against the seriousness of the

Natural Attitude and of tribal ontology. If we are without fundamental natures, then our social and historical identities are capable of being transmuted without an attendant loss of status as human.[13]

Human identity, existentially, is made and then lived. It is not inherited metaphysically, although it is inherited sociohistorically. The raw materials that make up any robust sense of social and moral identity—namely, values, principles, desires, commitments, and beliefs—are things that must be adopted by the individual. They are not biologically encoded into one's mental or character DNA. Still, such an inheritance is based on choice. Because of our radical freedom and the capacity to infuse meaning into the choices that we accept, we still have a choice to accept the sociocultural options bequeathed to us. Sartre's existentialism commits itself to the idea that prior to choice, the individual is a void.

Existentialism's advocacy of the naturelessness of human beings is quite a radical posture within the enterprise of Western philosophy, metaphysics, and philosophical anthropology, since traditionally a formal essence has been associated with a reference to the being of human beings. Sartre's rejection of a necessary human essence is liberating when viewed against the epistemic apodicticity of Western metaphysics that has grounded much of the problematic aspects of the Natural Attitude and from which our stubborn tribal identities stem.

To explicate the radical nature of Sartre's philosophical anthropology, it is important to revisit some of the special aspects of human identities against which it is found to be liberating. Traditionally essence has been posited as an answer to the question of what a thing is. It was considered to be the basic nature, or "structure," of a thing.[14] The thrust of this type of thinking is best exemplified at one end of the spectrum by the Aristotelian and Platonic/Socratic conception of humankind as essentially rational and at the other end by Sigmund Freud. The Freudian instinctual human is largely mired within unconscious libidinal and instinctual forces that regulate, and in some cases maniacally drive, his life.

A level of determinism characterizes a subject interpreted under the Freudian schema. This characterization for Freud is universal. It is an essence that holds for all human beings. There are dispositions that from the outset necessarily harness individuals and that fundamentally constitute them as specific types of species-beings. Individuals, therefore, are limited by the specific type of nature that they are possessed of. Though they may gain control over some of these dispositions (indeed, what was Freudian psychoanalysis if not a herculean effort to assist the individual to modify, mitigate, and undermine these impulses as they often represented themselves as neuroses?), they remain dogged by them as such. In other words, there is nowhere in essentialistic paradigms for an individual to be characterized as radically *self-transcendent*.

The Platonic/Socratic and Aristotelian tradition of positing rationality as the definitive essence of human constitution already delimits the individual because of a possessed metaphysical architectural design. Socrates would have difficulty explaining moral bivalence in human beings in a way that would satisfy most of us. In other words, given Socrates' view that all sin is caused by ignorance of the good, how could a rational person with knowledge of the good do both good and evil? Socrates could not entertain such a question given the ontological, epistemological, and metaphysical commitments that delimit his explanatory scope. We could chart a course right through Western philosophy, pointing to the mechanically constructed notion of Cartesian consciousness, the brutish aggressiveness of Hobbesian man, and the robotics of the wholly Kantian rational person. In all such systems robust self-creation becomes ontologically out of order, an anomalous state of affairs in several cases and metaphysically impossible in perhaps most.[15] As Edward Casey notes, to attribute an essence to man would be to make him necessary in some way.[16] Sartre's conception of humans as not possessing a fundamental nature is radical, not because it points to a plasticity about the human condition, but because it avoids codifying into a "human nature" any number of ostensibly displayed human behaviors or gestures such as aggression, generosity, and hostility. Theorists fixate on such traits and succumb to categorizations and classifications replete with hierarchical moral topologies and gradations; the traits of those occupying a certain part of the spectrum are codified and assigned moral and metaphysical status as tropes and archetypes typifying the normal and the supernormal. By default, anything outside such categories becomes the abnormal. To some, frenetic dancing with sexual gyrations is not just another expressive dance form, it is symptomatic of a perverse character—it betrays the theoretical constitutiveness of a rational creature and all that might be contained in that feature: control, repression, and rigidity. There is no point, Casey writes, in positing as part of man's essence every particular feature we observe in him.[17] This is clearly something that Sartre avoided, and according to William McBride, he had the courage never to yield to the temptation of simply stipulating certain salient behaviors as constituting the core of an allegedly fixed transtemporal human nature.[18]

Sartre's philosophical anthropology depicts a picture of human beings as tabulae rasae, not in John Locke's epistemological sense, but in the fundamental sense of their natures as a construction properly of their own making. Individuals are the creatures who make their own natures. They are nothing else but what they make of themselves after they are thrust into existence. They are a series of possibilities and projects, and since their existence precedes their essence, they are responsible for themselves.[19] If there are no a priori, preordained universal values for the nature human beings supposedly have, if they can freely choose to be rational and irrational, benevolent and malevolent, and if there is no transcendental deity to act as the metaphysical and moral arbiter in clashes between their nature and the purported acts committed against said nature, then they will recognize the entire contingency and malleability of their situation. If individuals cannot betray an essence and a nature, then they are free to challenge the pseudometaphysical bondage that the Natural Attitude and strong ascriptive tribal identities place them under. Strong racial and ethnic identity appeals to a form of essentialism. The one-drop rule in America, which identifies anyone with the faintest history of African ancestry as black, is a case in point. Attitudinally, America views race as an objective, absolute, and innately imputed trait. The point has been made that since race is biologically unreal, its social reality reduces to ethnicity.[20] To become a new type of person involves scrupulously examining the conditions under which one's self-identity has been formed as well as changing one's belief system, value commitments, and moral principles. If the major thrust of one's self-identity is racial/ethnic and if the social stance toward such an identity is inflexible because of an essentialist paradigm governing it, then any attempt to alter the features of that identity is viewed with both skepticism and moral disapproval. Existential ontology is a direct challenge to this essentialist attitude toward tribal ontology. The guilt incurred because people think they betray the authenticity of an identity that they accept in a spirit of seriousness dissipates in light of the possibilities they contain and the projects through which they realize themselves.

At heart, then, persons as members of the human species are the novelists of their lives and the engineers of their projects. As self-made and self-making entities, they realize that their lives are unending struggles to be what they have to be.[21]

If the existentialist self embodies drama, then it certainly cannot resist Unamuno's exalted declaration, "I came into the world to create myself."[22] Ortega, Sartre, and Unamuno view persons as fictional characters who spend their lives creating. Linked to this view of self-creativity is the awareness that choosing to become one type of self often involves abandoning another type of self. This awareness, too, brings forth a rejection of the view that abandonment results in the betrayal of some immutable nature. Individuals, as Sartre insists, can choose a future over and beyond what they are.[23]

How is this type of ontological freedom possible? The human in the existentialist framework is a self-surpassing being who is always in the making and who never reaches an end, or self-completion. Any imposed standpoint of completion is bad faith because it is negated and surpassed by our continuous becoming. It is surpassed because of our capacity as self-transcendent beings who are able to envision new projects and to realize our vast array of possibilities. It is further surpassed because we can instantiate our projects and possibilities into the world. Becoming is possible because on principle being and modes of being are heterogeneous.[24] We possess a trait that also allows us to embrace this ontological leverage and override the binding aspects of tribal ontology: we possess imagination. In fact, we are impossible without imagination, that is, without the capacity to invent for ourselves a conception of life, to "ideate" the characters we are going to be.[25]

Above the reality of our situation at the moment, we can envision a different situation, a situation that is just as meaningful and revealing of commitment as the one we are now a part of. This is because situations are not brute facts. Rather, they are intentionally constituted through the projects and values whereby we lend significance to things.[26] Two prisoners are in a different situation if their fundamental projects differ. The one who relates to the world as something to savor in all its variety is not in the situation of the one who regards the world as itself being a prison from which to retreat into his inner self. A situation is defined "by the 'coefficient of adversity' it presents: hence it is a function, not a cause, of the projects a person has adopted."[27]

David Cooper makes the point that at the heart of existential phenomenology lies the conclusion that the contents of the human world are articulated in terms of the significance they have through the intentional projects in which we engage. Our relation to this world is not that of substances causally interacting with others but what Heidegger calls "care." He writes: "I am not free, as the Stoic would have it, because I am an inner citadel protected against outside incursion by impregnable walls. Rather, as Merleau-Ponty puts it, 'nothing determines me from the outside . . . because I am from the start outside myself and open to the world.'"[28]

For the new type of moral man and woman of the new millennium this is the voice of freedom. No stance is more anathema to racial/ethnic tribal ontology than the above statement.

In the Natural Attitude, significance to a large extent is inscribed by the dominant social currents that are then maintained by a filtering process: Differences do not merely become insignificant, they can threaten the significance of all that has been deemed significant. Significations in the Natural Attitude are conceptual realities that must be lived: personal identities, preferences, and identifications must all be scaled down to fit into the neat conceptual shapes that order lives and idealize aspirations, possibilities, and the unrealized projects the individual may harbor. This idea of shrinking and scaling the self to fit into the ideated classifications of the Natural Attitude is a theme that concerned Unamuno very much. The feeling of surpassing the established limits of the self is an aspect of his vision that illustrates his strong sense of reality. He conceived of the human self as more than the definition made of it. The self at some point begins to exceed its definition. Paul Ilie writes: "After all, an idea about the self can only take into account what the self is up to the moment of the idea's formulation. And yet the self continues to expand beyond that moment, thus destroying the definition."[29]

A self that is becoming and creating itself and thus exceeding its "definition" is potentially a peremptory strike against tribal ontology. This becoming and self-creativity is ontologically problematic and disrespectful in relation to that which defines it. It stands as a corrective. But what of those who fail to effect such a corrective? I think of Paul Schmidt's assessment of how we as individuals try to structure and freeze our existing self into the image of some definite self so that we can say, "I am such and such."[30] Meaning then becomes subsumed under the public and collective meanings of the dominant hermeneutic model functioning within the particular matrix of the Natural Attitude.

Within existentialist ontology, however, meanings are not conceptual forms that interfere with life. If an existentialist self is one that grows from experience and knowledge, then it cannot be formalized. This knowledge and this experience are uniquely mine, but not only that—they are chosen by me. The judgment pronounced has to be mine. Even if I mimic the judgment of another, it is still a choice to do so. The meaning I affix has to be mine. The experience of tasting this food, the chance meeting with a stranger who resembles my father, both hold a meaning. But it is not the meaning of the prime minister of country X, and it is not her responsibility to interpret its meanings. My consciousness processes this experience of this meeting into a here-and-now value judgment. I cannot taste the food of another, and I cannot read the face of the stranger in the way that my friend who is with me and who has never seen my father might. Without a great stretch of the imagination, we can extend such experiences to capture a plethora of interpretations that lie outside the province of the interpretive schema of the Natural Attitude. The Natural Attitude might—depending on the meaning I choose to attach to such experiences and depending on how successful I might be in articulating them—label them as anomalous, decadent, unrealistic, and foolish. I could get thrown into an insane asylum if such meanings as I affix are seen as not just idiosyncratic but also subversive.

But as much as I might suffer existentially from this peremptory strike against me, it is still I who have the power to determine meaning. It is the meaning, then, of our experiences and not the ontological structure of the objects or situation in itself that constitutes reality. Alfred Schutz wonders how persons could, under the weight of the Natural Attitude, experience their own actions within and upon the world. He finds the answer in the subjective meaning persons bestow upon certain experiences of their known spontaneous life. This meaning is the result of a past experience looked at from the present Now with a reflective attitude. Only experiences whose constitutions can be questioned are subjectively meaningful.[31]

In a section on the past in *Being and Nothingness,* Sartre explains that it is I and always I who determine the meaningfulness of any meaning I choose to affix to my past, my present, and the existential situations of my life. This is accomplished by action. Who shall decide whether the period which I spent in prison for a theft was fruitful or deplorable? I, according to whether I gave up stealing or became a hardened criminal.[32] Meaning is a subjective affair between individuals and their projected ends and their immediate environment or world. Meaning is fluid, contingent, and the primary responsibility of individuals. With this in mind, a discussion of radical freedom and the inescapability of choosing prepares us for the responsibility ahead: self-pronounced (not fixed and written in the nature of things) meaning coupled with a life of action that is ontologically liberating and a major criterion for any meaningful attempt at robust self-creation or moral re-creation.

AN EXISTENTIALIST ACCOUNT OF FREEDOM: HUMAN REALITY REVISED

In the absence of a fixed nature, in the absence of any God to embellish the world and its inhabitants with objective values that they must adopt by virtue of being humans and possessing a specific human nature with specific requirements, humans are condemned to freedom. In the absence of any prior meaning to life, in the metaphysical blank slate that characterizes a universe of humans without goals, projected ends, visions, and projects, humans are condemned to create a human community replete with values of their own making with the full realization that the meanings of those values are meanings that they will and must choose. Sartre writes:

> If existence really does precede essence, there is no explaining things away by reference to a fixed and given human nature. In other words there is no determinism, man is free, man is freedom. On the other hand, if God does not exist, we find no values of commands to turn to which legitimize our conduct. So, in the bright realm of values, we have no excuse behind us, nor justification before us. We are alone, with no excuses.[33]

Individuals are abandoned and thrust into the world without innate survival mechanisms. They must make their worlds. They are free by compulsion and condemnation, not by choice. Though they did not create themselves, once thrust into the world, they are responsible for everything they do.

Man is not only free. He is freedom.[34]

To exercise this freedom individuals must act. Individuals are nothing more than an ensemble of their acts.[35] As distinct from mere wishing, feeling, and desiring, it is the potency of acts and actions in an efficacious human being that sets the wheels of the real universe in motion. This is a very important point for Sartre, and it is one of many ways in which he articulates his unique idea of freedom. In a world with a priori values or the design of some Supreme Being, desiring, wishing, and mere wanting might be sufficient to arouse the response of such a being. Prayers, incantations, pleas, and desires then would have causal efficacy because they are part of a necessary chain of events that would lead to the manifestation of certain events in the world. In the absence of such a cosmological feature, action is the criterion for the emergence of a human universe. All things will be as human beings will have decided they are to be, and there really is no reality except in action.[36] These actions, of course, have certain consequences in the world. But individuals are not irredeemably defined by the consequences of their actions nor by those of others for two reasons. First, they are always free to pursue other actions endorsed by the values that they hold and certify through their intentions. An action is on principle intentional. Action requires that one intentionally realize a conscious project.[37] In the absence of some divinely conceived machinery to imbue an action with its value (e.g., sex is only valid for its procreative purpose as decreed by God), the intentions of human beings become the only binding and legitimizing criteria for actions; thus, their intentions and subsequent actions are always in a position to overturn the meaning of a previous action and its consequences.

Second, individuals are free to interpret actions and their consequences. They are neither conceptually nor psychologically enslaved to the explanatory model offered. Explanation of behavior, says Sartre, is hermeneutical, not causal.[38] Intention in the existentialist framework is the fundamental structure of human reality. This means that we must go beyond the given toward a result to be achieved.[39] If that result is a new vision of the self, then we can see how self-creation and a resocialization of the self are possible. Against the contingently formulated identities one has inherited and accepted, an evolution of the self is projected and then realized through certain ends. This is always a possibility because of the basic ontological characteristic in one's makeup. One is a unique entity whose being consists not in what it is already but in what it is not yet, a being that consists in *not-yet-being*.[40]

The notion of not-yet-being is crucial. It will factor in as a prerequisite of rebelliousness later on. For now it stands as a corrective to several of the problems of the Natural Attitude and tribal ontology. From our discussion so far, it is obvious that, based on the contingency of values in our human-created and human-centered world and their malleability, the Natural Attitude—with its racial and ethnic categories, its insistence on authenticity by virtue of appealing to a consensus of stale traditions, its peculiar mores that become codified and censure growth and travel outside its confines—seems to betray a type of arrogance and a spirit of seriousness that is ripe for overthrow. The not-yet-being that I am is anathema to the rigid aspects of tribal ontology. The not-yet-being is always a threat to the rectitude and certainty of the Natural Attitude, as a middle-aged woman is terrified by a dream that she sees a likeness of herself as a wrinkled old woman. The likeness stands as a constant reminder of her capacity for aging. She will look like that one day if she chooses to remain alive. In the days after the dream, she behaves youthfully. She makes arrangements for a face-lift and rigorously applies collagen cream across her face, neck, and arms in a desperate attempt to halt aging. This, however, is something her freedom cannot prevent. Once she remains alive, once she rules out suicide as an option, then aging is part of the brute fact of human existence.[41] Similarly, the constraints spawned by the Natural Attitude try to annihilate the not-yet-being mode of my being. I as a not-yet-being always possess the capacity to overturn the impositions of the Natural Attitude by virtue of my becoming and of what I shall consciously become in my realized projects and visions. This becoming as a prerequisite for authentic self-creation is not fortuitous, it is not living without a goal or allowing oneself to be transported by currents over which one does not exercise some semblance of control. In this sense, the possession of not-yet-being is an intangible ghost in the wind, a destroyer of the inflexibility of certain aspects of the Natural Attitude. It can have no clearly demarcated identity because it has not yet materialized itself as a project.

Existentialism, obviously regarding this not-yet-being feature as a crucial part of human existence, properly formulates the logical priority of the future of human beings over their past and their present. Summarizing the existentialist ethos, Cooper notes that our existence requires the world that is intelligible only in relation to the future beings that we are on the way to becoming. We must first exist as "unsaturated," future-oriented loci of "care" and "value."[42]

Not-yet-being is a contrast to the idea of containment best captured in both the likeness and the concept of the photographic image. The picture I hang on my wall of myself laughing at a party reveals a surface gaiety that does little to bespeak the agony, boredom, and depression actually being experienced at the time. But the image contained there is a marker that others fix on. The possibility of becoming something else or of deciding to be something else lies outside the representational scope of that particular photograph. I think of Sartre's statement, "Man is not what he is." This means that I cannot be really defined in terms of what I might be at the moment (an autocrat, for example). I can always rise above this status and direct how I will become.

To launch, however, into a rich discussion of the factors that make this all possible, we will have to delve deeper into Sartre's notion of freedom, which I shall attempt via a discussion of his notion of *nothingness* and the triadic ontological components of human reality: *être-en-soi* (being-in-itself), *être-pour-soi* (being-for-itself), and *être-pour-autrui* (being-for-others). I will focus mainly on the for-itself. As a preface to the discussion, let us meditate on a crucial Sartrean edict that has been hinted at and will be fleshed out in the ensuing discussions: My ontological structure is not to be what I am and to be what I am not.

Of these three components (being-in-itself, being-for-itself, and being-for-others) the least interesting is being-in-itself. Sartre's well-known way of describing it was that it simply *is*. Being is what it is. In other words, it translates into a sort of crude brute existence. It can never be revealed in its totality to consciousness but exists independently of consciousness and reveals itself to consciousness. Its primary characteristic is never to reveal itself completely to consciousness.[43] It is beyond affirmation and negation. It simply is, the way a rock simply exists qua rock. Its being is not in question for itself. It has no identity that can be modified or changed as a result of its own manipulations.

Human reality basically is being-for-itself. The genesis of this dimension is to be found in several factors. One is that if existence really precedes essence, then I can find no trait or characteristic that will truly define me as a human being. My identity is always in question. I am Caribbean, I am a man, I am a philosopher, I am the owner of a truck, I am a son, a brother, and so on. I am other possibilities and situational realities, but none of them captures me. I am not one with myself. As William McBride suggests, the self is at base nothing but a capacity to put into question all that is alleged to be unalterable.[44] Individuals possess the ability to put things into question and to differentiate. Human consciousness can never be reduced to the self-identity of being-in-itself.[45] The for-itself is a being that is not what it is and that is what it is not.[46] Whatever the for-itself is, it might also be otherwise. If you fall into the temptation of characterizing yourself exclusively in one area of your self-identity, then you could also be characterized in other areas that fail to warrant your attention. Remember too that the not-yet aspect of your being that holds the possibility of a future self may also be used in manufacturing a future for-itself. That for-itself also might be otherwise. David Norton thinks that the "might be otherwise" is not an illusion but a constitutive characteristic of the for-itself. He suggests that "the otherwise" is *in* the for-itself, and for-itself is the being that "is what it is not, and is not what it is."[47] Being-for-itself can never be a pure being-for-itself, since it also exists as being in situation. Being exists not only in the immediate situation but as past situation, as having-been and yet-to be. The for-itself lacks a unity, or perhaps it has a unity that is severely fractured, and so the for-itself can never know itself in unity, in totality, in a face-to-face confrontation with its varied modes. What we come to realize, then, is that human reality is its own nothingness. In other words, the self is capable of questioning everything that is said to be given and immutable. It can create itself in many ways. Nothing that you might fix within the sphere of your character, personality, behavioral traits, and ostensible dispositions is reducible to anything that could be termed an essence of human nature. Out of the onto-logical reality of the nothingness of the for-itself lies the power of negation or nihilation. Being-for-itself is negative. Negation is a power point of affirmation. The judgments of the for-itself and its situational contingencies can be negat-ed and surpassed, reified and modified. Sartre writes, "The for-itself is always something other than what can be said of it."[48] The for-itself is the one that escapes this very denomination, the one that is already beyond the name given to it, beyond the property recognized in it.[49] This is freedom. This power of nihilation is affirmative. Sartre says, "The for-itself is free and can cause there to be a world because the for-itself is *the being which has to be what it was in the light of what it will be.*"[50] Freedom of the for-itself is always engaged. This means that we can only apprehend ourselves as unconditioned or radically free choices. Freedom is realized as a projection of my total possibilities and proj-ects. Because of the nothingness of my being, I can always, however, nihilate any of my projects, make it past, and project another.[51]

Freedom is nothing other than this nihilation. Freedom as choice is also change, which is defined by the end that it projects, "that is by the future which it has to be."[52] In deploying the technical and philosophical concept of free-dom, Sartre intends to represent autonomy of choice.[53] This choice, however, must be complemented by acting. In point of fact, Sartre views this choice as identical with acting. Exercising a mere intellectual option in one's mind with-out any corresponding application in the world is an exercise in futility. He writes: "It is necessary, however, to note that the choice, being identical with acting, supposes a commencement of realization in order that the choice may be distinguished from the dream and the wish."[54] This, of course, is all consis-tent with Sartre's attempts to eschew a human nature and his commitment to a world that is virtually empty apart from the contents of human contribution. Action is the surest way to bring anything resembling causal efficacy into the world. The world stands incomplete before me. A world replete with meanings that I inherit represents only a simulacrum of the potential for further mean-ings and values. My actions and creations contribute to the architectonics of a world that belongs to me as much as it belongs to those before me who have molded it in their image. In this way my exercise of freedom and my projec-tion of ends *ought to* cause me anguish.[55] I realize that in a world in which there are not any preordained decrees, values, goals, and ends, when I decide on a value and choose it and effect it as an end in the world, it carries what I would call normative import; that is, it suggests what I estimate ought to be done and the way things ought to be. My action carries such import because in some sense I am implying that such-and-such a value or such-and-such an end rep-resents the ideal way of living. My actions are in some sense seductive because in a world in which there is a plethora of possibilities from which to choose and in which no one need out of necessity choose *any specific option* (indeed one could choose not to choose any option at all), I hold the power to make such-and-such a value seem attractive, tempting, glamorous, and normatively desirable. I therefore carry the weight of the world on my shoulders. I am responsible for the world. Sartre writes: "We are taking the word 'responsibility' in its ordinary sense as consciousness (of) being the incontestable author of an event or of an object."[56]

Undoubtedly this sense of anguish that I and others feel is questionable. I wonder if the advertisers of milk and Ivana Trump feel anguish when, on the pages of a national magazine advertising that milk is rich in calcium without all the fat, Ivana declares: "And dahlin' you can never be too rich or too thin." In light of the anorexic disorders and the rampant avarice and vulgar materialism expressed even in young children who demand that their low-wage parents fork out money for expensive Nike shoes and Nintendo games, one wonders if such promoters, along with countless others involved in marketing and distribution strategies, feel the anguish Sartre writes about. A more likely possibility is that often individuals feel a sense of titillation and power as a result of this capacity they possess. If this is predominantly the case, I think that Sartre's point is still left intact. We may take Sartre's notion of responsibility and anguish as normative. That is, it *should* be the case that human beings should feel this responsibility and should be inclined to reflect deeply on their projects and ends in light of their seductiveness. Sartre's claim is not dependent on individuals' subjective feelings but is an objective philosophical observation about (the nature of) responsibility in situation.

Fundamentally, then, when we talk about choices, we are talking about ends—the ends one chooses and the ends that characterize one's being, so to speak. In choosing such ends, one confers on them what Sartre calls *transcendent existence.*[57] Individuals define their own being in and through their participation. They decide to define their being by their ends, ends that are attainable through action. When we speak of an existentialist self, then, we are talking about a self in action—a self that ontologically communicates in the world primarily through action that holds powers of transformation. Every project of freedom is an open, as opposed to a closed, project.

Despite the fact that freedom is a fact of human reality, it is not impervious to threats either from the individual or from others. To take the first, let us introduce the fact that I am a being-for-others. That is, upon reflection I realize that I am a consciousness for others. I am perceived, identified, and judged to be a certain kind of entity by others. I am many types to others. To my mother I am sensitive and fragile; to certain friends, strong-willed and driven; to my lover, nurturing and possessive; to Americans, a black man; to

Caribbeans, a brown-skinned man without a race. Another person—an Other—possesses freedom, and his freedom may threaten my own freedom. The existence of the Other represents a limitation on my freedom because I am not free from the determination of myself as an object for the Other. The Other is not a for-itself in his appearance to me.[58] He appears before me as an impenetrable consciousness. I am not able to apprehend for myself the self that I am for the Other. This means that because I do not inhabit the consciousness of another, I can never fully calibrate exactly how I am perceived by others; I can never know the reality of myself that I am for them. Likewise, I am unable to apprehend on the basis of the Other-as-object that appears to me what the Other is for himself.[59] I cannot penetrate and inhabit his consciousness and the being that he is for himself. I cannot experience the Other and know him in the way that he experiences his reality and knows himself. We can see that one of the basic outcomes of this dilemma is that each individual begins to seem like an object before the Other. We begin to reduce each other to beings-in-themselves. Sartre brings our attention to this solipsistic dilemma by his concept of *the look,* or *le regard,* which is also a sort of theatrical philosophical amplification of the concept of being-for-others. The look is basically the primordial revelation that another person is, like myself, a subject rather than simply one more object. It comes about through my realization of the permanent possibility of my being seen, being looked at, by that Other.[60]

In point of fact, if I may be permitted a minor relevant aside here, I would say that while the Sartrean characterization of the look in its entire scope lies beyond the purview of this book, in its fundamental outline, much of it is metaphorically extrapolatable to those aspects of the Natural Attitude that I find problematic. Consider the following characterization of what the look essentially represents: "By the Other's look, I am fixed within the world; things no longer have a simple relation to me; rather I and my situation are related to him as instruments. Further, I am aware of this and recognize myself as now being in the world with my possibilities objectified and fixed by him."[61]

At all times, we must remember, we are free. Part of what is represented by this freedom is negation of the given, even if, I submit, such a negation is at best an internal psychological stance or an attitude expressed in the life of the mind, which may not find immediate expression in everyday life. George Stack identifies the significant characteristic of my encounter with the Other as a reciprocal relationship of negation. When recognizing the Other, he is determined as an object. My own recognition of the Other is a recognition also of myself as an object in the consciousness of the Other.[62] Stack cites Sartre's argument that being-for-others entails a dual internal negation insofar as one would seek to act upon the internal negation by which the Other transcends my transcendence. Even if such acting upon the freedom of another were futile, the entire process, Stack argues, is obviously dialectical. He writes: "Precisely in the very recognition of oneself as transcending the transcendence of others one sees oneself in a social milieu which is quite different from our immediate experience of beings-in-themselves in a world."[63] Knowledge of myself as an object-for-others is meaningful and already humanized. Stack writes: "Sartre's entire analysis of the existence of others and my being for them reveals a social dimension of human relationships characterized by the interplay of individual consciousness and individual bodies. . . . Sartre no longer speaks of the world for *my* consciousness, but of the world in which I am an object for others and others are objects for me."[64]

In Sartrean ontology a firm simultaneity must hold: human reality is both being-for-itself and being-for others.

I think that there is something profoundly democratic in the midst of existentialist participatory metaphysics that one would normally designate as the provenance of a God or of an Atman. Despite the fact that the for-itself is not the foundation of its being and despite the fact that its own freedom constitutes and points to its own limitations however it might conceive of and constitute itself, it is not done in terms of a human essence that is given a priori. Quite the contrary. Sartre writes:

It is in its efforts to choose itself as a personal self that the for-itself sustains in existence certain social and abstract characteristics which make of it a man (or woman); and the necessary connections which accompany the essential elements of man appear only on the foundation of a free choice; in this sense each for-itself is responsible in its being for the existence of a human race. But it is necessary for us again to stress the undeniable fact that the for-itself can choose itself only beyond certain meanings of which it is not the origin. Each for-itself, in fact, is a for-itself only by choosing itself beyond nationality and race just as it speaks only by choosing the designation beyond the syntax and morphemes. This "beyond" is enough to assure its total independence in relation to the structures which it surpasses; but the fact remains that it constitutes itself as beyond in relation to these particular structures. What does this mean? It means that the for-itself arises in a world which is a world for other for-itselfs. Such is the given. And thereby, as we have seen, the meaning of the world is alien to the for-itself. This means simply that each man finds himself in the presence of meanings which do not come into the world through him. He arises in a world which is given to him as already looked-at, furrowed, explored, worked over in all its meanings, and whose very context is already defined by these investigations. In the very act by which he unfolds his time, he temporalizes himself in a world whose temporal meaning is already defined by other temporalizations: this is the fact of simultaneity. We are not dealing here with a limit of freedom; rather it is in this world that the for-itself must be free; that is, it must choose itself by taking into account these circumstances and not ad libitum.[65]

This metaphysical license for self-creation and self-reorientation is not, however, sufficient to goad one into action. Indeed if human reality is characterized as freedom and if one's situation in the world is one of radical freedom or abandonment, then this piece of facticity, so to speak, is a bit of information that one can overlook, negate, and refuse to participate in. Humans can and often do refuse to recognize their freedom despite the fact that they cannot choose not to be free. Sartre's intuition of human freedom must at all times be understood as two-sided: freedom as a fundamental fact about the human condition, and freedom as an often suppressed and always threatened asymptotic objective of human activity.[66] Sartre, for whom freedom was the supreme value and the basis and prerequisite for all values, is unequivocal on this point. Sartre writes:

> Human reality may be defined as a being such that in its being its freedom is at stake because human reality perpetually tries to refuse to recognize its freedom. Psychologically in each one of us this amounts to trying to take the causes and motives as things. We try to confer permanence upon them. We attempt to hide from ourselves that their nature and their weight depend each moment on the meaning which I give to them; we take them for constants. This amounts to considering the meaning which I gave to them just now or yesterday—which is irremediable because it is past—and extrapolating from it a character fixed still in the present. I attempt to persuade myself that the cause is as it was.[67]

This admonition is crucial, for I think that here Sartre has identified human complicity in sometimes religionizing, reifying, and hypostatizing tribal ontology and the problematic aspects of the Natural Attitude as I have described them. Attitudinally and by default, some of us against our better judgment maintain the delimiting and antifreedom aspects of the Natural Attitude. We in effect confer too much ontological respect upon those meanings, values, and principles that we inherit and uncritically accept. It is true, for example, that we do not choose our immediate culture, or what I may term *the value-bearing milieu*. We are, however, responsible for the reluctance to remove ourselves from the authoritative hold they have on our moral lives. We are responsible for exercising critical moral reason over our lives and deciding which cultural features of our socializing world ought to be dispensed with, realizing, of course, the enormous difficulty of such an enterprise and perhaps the ultimate impossibility of successfully completing this moral campaign.

An *ontologically disrespectful,* or, more charitably, an ontologically iconoclastic, attitude is not vengeful, destructive, or nihilistic. Such an attitude undermines the spirit of seriousness from the reified tenets that regulate one's life. In recognizing one's freedom and one's capacity to invest this superstructure with a meaning of one's own, one possesses a degree of power—not power in the coercive sense but in the sense that one's freedom, and therefore one's executed action in the world, is what I would call a form of *ontological revisionism.* That is, one can restructure one's being radically. There is a great deal of evidence to substantiate the point that I am making. It relates to what Sartre would call *the lived experience,* or *le vécu.* Consider, for example, those individuals who at some level realize the leveling aspect of living an uncritical national identity, and those defined in strictly racial terms in ways that overshadow other meaningful aspects of their identities who in a spirit of defiance attempt to problematize and then refute the logic on which such categories are spuriously built.[68]

If freedom is two-pronged, then it should be perfectly clear by now that taking up this freedom into an active life plan is not automatic. If so, then the process of self-creation and resocialization of a self molded by others can be stymied. What then motivates the individual to action? What factors force her to recognize this freedom and to live it in the existential sense in the service of a life that she chooses?

I am going to suggest that specific features of her condition spur her in the project of acting on this freedom and thus accomplishing some form of self-creation. What I aim to do next is to unearth a fundamental state of lack within human reality. This state of lack and its pangs of ontological hunger can act as a possible motivation for the human subject to embrace and enact this freedom in the construction of a self in becoming. In so doing, the individual will come to see a certain truth about her position in the world: a nakedness about the state of her consciousness that has been clothed in postulates, edicts, meanings, and values other than her own. She will see the prejudices, conformism, and cultural accouterments that have all been taken for a staid but false representation of being.

ONTOLOGICAL LACK AND REBELLIOUSNESS

At the heart, or one could say the stomach, of much existential thought is the notion of lack. This lack is identified in many ways by several of existentialism's progenitors. Nevertheless, the indisputable observation one makes is that human reality is plagued by a fundamental sense of incompleteness and a yearning for being. It might announce itself as a yearning for something higher, such the existence of life on a more exalted and majestic plane, in order to transcend the mundane routine of everyday life.

Two basic themes in Gabriel Marcel's profound and probing *The Mystery of Being* speak to this sense of lack in the self and ground his theory of becoming and self-actualization. According to Marcel, most individuals experience a deep sense of ontological exigence. It is not a desire "but an interior urge which can be interpreted as an appeal: There is a demand for the existence of being."[69] This urge is an exigence for fullness. In truth, much of what concerned Marcel throughout his life was the way in which a postindustrial society tended to define human beings in terms of their functions. People in essence become the functions and the roles assigned to them, with the attendant loss of a deeper connection they might have with themselves and their fellow humans. Individuals find that they simply cannot put their hearts into their functions.[70] The consequences are felt compellingly in the form of a lack of something, an impoverishment and an aridity.[71] It is as an appeal from the depths of one's being and an "urge" (élan) toward an affirmation of that being. It exists in everyone. Marcel saw it as an intrinsic human characteristic. We desire a fullness that is not quantitative in design. He describes this fullness as the urge, or longing, for being. This fullness that stems from a pervasive lack, however, stands as the contradiction of the "hollowness of a functionalized world and of the overpowering monotony of a society in which beings take on more and more the appearance of specimens which it is increasingly difficult to differentiate."[72]

The functionalized world in which individuals find themselves enmeshed can be said to represent a pseudoreality that is presented to the will before the latter can even exercise its proper function. There is for Marcel a profound reality that is denied personalization and a form of personal "being toward which one feels an exigency."[73] Patricia Sanborn makes the interesting claim that while Marcel believes that ontological lack has to be transcended in order for the self to be, he is not readily forthcoming with a phenomenological account of ontological sufficiency. What is important about Marcel's notion of exigence, however, is that it acts as a catalyst toward a deeper and more satisfying sense of self. Sanborn argues that if every individual has within her a basic push toward selfhood, then the appeal must break through her functionalization and force recognition.[74] The dissatisfaction and the sense of lack, at first a reaction against the world and others, eventually pushes us to focus on our lives. We become aware of a gap between what we now are and what we can be. We sense that by a movement of conversion we can approach the latter state. This awareness is based on the fact that we each have a vague sense of who we are. Accompanying this sense is an urge to move beyond what we are now.[75]

Sanborn's analysis strikes me as correct. If it is true that Marcel refrains from supplying the details of sufficiency, he has at least not taken its realization outside the scope of human possibility. This possibility, which Marcel grounds in a spirit of restlessness, is one that I will take up later and put in the service of the ontologically rebellious self. Marcel's idea of restlessness depicts the individual as a wayfarer, a voyager always on the way. He says that there is never any rest for us, there is no final high terrace to which we can climb. Our condition in this world is that of "a wanderer, an itinerant being, who cannot come to absolute rest."[76] We are wayfarers always moving toward a goal that we both see and do not see. Marcel, arguing that most people are strangers to their own depths, locates the grandeur of the individual within this ontological deficiency or lack. We are not diminished by this lack and this ignorance of our own depths. It is this sense of incompleteness that makes our humanity so rich and indeterminate. People are always in the making, always becoming. It is this lack and the hunger born from it that drive us to become.

Philosophy remains for me an enduringly beautiful and sumptuous enterprise because of the many ways in which daily life reinforces its quest for deeper meaning, truth, and heroism. My friend Kevin, in a conversation about my notion of an ordered moral becoming that leads to a moral cosmopolitan identity, once asked me, "Who in the world has time to become?" Certainly not he; and if not he, then no one else but myself. This comment I regard as ironic since it long predates a small but persistent dilemma he faces in the challenges of balancing fatherhood, career, and a nostalgic commitment to maintaining some semblance of the life of the mind. In our many warm and wistful conversations he often confessed that as much as he enjoyed married life, fatherhood, and the good fortune of owning his own company, he yearned for and appreciated moments of solitude when he had the opportunity to commune with his beloved journal. It is in the journal that some of his strongest quests for becoming are identified. It is there that the not-yet aspect of his being presents itself like the desperate, pleading cries of a fetus longing to be born. The journal and the moments of solitude reveal the exigency, the depth, and the deficiency. Yet it is a depth that I suspect he cannot deeply acknowledge since the fundamental requirement for its fulfillment—time—is distressingly scarce. I do not take this tension in his life, however, as proof that conscious or moral becoming is futile. Rather, the desire for it and its inescapability in one form or another are phenomena rooted deeply in the human condition. I interpret Marcel's notion of the deficiency and the lack as heroic or a form of grandeur because it acts as the ultimate catalyst in further self-creation and re-creation.

Tribal ontology, with its ready-made forms of racial/ethnic ascriptives, covers up this lack, conceals it from wayfaring beings. We are force-fed a diet of false essentialisms. Tribal postulates do have this essentializing force. "But our ethnicity is the essential nature of who we are," Kevin announces to me from time to time as he tries to balance the identities he holds as South African and Jew. Such is the nature of the hypostatizing force of tribal bequests, that they make us feel that there is nothing beneath them. An inheritance is, after all, something that one freely acquires. Nothing efficacious is required of one. No earning need be done. It is yours. The tribe hands us its frames of interpretation, its values, and its model of an authentic humanity. We are spared the responsibility not just of judging the values and the model of the tribe but of creating assemblages or models of our own authorship. The assemblages have to be earned by a willingness to go beyond the givens of the tribe. In going beyond, we see the infinite capacity to be more than our participation in the tribe. In going beyond, we bear witness to the enormous space, the void, that demands our courageous participation.

Perhaps no philosopher in the existential pantheon offers a more exalted paean to the ache of this lack than Unamuno. Meditate on the following extract:

> The visible universe, the universe that is created by the instinct of self-preservation, becomes all too narrow for me. It is like a cramped cell, against the bars of which my soul beats its wings in vain. Its lack of air stifles me. More, more and always more! I want to be myself, and yet without ceasing to be myself to be others as well, to merge myself into the totality of things visible and invisible, to extend myself into the illimitable of space and to prolong myself into the infinite of time.[77]

Unamuno identifies this lack as a hunger for immortality, which he thinks is the basic quest for human beings. Gaining fame and recognition is a way of achieving a sense of immortality that relieves our ontological angst. This hunger is not an abstract feeling. It is a concrete hunger.[78] Unamuno declares that self-perpetuation is his task and that we "aim at being all because in that we see the only means of escaping from being nothing."[79] This lack that breeds a hunger within us cannot be formulated in conceptual propositions susceptible of rational discussion. It simply announces itself in us as hunger announces itself. He writes: "Neither can the wolf that throws itself with the fury of hunger upon its prey or with the fury of instinct upon the she-wolf, enunciate its impulse rationally and as a logical problem."[80] The presence of ontological hunger in Unamuno's philosophy leads ultimately to a gargantuan spiritual cannibalistic feast. The characteristic of true individuality, he notes, consists "in nourishing oneself with other individualities and in giving oneself to them as nourishment."[81] A poet in one of Unamuno's novels announces: "I do not want to devour others. Let them devour me. How beautiful it is to be a victim! To give oneself as spiritual food . . . to be consumed . . . to dissolve in the soul of others."[82] In *Niebla,* a character entertains the idea of devouring oneself. Still another character declares that "cannibalism is the perfect thing, believe me, anthropophagy. Man can only live off other men . . . we must eat souls, which are . . . most painful to digest. Feed on them and give your own as food."[83] Unamuno's identification of the self as a bottomless pit and an insatiable force speaks eloquently, however, to the tragic paradox of the human situation: our endeavors only leave us hungrier. Ontological fulfillment is a lifelong process that has no end because for Unamuno we have no end and no sense of completion and satisfaction here on earth. The hunger prevails as more and more through our becoming we exceed our definitions and the limitations placed on our excessive appetite by a watchful civilization. I think of his dramatic metaphor, "Human society is nothing but a theatrical company . . . and the social self is nothing but a hypocrite."[84] Unamuno, like Carl Jung and the Buddhists, is sympathetic to the notion that the self is a hazardous construction and sees selfhood as a sort of heuristic abstraction.[85] This means that it is fundamentally interpretable, or open to interpretation.

Similarly, Ortega appeals to this notion of lack that manifests itself in several ways in the life of the individual. In *Man and Crisis* he speaks on more than one occasion of the hunger in the individual to be and to submit to the desire to be as one is, to realize one's most highly individual "I." It was Ortega's concern that the authenticity and the depth, so to speak, of the individual's soul was becoming lost under the weight of others' postulates, edicts, ideas, and banner of respectability. My opinion, he says, consists in repeating what I hear others say. But exactly who is that Other or those Others to whom I entrust the task of being me?[86] Reacting to much of what I have found to be problematic about the Natural Attitude that imprisons individuality, Ortega laments that "people" is an irresponsible "I," the "I" of society, the social "I." When I live on what "they say" and fill my life with it, I have replaced the "I" that I myself am in solitude with the mass "I." I have in effect made myself people. Instead of living my own life, I am deciding it by changing it to otherness.[87]

Ortega accomplishes two things here. First, he identifies the underlying factors that often exacerbate the sense of existential lack in human reality (which one could reasonably see as a natural ontological feature of human reality) or that actually cause this sense of lack. One's sense of self, or the innermost depth of one's being, becomes buried under the weight of social postulates and naturalized forms of living that bear little resemblance to one's own personal constitution or one's desire for a new self. But lacking the culinary substance to satisfy the hunger of ontological exigence,[88] the social accouterments quickly dissipate, leaving a famished and perturbed soul.

Second, Ortega highlights the genesis of ontological rebelliousness that I shall bring into sharper relief later on. The compulsory social garb that is too small for one's spiritual appetite or just ill suited for the idiosyncratic and peculiar nature of one's constitution is thrown off in a spirit of defiance in much the way that an eleven-year-old twin—on the cusp of adolescence and therefore struggling for an autonomous identity—declares that she is sick and tired of being dressed like her sister. Ortega's articulation of culture as interfering with the individuality of man strikes me as too dismissive in a general sense. He ought to have made a distinction between the nurturing aspects of culture that encourage one to choose one's own conception of a good life (this is what is supposed to be embraced by liberalism) and the pernicious aspects of culture that seek to authoritatively bind one into a supraimage. Nevertheless, I take Ortega's articulation as essential in identifying the mistake many make in lazily adhering to the notion that what we have identified as ontological lack is something that can be quickly satisfied by the collective diet provided by dominant elements of culture.

The notion of lack also plays a role in Sartre's phenomenological and ontological account of human reality. Lack appears in the world only with the upsurge of human reality.[89] Identifying lack in the for-itself, Sartre states that what it lacks is a certain particular and concrete reality. It lacks something for something else as the broken disc of the moon lacks that which would be necessary to complete and transform it into a full moon.[90] Just as the crescent moon lacks a fragment of the moon in order to be a full moon, so the for-itself lacks the in-itself, or, we could say, a dimension that would lead to fullness or wholeness analogous to the fullness or wholeness of the moon. Every consciousness lacks something for something. Lack does not come to it from without, like the crescent moon versus the full moon. The lack of the for-itself is a lack that it is.[91] This lack, in Sartre's system, is the foundation of its own nothingness. Lacks are human, and human beings are constantly in the position of lacking. In other words, lack is a fundamental part of our makeup as human beings. Our attempts at trying to make good our lack are an important aspect of our existence.

What I am particularly concerned with, therefore, are the ways in which this sense of lack, despite its varied conceptions in existentialist literature, is actually experienced on some psychoemotional level by individuals in their existence and the implications this must have for their lives. I say this as a postscript to the idea that freedom is two-pronged and that it is not always immediately embraced as the ontological reality it really is in our lives. If this lack is experienced and felt deeply, then it might be the factor that pushes one into ontological rebelliousness and robust self-creation. I submit further that ontological hunger, or the hunger for being, is a propelling feature that will wake the individual from her self-imposed slumber regarding her freedom. It is a catalyst. The individual recognizes that her functionality, her roles, and the various vestiges of garb that have been customized for her to wear by a collective and impersonal army of designers cannot form the substance for the fulfillment she craves. Ontological hunger is the motivator that will force the individual to take that first step toward embracing and recognizing her freedom and then putting that freedom to a project part of whose outcome will provide some form of ontological fulfillment. The lack, therefore, forces one in many ways to eclipse the "natural" functions of one's existence and, perhaps for the first meaningful time in one's life, to apply creativity and imagination to the business of metaphysically earning one's own unique existence. Part of what triggers this hunger might be a habit of simply getting stuck to the given that one has been reared on, despite the natural tendency or proclivity for becoming, which, as I have argued, is an embedded feature of the human condition. Ontological hunger is a way of getting unstuck in much the way that the baby eagle stuck on the mountainside must learn to flee its environment after being weaned by its mother and after the tiny shreds of meat she now occasionally brings become insufficient for an expanding omnivorous appetite that can only be satisfied by it own efforts.

The surpassing of the assumed so-called naturalness of our existence—the willingness to eclipse the natural functions of our prescribed roles and other aspects of our existence in the way that aestheticizers of the body eclipse the natural function of the ears, nose, navel, and nipples by piercing them with ornaments and sexual adventurers eclipse the functions of various parts of the body including the anus by eroticizing them—is the option of the moral becomer who feels this lack. The ontologically hungry must learn to redirect the trained and "naturalized" parts of their souls (so to speak) to new and daring tasks. In Sartrean terms one could say that many of us engage in the blind pursuit of being by hiding from ourselves the free project that is the actual pursuit. We, in effect, become passively obedient to every task.[92] If in fact we are, as Sartre says, responsible for our existence, and if freedom is an indisputable ontological condition of our existence, then it is my intuition that ontological lack and hunger are the phenomena that empirically force the individual into embracing this freedom and positing consciously a series of ends and projects for herself. Like the child who walks for hours without realizing that she has a bleeding cut on her foot until a friend points to the wound in amazement and then is possessed with an urge to tend to the wound and stop its bleeding, the ontologically hungry person, upon perceiving this lack, is compelled to take on the project of actual meaningful living.

In the aftermath of acknowledging the profound lack in her existence and the attendant call to action, the individual is ready for what may be called *ontological rebellion*. Ontological rebellion is not just an exercise in fulfillment of a whimsical nature. It is the partial requirement for throwing off the bequeathed and worn armor that one has uncritically taken to be the very real and metaphysical stuff of one's life—the accouterments that form the fabric of one's soul, the leitmotif that forms the supposed necessary linkage between oneself and one's fellow human beings: One's ethnicity, one's racial designation and identity, or the unquestioning patriotism that one feels is what, it is said, essentially makes one the most authentic type of person. Ontological rebellion does not just prevent the individual from acting like a programmed robot that absorbs the stereotypes that are supposed to typify his or her kind: the white adolescent South African boy who must insistently accuse his black classmate of plagiarism when the latter consistently defeats him in debates; or the Asian college freshman who, because he is ashamed of his parents' Chinese accent, speaks in an excruciatingly slow, moderate, and overly precise way. In affecting a style meant to undercut a stereotype, he merely reinforces it because of the extremity and uneasiness of his attempts.[93] Ontological rebellion will prove that the underlying factors to which the individual is responding are not just false in some cases but also are largely irrelevant in the context of two factors: one is his here-and-now uniqueness, his "nobody else like himself" mode of existence and the myriad responses he can actually effect in the world; the other is a powerful ontological feature of his human condition—the not-yet aspect of his being, the sense that regardless of how he finds himself predicated, there are alternative ways (of varying degrees and scales, depending on a host of factors) of being and existing in the world. Rather than construct a self that is largely reactionary and stands as a clinical corrective to a falsely perceived anomaly—as was the case with the Asian college freshman—the ontologically rebellious individual constructs a self that is grounded in a spirit of creative possibilities drawn from a hermeneutics he chooses to adopt in relation to such experiences. Here at this juncture the individual can put a very crucial aspect of chosen freedom in the service of ontological rebelliousness. To the extent that he understands this freedom, not as some sort of original choice or leap of faith, but in terms of powers of withdrawal—of refusal, of beginning something else—then it becomes, as Cooper describes it, a movement of escape.[94] The exercise of such powers requires an indifference to what people say, that is, when people are representative of the "they."[95]

According to philosopher Paul Schmidt:

> Ontological rebellion involves a diametrical shift in orientation aiming at rejection of very basic internal modes of existing within the concrete individual. Ontological rebellion enters the realm of possibility only after a metaphysical rejection of the concept of a fixed human nature and a historical rejection of legal-political systems. It is the most drastic form of rebellion, not just as change in one's manner of living arising from the rejecting of external social and natural conditions but an altering of the core of one's being. Having rejected metaphysical truths and social-historical principles, man now exhumes the depth of his being to reject himself, again and again, seeking to create himself.[96]

This conception of ontological rebelliousness bears close resemblance to the Brazilian theologian Leonardo Buff's conception of the actual human condition. He writes:

The Human being is a knot of relationships and throbbing in all directions. Humans are not focused on this or that object but on the totality of objects. Hence they are forever abandoning anything stuck and unlimited, and they are always protesting and challenging closed worlds. What lies within them is not simply being, but being-able-to-be. They are projection and striving toward an ever-more, toward an unknown . . . and the not-yet.[97]

The idea of the not-yet is central to the project of self-creation and ontological rebellion. The not-yet is the vast array of possibilities. The not-yet could stand as a presence, vague at times but nevertheless a firm and unshakable presence, suggesting to us that a radically different project of ourselves can be devised. Hence the lives of immigrants are fascinating because of the way their often radical upsurge into a different world topples the false pseudo-ontological foundations of their previous lives. Do the faculty members of Morehouse College in Atlanta really care that the new assistant professor of chemistry was an untouchable in his native India? Do many of the students, ignorant of world cultures and their typifications, care? The re-creation of the untouchable's life is an invocation of the existentialist theme found in Jaspers and Kierkegaard: The individual cannot be fully understood under universal categories since he really is inexhaustible in the endlessness of his concretion.[98] The outcast in one country has rejected his seemingly most intractable trait. Thus we see the inextricable link between the notion of an existential freedom and ontological rebelliousness. Sartre, as stated before, argues that the individual is not what he is. He cannot be defined in terms of what he might obviously be at the moment, because he can rise above this designation and channel the course of his becoming. One in essence transcends the "thingness," or ready-made object, that one is for others and that one is ontologically designated to be by the Natural Attitude. In other words, authentic creativity becomes dissimulated under the debris of the Natural Attitude. In transcending this, one comes that much closer to the task of resocializing the self.

Ontological rebellion has as one of its primary aims the attainment of a *metaphysics of the concrete,* that is, the autobiography of one's feelings.[99] A metaphysics of the concrete demands the turning of all of one's powers of observation in search of one's individual structure. The first-person grammar is the language for such a task, which stands in sharp contrast to the traditional metaphysics of the abstract. The latter was a history of systems presenting structures of universal scope applicable to the totality of existence.[100] The analysis of the structures of the concrete has its locus only in the individual. According to Schmidt, the language of the concrete is marked by four features: the first person singular; the unity of a present-time-to-me, which is a single whole made up of other single wholes; the living-space of my-feeling and my-bodying; and the expression of my concreteness in my-bodying.[101]

An ontological rebel in many ways is already a metaphysical rebel in one important respect: that of a fixed human nature. Sartre already provides many of the philosophical tools needed to legitimate a spirit of rebellion. Schmidt is generous in pointing out ways in which Sartre amplifies his project (although ultimately he thinks Sartre lapses into universal abstractionism). He notes that Sartre's radical concept of being-for-itself destroys in one swoop the apparatus of description via qualities (universals) each of which is what it is. Sartre gives us a being in whom change is not a mere shifting of qualities (universals) but a thickness of possibilities.[102] To the extent that being achieves a full congruence with all its facets and recognizes itself in all its peculiar dimensions and thereby frees itself from any hidden controls, Schmidt argues, one's actions will flow openly in accord with who one is.[103] Those actions are crucial in this phase of *being reorientation*, which is the goal of ontological rebellion. Action that is autonomously undertaken in a spirit of sincerity with respect to one's immediate experiences and the attention one pays to such experiences leads to a rejection tantamount to a drastic attitudinal shift. The dissolution of a deep-seated habit, Schmidt argues, will drastically alter the character of a person. He warns, however, that this dissolution could leave a person in limbo, which could be positively felt as a wider freedom of action no longer restricted by that habit, or negatively felt as a threat to the security of past regular behavior.[104] He admits:

My own response was positive, a freedom to embark on fresh paths of experience. Such fresh experiences provide the generative matrix for new valuings, new attitudes and habits. With the dissolution of the habit, a rigidity of character disappears and I am left with a wider appreciation of alternative life patterns of others. So rejection leads to a wider receptivity of alternatives. In this particular case, in which the rejection led to the view that ethical claims can be individual in intention, I found myself in a position to embark at once into new experiences since I alone choose my values and am alone responsible. There was no longer any need to persuade or wait for others; no need to consider the universal intention of the ethical judgment. This phase of my ethical rebellion produced a new sense of adventure, risk and freedom, the new "responsibility" vastly increasing the vitality of my existing.[105]

Many of the risks Schmidt talks about are connected with an interesting tale of intellectual and personal independence in which he transcended his dependencies on analytical and universalistic modes of thinking as a trained professional philosopher, sought a divorce, and distanced himself from the small-town mentality of myriad locales during his odyssey as college professor and department chair. His notion of ontological rebellion, legitimized via metaphysical rebellion, which he borrows from Camus, mandates the overthrow of all rules and laws as they bind and curtail the free movement of one's being. It is anarchy, he admits. But anarchy, as far as he is concerned, is not synonymous with chaos, destruction, and terror. Anarchy can lead to a loving, a sensitivity, and a communicating far more open, peaceful, and shared than any relation determined by rules and laws.[106] This is a controversial proposition that my intuition does not respect. However, I will not argue against this notion here. I wish to emphasize the faith Schmidt places in the sense of life of the onto-logical rebel who frees his being from the shackles of enculturation, social facts and currents, and binding edicts that seek to mold and shape the substantive aspect of his psyche. Schmidt argues that ontological rebellion not only bestows upon one a concrete freedom to choose the mode of one's existence but also grants one the freedom from all mechanisms that tend to make of an individual an object, an in-itself. One is granted the freedom for overcoming oneself, "a will to power within one's being for transcending one's being."[107] Sartrean nihilation rules! Ontological freedom refers, then, to a rejecting that is prima-rily internal to a single existent, "not against another, but monadic, within the fiber of my being."[108]

Schmidt writes of some of the direct effects of his ontological rebellion and the concomitant freedom he enjoyed. Referring to Thoreau, Margaret Fuller, and even Plato, he says:

> These Transcendental Idealists gave me the courage of their independent lives, each choosing his own way, each aiming at a purity of action that had meaning to him or her, given by ideals that functioned concretely in their lives. So I learned that I could choose my own pure ideal way and I did. I gave up studying physics and chemistry, choosing philosophy against the practical advice of all, choosing ideals of love and friendship, truth and beauty, nature and reality, simplicity and orderliness. These ideals were fine in the abstract, but how to embody them in my concrete existing as I faced the draft of World War II. Totally ignorant of conscientious objection, I enlist-ed in the Air Force to fly. Before active duty I enjoyed six months of initial explo-ration of these ideals in my existing, enough to solidify them in my being. Surpris-ingly enough, even during the period of active duty I was able to accept military orderliness and simplicity, form friendships, explore nature in different geographical places and pursue truth in reading at Air Base Libraries each evening.[109]

Schmidt's story is an example of ontological autobiography, which is the practice of ontology, or the search for being, in the form of self-narration. It is a form of self-exploration that is not tantamount to a quick psychological self-inventory but instead is a way of validating immediate perceptions, evaluations, and one's take on a situation at the moment. In short, ontological autobiogra-phy completes the process of portraying one's radical singularity. I think of Sartre's analysis of the Jew: "I am unable to feel myself as a Jew or as a minor or as Pariah."[110] Extrapolating the examples to fit a more personal mold: When

I bite into the delicious candy, do I experience it as a Caribbean man? When the funkiness of Louis Armstrong's trumpet inspires a thought I have about becoming, what sort of response is it? It may be similar to that of another, but it is mine and mine alone, incommunicable in its totality and not fully comprehensible even to me. Viscerally it is unlike those of another. Ontological rebellion and its material expression, ontological autobiography, grant us the power to validate all meaningful aspects of our existence while leaving us as the final authority in determining what is meaningful. It can allow us to implement the phenomenological method of bracketing and in so doing come to reject the false categories, artifices, and normative structures that legitimize authenticity and morality in our lives. Meditate upon the following scenarios as a way of understanding the situation.

Scenario 1: The Holocaust Survivor

I am a Holocaust survivor. I am standing in an art gallery admiring what I think is a beautiful painting of a young girl looking wistfully at a gravestone. I am moved by the painting, by the gloominess of the hills beyond, which contrasts with the bright red of the girl's dress. Beside the gravestone is a water hole, deep blue. I find myself weeping. It is just too much. On her face is written the pathos of a monumental history: it is a canvas on which hundreds of stories, histories, and unbroken dreams have been written. She looks too young to be full of so much wisdom. A man approaches me and says, "Yes, you are moved. I am too. It is by a great Nazi artist."

But it is still a great painting, I find myself saying to my friends, who are aghast at my response. No Jewish person, upon learning who the painter is, would continue to lavish such praise upon it. "Your continued fondness in light of the knowledge of its origin is immoral," I am told repeatedly.

They will not understand, I think to myself, and then reflect on the weirdness of life. A few days after my experience I saw a movie in which an old Holocaust survivor had come upon a postcard with an oil painting. The postcard had been done by Adolf Hitler. He kept repeating to everyone, "There is something here. He has captured something here that is truly amazing." The postcard became his most prized possession, and he burned it when his youngest son died of cancer.

Scenario 2: Jean Genet and the Attraction to the Perverse

Jean Genet, the French novelist and criminal, talked of being sexually attracted to Nazi officers at the same time that he was repulsed by their ideologies and the moral atrocities they perpetrated. Committed to civil rights principles, racial equality, and the ethos of the hippie movement in America, he recounts his sexual arousal and fascination at the sight of the policemen in their black boots beating down rioters in the streets, all this while despising them and morally condemning them with every fiber of his being.

Scenario 3: The Beauty of War

I am standing in a field that was scorched and ravaged by an attack from a neighboring country. The field, once embellished and surrounded by temples, mosques, and beautiful homes, is now surrounded by piles of rubble and debris. But for just one moment in the midst of all this war I felt something, I saw something beyond the terror and the loss and the devastation. In the months since then, no one has been able to share what I felt. Most recount their sense of loss, of fear, of anger. A few have said that they feel we deserved it because of our selfish and lavish lifestyles, which just were not right when across the border others lived in misery and poverty.

A few months later, leafing through a book in a bookstore, I came across a writer who I feel captures what in my being I struggled with when he writes that war can be beautiful because "it initiates the dreamt-of metalization of the human body. War is beautiful because it enriches a flowering meadow with the fiery orchids of machine guns. War is beautiful because it combines the gun-fire, the cannonades, the cease-fire, the scents, and the stench of putrefaction into a symphony."[111]

Because ontological rebellion is a way of opening up oneself to new experiences, it is ideally suited for providing a very critical space within which to heuristically judge one's life and experiences: the rebellion ideally bridges the chasm between the radical singularity that one is and the containment against which one must struggle. Ontological rebellion is achieved via narration, not proof or explanation. As the scenarios are meant to suggest, the disparate elements of one's being cannot be ruled and bullied by the artifices and dictates of the Natural Attitude. One way of interpreting the scenarios is to suggest that they could capture what Friedrich Nietzsche would call *the capacity to feel unhistorically.* Commenting on the need for human forgetfulness in the second of the *Untimely Meditations,* he writes:

> In the case of the smallest or of the greatest happiness, however, it is always the same thing that makes happiness: the ability to forget or, expressed in more scholarly fashion, the capacity to feel unhistorically during its duration. He who cannot sink down on the threshold of the moment and forget all the past, who cannot stand balanced like a goddess of victory without growing dizzy and afraid, will never know what happiness is.[112]

The scenarios, I hope, will allow us to do more than look at the existence of paradoxes in human responses and evaluations. To the extent that such paradoxes are brought to light within the lives of moral agents, this should suggest the incompetence and triviality of dismissing outright the legitimacy of here-and-now experiences and the error of characterizing them as sick or twisted because they fail to register "authentic" responses, that is, responses that are not encased within some majoritarian interpretive paradigm. They point to something deeper that identity designations (racial/ethnic/national) of the Natural Attitude just cannot do away with. Such identities, again, are often smug, arbitrary, sociopolitically contrived, and inappropriate for the actual psychoexistential state of the individual. The responses, however, are not. They are profound and emerge from the depths of an existence that is not analogous to what we mistakenly take as examples of being: social identities. Ontological rebellion taken far enough leads to new forms of self-ownership that are vital for any resocialization of self and for the project of self re-creation. The ontological rebel, then, is iconoclastic, irreverent, and a risk taker. Such features of the self are important ingredients for those who identify themselves as moral cosmopolitans. The scenarios, to the extent that they capture the ways that emotional and aesthetic responses often fall outside neat and tidy moral paradigms and socially sanctioned ways of viewing the world, qualify as ontologically rebellious sketches. Rendered in autobiographical ways and accompanied by a degree of forgetting—that is, forgetting the stultifying mind-set of the Natural Attitude—we see that individuals can locate within themselves unique and unforeseen ways of experiencing their worlds and the reorientation of being. When we speak of a reorientation of being, a breaking of the internalized modes of external authority within, we get an idea of what ontological rebellion looks like and how it is crucial for any meaningful attempt at authentic self re-creation.

EXISTENCE AND THE THREAT OF THE OTHER: OVERCOMING RACIAL IDENTITIES

Now we must face a very practical and concrete issue head on. What are we to do when the existence of the Other or the edicts of significant others pose a serious threat to our projects? Sartre acknowledges that the Other's existence does effect a factual limit to our freedom, since the upsurge of the Other brings about certain determinations that we are without having chosen them.

Here we are, Jew or Aryan, handsome or ugly, with no hope of apprehending these meanings that we have outside and no hope of changing them.[113] We inherit, Sartre tells us, a world of meanings and signs that we did not create. We come into the world basically as secondhand consumers, and these characteristics define us as being-for-others. In our unique model of existing, we can't feel ourselves as these things as we are perceived by the Other. Sartre instructs us to react against such interdictions, declaring, for example, that race is simply a collective fiction. In doing so, we encounter total alienation in being something that we have not chosen to be. Good Sartrean counsel would address the fact that although we do not choose to be for the Other what we are, we can try to choose for ourselves what we are for the Other by choosing ourselves such as we appear to the Other.[114] This we can choose as an end for ourselves, as a fundamental project. Although we have at our disposal a plethora of ways of assuming our being-for-others, we are not able not to assume it. Despite the panoply of choices that we make in responding to our status of being-for-others, we are still in some way forced to grapple with this undeniable ontological phenomenon. Even indifference to it is still a stance toward it.

There are a number of empowering ways in which we can face the tension between that aspect of the for-itself with which we identify and the being-for-others that we are in a social sense but that undermines those aspects of ourselves that we identify as authentically ours. I am attracted to the idea of transforming one's being-for-others in such a fashion that the way others eventually see one will bear closer resemblance to the for-itself that one has incorporated into one's sense of self. I am, therefore, interested in the coercive possibilities and powers of the for-itself. I hope that eventually we can arrive at a situation where the split between the two ontological spheres of the for-itself and being-for-others is undermined. The Other would then be more likely to see me as I authentically see myself. I believe that this is what much of feminism and black liberation has been about.

Consider the plight of the black woman who knows herself to be brilliant but who in the presence of certain white racialists and/or racist individuals must comport herself in ways that appease their expectations. That is, she must underplay her acute intelligence and be deferential in intellectual discussions while in their presence, lest her boss, who happens to be such an individual, becomes intimidated and finds a reason to refuse her a promotion she deserves. She may navigate between these states of frustrating tensions by playing the game and acting out a role while trying to maintain self-respect and some semblance of allegiance to her values. She may dismiss the reality of the being-for-others that she is, refuse to grant it any ontological seriousness and value, adhere to a standard of loyalty to that portion of the for-itself she incorporates into her sense of self, and bear the consequences proudly, maintaining all the while that the integrity of being true to her deepest vision and deepest sense of self is worth the punishment meted out in a world dominated by those for whom she is a certain type of being. Is this a form of bad faith? I think the worry over bad faith is both irrelevant and unhelpful in much the same way that I have regarded as often trivial and unhelpful the Christian judgment of sin against a certain type of behavior from the viewpoint of the person who is being besieged with the label. In a spirit of ontological rebellion, such an individual would not be put off by the term of bad faith but rather would seek creative measures to respond to the demands of her immediate experiences and the remedies suggested by such experiences. Such remedies may turn out to be forms of good faith, or they may not. My point is that as a roving, independent, and autonomous creative creature, the ontological rebel sees the notion of bad faith as irrelevant to her life.

In many respects, I would suggest, one is actually not the being-for-others that is often claimed. In fact, in many cases one's being-for others is a constructed fiction that really has no relation to the reality that one is. When I speak of reality in this sense, I am speaking of the for-itself as the one who makes herself be, as the one by whom there really is a world, and who is compelled to decide the meaning of being. Again I am describing the for-itself in concrete personal terms rather than as a metaphysical entity. The being-for-others that the black woman is—that is, an intellectually deficient and less-than-human creature—is a delusional construction in the minds of certain racists, who may have the power to create policies and social edicts that are founded on those fantastic constructions. Over time those constructions take on the demeanor of normality and rationality. However, any free-choosing aspect of the for-itself that defines itself within the delusional and fictional boundaries of a false being-for-others schema is plainly complicitous in perpetuating a lie. In other words, if you grant too much legitimacy to the personification of yourself that others have anomalously, you are responsible for according a degree of reality to a place where no reality exists. It is obvious that Sartre has given us some emancipatory tools to deal with this existential dilemma faced in any encounter between the for-itself and the being-for-others. Yet I think that the concept of being-for-others is a much more complex and less straightforward phenomenon than Sartre wants to make of it, at least in *Being and Nothingness.*

In cases where one's being-for-others is both an ontological lie and an existential pathology, one needs to speak more in terms of living beyond being-for-others in the name of real and radical freedom. That is, the entire oppressive project of choosing myself such as I appear to the Other is to be abandoned.[115]

In effect one would not be evading one's freedom and embodiment, but, rather, showing that one's embodiment simply misses the anomalous criteria of the being-for-others standard. By suggesting that one lives beyond being-for-others, I mean that there are moments when one's being-for-others is a pathological lie. I believe that, for example, the entire predication of race in this country rests on false categories. Race has already been proven to be biologically unfounded; that is, the concept of race as a biological category and a natural kind is untenable. When race is propagated falsely as something that is metaphysically real, as is certainly the case in this country, when the racial purity is measured against a one-drop standard that categorizes all persons with a hint of African ancestry as black, and when it is impossible for any woman classified as black to bear a child who could be classified as white, one begins to realize the extent to which our social reality and our sociopolitical institutions are the products of conceptual hallucinations. But these hallucinations are normalized and granted epistemological validation by the culture at large. Reality has been grossly misinterpreted, and those who detect the cognitive aberrations or, worse, those who actually figure out what the correct interpretation is, are labeled confused, paranoid, whiners, complainers, race obsessed, and troublemakers. Philosopher Charles Mills regards white misunderstanding, misrepresentation, evasion, and self-deception on matters related to race as "among the most pervasive mental phenomena of the past few hundred years."[116]

OVERCOMING RACIAL ASCRIPTIVES

In "Race, Life, Death, Identity, Tragedy, and Good Faith," philosopher Naomi Zack carries forth the task of ontological rebellion in a very insightful and empowering way.[117] Deconstructing the notion of race, she argues that racial identification is a third-person description with a built-in distance from a self. She ultimately advocates the shedding of one's racial identity as the only meaningful way of fighting racial injustice.

Zack demonstrates the false metaphysics upon which race is predicated. No genes or chromosomal markers for any of the designated racial groups have been identified. There are no verified correlations between so-called racial biological traits. She argues that empirically assumed biological traits of race are actually a changing range of biological traits that are no different from other biological traits except that they happen to have been selected as racial.[118] Race exists in the minds of those assigning racial ascriptions, not in the bodies of the racially identified. She argues that the biological characteristics of whiteness are insufficient to empirically ground a concept of race. Shedding one's racial identity involves regarding one's physical characteristics as what they are without adding false racial qualities to them. She writes:

> For example, brown skin, in any of its particular hues, is exactly what it is visually perceived to be in the normal course of human visual perception and its racialization is a false addition. One may, in good faith, look in the mirror and see a person with the shade of brown skin one has. To think one sees a "black person" or a "brown person"—or a black or brown man or woman, as gender is relevant—is in bad faith. That is, the racialization of one's skin color is part of the cultural mendacity of the con-

struction of race. Assuming the word "brown" as a description of a person's skin is not itself a racial term, the brownness of a person's skin does not have the biological force to operate as an attribute of the entire person, for example, her internal organs, bones and nerves, not to mention her emotions, thoughts and actions.[119]

Racial identification falsely has as its goal the biological body as its subject. Race is thus oppressively attached to human biology, but race is not itself biological.[120] To be racially identified is also to be *wrong* in contrast to those who are not thus identified. Identification refers to how others categorize one and does not necessarily encompass the view of oneself that is connected to one's decisions, choices, will, and action. One's view of oneself, which includes how one is identified, must include some sense of one's agency. Because oppression limits agency by curtailing the liberty of those oppressed, Zack argues that a nonwhite racial identity cannot be accepted as a foundation for identity if one chooses freedom.[121] Nor can a racialized person effectively resist racism from within a racialized identity. This, she states, "is perhaps a great irony about racialized existence: one accepts that others have said one is *this;* one sees that one is not *this;* one's resistance in action requires some affirmation of oneself as *this* one is not."[122] Zack argues that many who are racially identified accept the identification and admit among themselves that they are thereby wrong. They do not, however, realize that the wrongness can be repudiated if the identification is not accepted.[123]

What I find particularly interesting about Zack's critique and rejection of racial identity is the fact that she attempts to prove its ontological uselessness by appealing to the unavoidability of death in the life of any and all subjects. She argues that the existential question that is raised by the powerful reality of race is: "How relevant is race to a life that in each case is some human being's *my life?*" Zack's creative approach to this problem is to admit that no one can ever know where she is in her life because death is an ever present possibility. If one dies tomorrow, then one's present would be rearranged as one's end. Death is a powerful event that tends to strain out any of the relevance to life that lies may have regardless of the cultural power of those lies. Zack writes: "When I think about the inevitable catastrophe of my death, it simply does not matter to me that my too-short life will have been racialized."[124] Biological death is simply a part of the natural order of things. But to a human consciousness that involves life-plan decisions, will, and action, death is perceived as a drastic cessation of the metanatural human order. Death, therefore, eliminates the continuation of agency, which most individuals would rather have continue. She writes:

> Existentially, the awareness of the inevitability of death, . . . in rupturing the virginity of life, creates what existentialists have called existence.

The return to my own life—in the sense that applies to everyone's own life—as an agent, and as the only agent in it from the only possible existential point of view on it, namely my own, after the acceptance of my inevitable death, which could happen at any time, may catapult me into the here and now. Existential literature, Zen Buddhism, and the wisdom of popular culture tell us that the realization of the evanescence of life can make the experience of being alive more intense. . . . .

[T]here is an existential return to the here and now after the realization of death's inevitability and readiness, which, assuming that one does nothing except wait for death, would seem to entail a fresh commitment to one's own life, or a realignment of one's fundamental attitude toward one's life.[125]

Zack contends that this change in attitude, or upsurge, results in greater freedom as an agent and a higher value placed on such freedom, which makes limitations on agency less tolerable. To experience oneself as a member of an oppressed race in the existential return-to-life after awareness of death constitutes an intolerable constraint on freedom. Oppression experienced from the inside is paralyzing and depressing when what an agent needs after this existential return to one's life is "either an irrepressible upsurge of some kind, or a lightening up of engagement."[126] A free agency of this sort can only be assumed by a racialized being if she casts off all racial oppression in her own first-person identity. In so doing, the agent "casts off racial identification, and race insofar as it pertains to her. The perpetual moment of freedom is therefore raceless. Race has nothing to do with *my life* in the existential sense of identity."[127]

In Zack's analysis of the transcendental efficacy of the awareness of death's inevitability, we see a particular type of attempt to capture what may be called a metaphysics of the concrete. Zack's analysis is quite telling because her attempt to invoke a natural occurrence such as death, as opposed to a set of manufactured human-constructed paradigms, to explain the psychic disposition of the individual toward her own life is most authentic. I think that it comes close to being a pure experiential and bracketed account of the way the individual can anchor herself to a unique awareness about her state of existence. It is this unique awareness that makes race irrelevant to one's life. In this mode of awareness one has attained freedom. It is not freedom as a reaction to something imposed; it is the freedom to be independent of social constrictions. Like an odor or a song that abruptly brings back a memory in place, the upsurge that results from the return to one's life as a result of this awareness of death dislocates the authority of the Natural Attitude. Structures that had previously dominated one's psychic makeup, responses, and reactions fall, and in their place is what I think Zack and many existentialists and undoubtedly much of Indian philosophy try to articulate: a purity and untarnished glimmer of the unadorned uniqueness of one's life, a uniqueness that is perceived at specific moments, such as the birth of one's child, falling in love, and, as Zack argues, death.[128]

If the upsurge or return to one's life brought about by reflecting on death deepens the ontological rebelliousness of the individual, then so do key existential aspects of one's life. One sees cases of ontological rebelliousness in certain movements in America that would seek to reject specific racial categories. In the *Newsweek* issue of 8 April 1996, in an article called "Don't You Dare List Them as Other: Multiracial Americans Seek Full Recognition," the white mother of a child whose father is black is reported to have rejected the schools' classification of her son as black as well as the Census Bureau's labeling of him as white. She has formed Project RACE (Reclassify All Children Equally) and contends that "the government doesn't have the right to act as the racial police and tell my child he has to choose one of his parents or else be an Other." The mother protests that her son is multiracial and resents being told by school officials that he could not be classified as both. In Michigan, a black mother of two multiracial children helped lead a successful drive for a multiracial category on statewide forms, making Michigan one of seven states that allow such a listing. The article explains that such pressure has forced federal officials to reassess the federal government's nineteen-year-old policy of dividing the population into four races (white, black, Asian, and American Indian) and two ethnic groups (Hispanic and non-Hispanic). On 27 October 1997, a *New York Times* article ("White House Adopts New Racial Categories) reports that the Office of Management and Budget has decided that respondents to the 2000 census will be permitted to check as many racial categories (black, white, Asian, Native American, or Pacific Islander, as well as Hispanic and non-Hispanic) as apply, but there will be no mixed-race category. The newspaper reports that the federal government has not decided what to do with the new data. And in states where children can check multiple boxes, the one-drop rule will still apply if "black" is checked.

Another article, "In Living Color," in the *Newsweek* of 15 May 1997, fresh on the heels of Tiger Woods's success in the golf world, reported on the growing number of interracial student organizations on American college campuses. Sheila Chung, a student at the University of California, Berkeley, calls herself "Korgentinian" for Korean and Argentinean. Some of her friends, according to the report, identify themselves as "China-Latina" or "Blackanese." Tiger Woods himself objects to being called African American. As a boy he created a neologism, "Cablinasian," that combines Caucasian, black, Indian, and Asian. Woods emphatically states that he embraces all sides of his family's ancestry without compromise and that to be identified by any one of them is to deny a part of him.

The self-imposed hybridization that these recent phenomena speak to is a form of ontological rebellion and a direct repudiation of the cruel metaphysics of race in America. The question of their authenticity as antidotes and the nature of their political and social implications are separate issues. I mention them, however, because they point to creative ways that people of color seek to transcend the pernicious limitations placed upon them by challenging the one-drop rule in American racial classifications and more generally the reification of race as a natural category when it is not.[129] Zack's approach, as well as the existentialist ethos in general, strikes me as a very powerful antidote to many of the limiting aspects of tribal ontology. Part of what it means to be a new type of human being involves having the courage to identify the pathology and perniciousness of the foundations on which one's bequeathed identity rests. These individuals are taking moral charge of their lives and infusing them with assemblages of their own making. Who one is involves the construction of others. But that is not an unalterable situation. To re-create the self as an edifice of one's making, to assemble it with a new set of value premises, and to address it with a new moral vocabulary is to morally politicize the self in a way that is truly heroic.

An existentialist approach to the problem may strike some as apolitical, or not political enough. I share with many of the existentialists and with philosophers like Judi Krishnamurti, however, a reverence and concern for the individual qua individual. Furthermore, it seems to me that since politics and societal concerns are generated by individuals, any redress on a deep and generative level must start with the individual, and with individuals in general. A concern for the politics of the soul, therefore, is a prerequisite for any meaningful change in the structure of society. Existentialism's view of the human as a metaphysical blank slate, coupled with the ontologically rebellious spirit it encourages, does not constitute a blueprint for self-creation. It does, however, place the capacity for self-creation within our range of choices, and it delegitimizes the false framework upon which our previous inherited identities were imposed. It also places the power to name meaning back where it belongs: with the individual. Since our status as human beings in a social world is ontologically ambiguous, as I have argued, then no external sociopolitical or cultural naming agency can have the final authority nor the temerity to assign labels to us as if we were ontologically determinate entities. The rigid designators I have referred to have determined the quality of our inner lives. This seems to be the strongest type of domination. Yet the process of undermining the constraints and false categories that shackle the contemporary self is an arduous one with very few foreseeable tangible results. The life that one lives while attempting ontological rebellion and liberation, and afterwards, may be a life of the mind in which one's ideas and self-concept can find no immediate validation and confirmation in the outside world. A state of incongruence is therefore visited upon one because there may not be an existential reality that is susceptible to one's newly constructed vision. Zack underscores this point. Arguing for a new notion of a separate mixed-race category as a way of undermining the purity of race, she states:

> To write about one's mixed-race identity is as much to invent oneself or one's racial group, as to describe them. One invents oneself on paper, as part of a theoretical inquiry, because outside of one's activities as an intellectual, that is, outside of the life of the mind, one has no secure racial existence. Mixed race is not recognized as an identity or form of culture by those individuals—the majority—who believe that they are racially pure. And, predictably, the self-invention of mixed race identity is precarious.[130]

If an existentialist conception of the self coupled with ontological rebellion aims at bringing about a resocialization of the self, and if ontological rebellion is a reorientation of being, then a partial existence within the life of the mind, one that has no formal or procedural validation in reality, is still a success. One has achieved some semblance of ontological efficacy.

David Hollinger notes that nowhere in the entire ethnoracial pantheon do individuals have more freedom to decide how much emphasis they will place on their ethnicity than within the Euro-American bloc. Euro-Americans of Italian, Norwegian, or Irish descent can ignore or affirm their heritage with great ease.[131] Another work points out the pseudotribalism operative in the mind-set of many white, middle-class Americans of third- or fourth-generation immigrant descent who manage to wring a great deal out of their ethnic affiliations without any great cost. These "white ethnics" tend to shy away from those aspects of communal life that impose obligations and get in the way of their privacy and individual expressivity. They do, however, tend to enjoy a "symbolic ethnicity," which is described as a subjective feeling of identity, rather than the truly robust form of social ethnicity one acquires and experiences by being a member of a specific community replete with commitments and forms of constraint.[132] Hollinger argues that when Americans are free to exercise their ethnic options, to associate with and disassociate from their affiliations at will, then we will have approached a postethnic society.

The capacity to associate or disassociate seems at first glance to be a form of ontological rebellion, but it really is not. As Mary C. Waters shows in her *Ethnic Options: Choosing Identities in America,* those characterized as voluntary ethnics, that is, those who affiliate and disaffiliate at will, still see ethnicity as a primordial biological status.[133] She makes a very interesting observation about a form of self-deception on the part of voluntary ethnics. In Hollinger's words:

> Waters' subjects' denial of the voluntary character of their own ethnic identities rendered them, in turn, insensitive to the involuntary character of the ethno-racial identities on non-whites: they see a formal 'equivalence between the African-American

and say, Polish-American heritages,' while often denying the depth and durability of the racism that has largely constructed and persistently bedeviled the former.[134]

Voluntary ethnicity cannot be a form of ontological rebellion because the radical reorientation of being that is central to this undertaking is absent. Those who may be described as voluntary ethnics are still holding on to a tribal superstructure that they deem central to their humanity, or at least central to the deepest sense of who they are. In reality this superstructure cannot be ethnicity, nor can it be race, because these features do not contain the types of properties that would have to be in place in order for such a strong identification to hold. In other words, this type of freelance exchange of ethnic options still betrays a deep commitment to the centrality of race and ethnicity in one's life. It resembles ontological rebellion only to the extent that one thinks one is autonomously choosing options of one's own, much like the child in the candy store believes he is free because he has twelve bars of chocolate from which to choose, never stopping for a moment to consider the possibility that his so-called freedom to pick any of the twelve brands is dependent upon his enslavement to chocolate in the first place.

The radical ontological rebel who throws off racial and ethnic tribal affiliations is not tempted even to consider ethnic and racial affiliations as the truly meaningful signifiers of human identity. Such a person, however—as is the case of those persons who in principle reject being labeled definitively by others and who choose other labels as a procedural way of cultivating identities that are not ethnically and racially specific—can carve provisional markers that might look like ethnic or racial markers, as in the case of "other" or "multiracial." The key difference between such a person and those who cultivate "symbolic ethnicity" is that the latter, as far as I am concerned, have already bought into and accepted ethnicity and racial affiliation as viable and appropriate moral human markers. The true ontological rebel rejects on principle such markers. He or she, however, might have little choice but to provisionally navigate within those markers while attempting to effect moral changes that seek to end the practice of referring to people first and foremost as ethnics and races.

A postethnic society, as far as the ontologically rebellious person is concerned, cannot be one in which racial and ethnic affiliation and disaffiliation are either possible or encouraged. Rather, it would be a society in which persons would strive to embrace other means of identifying, categorizing, and labeling persons; it would be a more enlightened society in which labels and markers would actually tell us something conceptually and morally interesting about persons rather than the mere pigmentation of their skin or the geographical region from which they came. Such features are often interesting, but they do very little to locate the moral attributes of persons or the core of their humanity.

The cosmetic and superficial gestures in today's culture that pass for individualism (rampant nihilism, styles, fashions, hair colors, and body piercing) are actually the marks of an abject conformity to what may be classed as various subcultures or groups within the mainstream of American life. A creative and positive individualism in today's culture would indeed be hard to accomplish. It would require a radical break with many of the traditions and conceptions of modern life and would wreak havoc with the conformism that is sold as individualism. But for the creative individuals wherever they may be, those who see themselves as eternal emigrants and who resent fixed standpoints, unreflective constitutive identities, and markers of completion as proof of a good life, the journey continues. Self-invention, they know, is their greatest gift from the gods; and if there are no gods, such power gives them an idea of what it would mean to be a god. Leaving behind what they were, they imagine a project and begin the process of overcoming themselves.

3

MORAL BECOMING, MORAL MASKING,

AND THE NARRATIVITY OF THE SELF:

NEGOTIATING THE COSMOPOLITAN TERRAIN

An individual is the meeting place of empirical possibilities.
—Elliot Deutsch, *Creative Being*

MORAL IMAGINATION AND SELF-TRANSFORMATION

Imagination is crucial to the undertaking of the creative individual who attempts self-invention. It points to expanded possibilities and ideates new forms of reality. It invites one to see oneself as an expression of alternative possibilities. To imagine involves taking a perceptual starter such as an image, a fantasy, an idea, a character, or an inspiring possibility and imbuing it with qualities that one wishes to make one's own. One's personal instantiation of the quality will invest it with the desired but absent qualities. Besides being instrumental in facilitating the day-to-day passage of roles in our lives,[1] imagination magnifies self-image and expands self-identity by allowing one to see oneself in a variety of ways. Karen Hanson writes that a man who sees himself in a variety of ways—as peacemaker, preserver of the past, passionless, nobody's favorite—thereby prevents a feeling of closure from entombing his self-image. One interpretation need not exhaust the object. In fact seeing oneself as ...(x), with x possibly standing for several things, is highly suggestive of alternate possibilities. And further, she says: "Imagination might most naturally be identified as the expedient which can take us beyond or out of the social roles we happen to inhabit. It seems the instrument which can implement a coherent yet creative transport."[2] The imaginer is a self-styled portraitist who finds that the motif of seeing oneself as x can be liberating, because imagination is hermeneutically powerful. The power of its creativeness, the new, the innovative, and the exciting are brought into existence. Imagination liberates becoming and is certainly a way out of some of the pernicious strangleholds of the Natural Attitude, especially when exercised by the ontologically rebellious. It accomplishes this liberation of becoming, not by conceptual analyses of the

Natural Attitude, but by literally lifting the self above the familiarity of the Natural Attitude. It soars on the strength of its vision. If one observes the innovative leaps made by board-game players, one sees that the tactical maneuverings that lead to success are often accomplished by imaginative leaps that have little to do with paying attention to the strategies of the opponent. I think also of science fiction writers, who literally lift themselves from familiar scientific paradigms governing their immediate and familiar world. To a large extent imagination is beyond strategy. Its new conceptions are starting points in and of themselves. If imagination is crucial for self-creation and identity, then it is also crucial for self-transformation. Above all, the would-be cosmopolitan is bent on the project of self-transformation. Philosopher Anthony Appiah notes that the fundamental thought of the cosmopolitanism he defends is the freedom to create oneself— the freedom that liberalism celebrates. It requires a range of socially transmitted options from which to invent what we have come to call our identities.[3]

Richard Shusterman writes that if self-realization is not defined by a fixed human essence, then self-transformation becomes a distinctly individual challenge. Wittgenstein confessed, Shusterman observes, that he went to war in 1914 not for the sake of the country but because of an intense desire to turn into a different person.[4] Self-transformation is a way of re-presenting a self that does not please us. Self-transformation becomes the guiding goal of the philosophical life. The main interest in life and in work is to become someone who you were not in the beginning.[5]

What is being described is more than the gyrations of an active imagination being put in the service of self-creation and self-transformation. We are describing a certain type of imagination, one I would describe as *moral imagination,* an imagination that leads to an ordered moral becoming and that recognizes the different candidates for the self and judiciously picks those that best provide the machinery for getting to the goal. In this case the goal is a cosmopolitan identity. Moral imagination in its active state will often call for a repudiation of one of more of the existing plausible candidates for self-identity. Benjamin Llamzon observes that it sometimes happens, as in the case of Martin Luther, that a man repudiates all that he ever was to turn over a new leaf.[6] Moral imagination, when accompanied by the "ruler principle in man," assists individuals in selecting those particular values and roles and making those decisions that best capture the way of becoming what they choose to be. No self can be predicated in human beings until the "ruler" in them acts. Individuals cannot act without awareness of their fields.[7] To be interested at all in choosing what sort of person to become among the possibilities open to me, I must already have decided that life is worth living and that becoming a certain type of self is worth my life's effort.[8]

To morally imagine a new ideated self and to seek creative ways of transforming such a self is to liberate oneself from the limitations of the labels of those with naming powers. An ordered moral becoming is a becoming that best prepares the individual for the type of moral identity he or she posits as a possibility in the world. Depending on the sort of identity one wishes to achieve, one might need to think in terms of the types of experiences and value centers—which would include persons, education, and communities—one ought to expose oneself to. If the type of person one wants to be is to be regarded as an achievement, then it will involve what Elliot Deutsch calls a sense of ideality. This means that what it means to be a person will involve a mapping out of ideal possibilities that are realizable along a continuum of achievement.[9]

An ordered moral becoming ideates a desired self that one thinks one ought to be. One ought to be this type of self because one is under the reasoned view that to be such a self represents a unique and rich way of being in the world. We have already rejected the typifications of certain models of identities crudely predicated on racialist and ethnocentric foundations because they treat the self as a closed, mummified entity and deny its becoming and evolution, as well as the concomitant new identity states that follow from this evolution. I favor the form of becoming that has a telos. What cannot be put in the service of this telos is a random or nomadic expression of becoming with no regulative stipulatives to guide it. The drunken driver on a highway and the sober yet unmapped and directionless driver cannot arrive at their destinations without objective and clear directions. Those who want to pursue unprincipled becoming have no protection against what they are trying to unbecome.

What do moral imagination and self-transformation accomplish? They allow us the freedom to use our lives to tell a particular story, a different story or narrative from the one that characterizes our lives. Indeed, I have been implicitly arguing that much of tribal ontology is a formulaic bromide that pre-programs the genres that make up the stories of our lives. It delineates what is culturally and sociopolitically out of order. It prevents radically different stories from emerging out of the contexts of our lives. Or, if such stories are squeezed from the life of an individual, tribal ontology, to the extent that it saturates public consciousness, robs them of their legitimacy and spiritual currency. The strength of the tribal ontology is that it mythologizes identities and then pathologizes those identities and stories that go against the grain of its myths. An ordered moral becoming whose aim is to weave a story different from the one bequeathed to one represents a way of stripping away the various fictions and myths through which one has been living. To tell a different story with the real stuff of one's life—one's commitments, projects, values, and desires—is to rely on and in some sense to presuppose the narrativity of the self.

THE NARRATIVITY OF THE SELF

The literature of the self as a narrative construct is gargantuan. It is not my purpose to provide an exhaustive survey of the extant literature on the topic. What I wish to do, however, is draw on those resources that discuss the most pressing conceptual features of a narrative conception of the self.

Shusterman, who defends a lived and practiced philosophy as a way of life, sees narrative as central to the task of self-constitution. If we help to determine who we are by the stories we tell of ourselves, then we are entitled to theorize issues of the self in our own voices and from our own experiences. He writes:

> Further, if philosophy is a personal life practice devoted to self-improvement through self-understanding, then certain details of one's life surely become relevant for analysis. Which details, precisely? That, of course, is also contingent, determinable only through concrete philosophical interpretation, though certain details (like gender and ethnicity) seem more apt to be significant than others (say, social security number or mother's maiden name).[10]

Shusterman identifies the problem of narrative unity as one of integrating the self's conflicting roles and stories and unifying the multiple transformations of character into a coherent sense of self. He locates the ways in which the question of his Jewish identity raises a problem of narrative self-construction: the underdetermination of self by narrative. He writes:

> For any open series of narrative events, given an indeterminate future in terms of which these events can be interpreted and also given the future revisability of past narrative interpretations, there will always be more than one narrative that can fit the facts of the individual. This plurality of comprehensive self-narratives raises the possibility of living as more than one self.[11]

Divergent narratives, on his account, shake one's fixed sense of identity and also deny any univocal sense of the meaning of any action.

Paul Anthony Kerby writes that life is inherently a narrative structure that we make explicit when we reflect upon our possible future. We are storytelling animals because we are already caught up in a story and already committed to meaning. Narration is a realm of intelligibility in which we are already involved, explicitly or implicitly. We ought not to be misled into thinking that the function of a narrative is to report the "facts" of our lives as they were. Following the lead of Paul Ricoeur, Kerby argues that to narrate experience is to refigure and tell it in a certain way and often for a certain end. Self-narration is both a receptive and creative-interpretive act. Narration excludes certain phenomena and dwells on others. It is unavoidably selective. It is receptive in the sense that others, as well as our experiences with them, are instrumental to the ways we narrate our lives. Our self-narration cannot be solipsistic. A mother cannot self-narrate her meaningful (or meaningless) identity as a mother without the attendant lives of her children and their narratives. But it is creative-interpretive in that no narrative comes ready-made or furnished with closed-ended meanings. Narratives are not endowed with automatic and objective formulae for interpretation. One will at some point have to make pertinent judgments about which phenomena—whether in the form of certain traditions, paradigms for evaluations, criteria for authenticity—may have to be excluded or reincluded in the enterprise of self-creation. Moral imagination emancipates one from conventions one has morally outgrown. Kerby underscores my notion of moral imagination when he emphasizes that the human subject is an unfinished subject that continually writes, develops, and often erases its own definitions and its own stories. Kerby says:

> What lies behind our self-conception is not some identical thing-in-itself (soul, self, spirit, ego), rather language as it derives from our sedimented history, especially the autobiographical language of self-narration. If I am a being who self-interprets, then it is to the interpreting itself that we should turn; no escape from this circularity by recourse to a self external or transcendent to this act.[12]

Without flogging the point to death, we can see how narrative account of the self in which narrative construction is open ended both underwrites the legitimacy of the naming capacity of the Natural Attitude and aids the process of becoming. The goal is an interpretation of narrative that honors its capacity to deliver us over the past as well as a medium of our aspirations and desires. We imaginatively express in the stories we tell ourselves and others a possible future with its joys and hardships and hence possible selves. Kerby continues:

> The stories we tell are part and parcel of our becoming. They are a mode of vision, plotting what is good and what is bad for us; what is possible and what is not—plotting who we may become. But in the telling we seem also to be immediately involved in generating the value of a certain state of affairs or course of action, of judging its worth, ethical or otherwise.[13]

Similarly, Charles Taylor, who emphasizes our capacity as self-interpreting animals, underscores the role that narrative plays in what I have termed an ordered moral becoming. Taylor sees self-identity and the possession of an orientation to the good as inextricably linked. Any sense of the good that a person has must be woven into the understanding of his or her life. This understanding is grasped as an unfolding story. We all grasp our lives in a narrative.[14] Taylor depicts human life as existing in a space of questions that only a coherent narrative can answer. In order to have a sense of who we are, we have to have a notion of how we have become and of where we are going. Narrative, on his account, has to play a bigger role than merely structuring my present. What I am has to be understood as what I have become. This sense of what I have become can only be given in a story. Taylor writes:

> And as I project my life forward and endorse the existing direction or give it a new one, I project a future story, not just a state of the momentary future but a bent for my whole life to come. This sense of my life as having a direction towards what I am not yet is what Alasdair MacIntyre captures in his notion . . . that life is seen as a quest.[15]

Taylor does not merely argue that our becoming unfolds in the drama of narratives. He contends that our identity is defined by our fundamental evaluations. These evaluations are self-referential and self-constitutive. They are crucial for our understanding of what is of value to us. They define not only who we are but also what we want. Narratives have a moralizing force and provide a heuristic frame or horizon on which all identities are predicated. This horizon allows us to determine what is good or valuable, what we endorse or oppose.

Becoming, as it unfolds in narratives and the attendant evaluations one makes in such unfoldings, leads to some form of soul maturation. My evaluations of the narratives through which my becoming unfolds lead me to *morally thematize my life.* I submit that moral thematization accompanied by skills such as moral imagination and autonomy is crucial for any hope of ordered moral becoming and any possibility of achieving a substantive identity ethos to replace others. To morally thematize my life is not just to interpret my past and its attendant stories with a view toward conferring some characterization of the person I am and the person I was. It is to organize my life in such a way that the moral quest I embark upon is guided by regulatives. Standing before becoming is a goal, a vision of the person I would like to be and think I ought to be. Moral thematization allows me to jettison the stories, interpretations, and evaluative paradigms that I have outgrown. It is instrumental in the formation of character because it regulates my values, aspirations, and moral behavior for the purpose of becoming a better person. To morally thematize my life is to begin to construct the new themes that my stories, life experiences, and narratives will dramatize. The stories are different from those that currently characterize my life. To live a morally thematized life is to live a life dedicated to certain values and commitments. An identity based on specific commitments, projects, and values is a moral identity. The would-be cosmopolitan who wishes to thematize his or her life finds that as a moral identity, because cosmopolitanism stands for a particular ethos and manner of engaging with one's fellow humans, it is richly superior to any ethnic, racial, or national identity, all of which rely on nonmoral markers that divide people into moral categories. Can one be a good Israeli Jew and be a supporter of mixed marriages between Jews and Palestinians?

To morally thematize one's life with the view of becoming a cosmopolitan is to embark on a normative quest one believes to be a spiritual and moral advancement over the ethnoracial categorizations that one had no part in naming and no power to eradicate or even substantially modify. One cannot single-handedly change the sociohistorical machinery responsible for maintaining the prejudices, attitudes, and criminalization of the Other. But one can certainly wring from one's soul the prejudicial contaminants leaked from a bloated cultural superego with which one finds it difficult to identify. In Freudian psychoanalytic terms, the cultural superego, like the individual superego, stands as the repository of specific traits, values, and beliefs. Its aggressiveness and the curtailments it places on individual expressivity can produce neuroses both individually and communally. Indeed, one can exert a discerning spirit that allows one to distance oneself from the prejudices and neuroses of others while recognizing that they are the cultural properties and values of others; and further, one is cognizant that one is being evaluated by others according to those values. A morally thematized life, in the continued spirit of the ontologically rebellious, must start with the explicit rejection of those cultural values that are anathema to the vision of one's moral imagination. Moving a step ahead of the ontological rebel, one formulates a definite plan of action to become the type of moral person one wants to be. In order to own one's becoming as a morally mature and autonomous person, one begins the process of breaking the mold of respectability and undermining the authority structure that one's culture has erected as a way of regulating one as a piece of cultural property. Part of what it will mean to become a new type of person is to contend radically with the historical accretions that have formed the person one is. I am advocating the destruction of the attitudes of group minds as they exist within the person, the group minds that are presented in the forms of racial and ethnic characteristics that attempt to function as moral features of persons, class prejudices, and national consciousness.[16] Moral thematization, to the extent that it captures some semblance of moral health, must engage in this type of filtering process. Failure to do so undermines the future possibility of the self one is struggling to write into existence. Whatever telos one is trying to capture will have to be written with a series of narratives that will be captured by both a process of unbecoming as one extricates oneself from the cultural and societal morass one has been entangled in and by the simultaneous process of becoming captured in the free and dynamic movement of a new self.

The teleological character of narrative is best captured by Alasdair MacIntyre in *After Virtue*. Although I do not endorse all of his commitments and conclusions, MacIntyre's delineation of the narrative nature of the self is rich and insightful. The foundation on which his thesis rests is the view that persons are by nature storytelling animals. MacIntyre agrees with Barbara Hardy that we dream, daydream, remember, anticipate, hope, despair, believe, doubt, plan, revise, criticize, construct, gossip, learn, hate, and love by narrative. It is because all of us live out narratives in our lives and because we understand our own lives in terms of these narratives that the form of narrative is appropriate for understanding the actions of others. Stories, he notes, are lived before they are told.[17]

The narratives that we live out have an unpredictable and teleological character, because our present is always informed by some idea of some future. The image or idea of future always presents itself in the form of a variety of ends or a telos. We find ourselves in the present either moving or failing to move toward this telos. The dialectics of unpredictability and teleology are inextricably linked to our lives. MacIntyre likens our fate to those of fictional characters who do not know what will happen next in their lives but who nevertheless have specific forms in their lives that propel them toward a future. There are always constraints on the way the narratives may develop. Despite this, however, they can continue in myriad ways.[18]

Regardless of how the narratives unfold or fail to unfold, they all exhibit the unmistakable uniqueness of the subjects' history. MacIntyre writes: "I am the *subject* of a history that is my own and no one else's, that has its own peculiar meaning."[19] Personal identity is the identity presupposed by the unity of the character that the unity of a narrative requires. Without this unity there would be no subjects of whom stories could be told. MacIntyre is here arguing against the notion that identity is something that is founded on the psychological continuity or discontinuity of the self. Rather, "the self inhabits a character whose unity of a narrative is embodied in a single life." It consists in asking: "What is the good for me?" which is tantamount to asking what is the best way for me to live out that unity and bring it to completion.[20] Ultimately, though, the unity of a human life is the unity of a narrative quest.

MacIntyre says: "Quests sometimes fail, are frustrated, abandoned or dissipated into distractions; and human lives may in all these ways also fail. But the only criteria for success or failure in a human life as a whole are the criteria of success or failure in a narrated or to-be-narrated quest."[21] In pursuing a quest, some conception of the good for the individual is required.

Rewriting the Self: History, Memory, and Narrative, Mark Freeman's work in philosophical psychology, explores the rewriting of the self, which Freeman describes as the process by which one's past—and indeed one's self—is figured anew through interpretation. He echoes Taylor's view of humans as self-interpreting animals and sees much of human experience as being characterized by a sense of secrecy and indeterminacy. Given our immersion in language, culture, and history, interpretation is a way of making sense of much that is unclear about our existence.[22] The primary things we subject to interpretation, such as our history and our past, are things that we ourselves have fashioned though our own reflective imagination. A precondition for a rewriting of any self is some sort of self-understanding. Rewriting the self is not just an interpretive process. It is also a recollective experience. Like Taylor, Freeman endorses the notion that as we explore and survey our histories and our contingent makeup, we make some sort of evaluative judgment about who and what we are. He argues that any vision one holds that accommodates a view of the sort of person one would like to be must also take quite seriously this recollective and interpretive stance to one's own life. One cannot fashion a new self and aspire to a self one is not yet without understanding the elements, as varied and complex as they might be, that have formed the *this* one finds oneself to be at present. This interpretive and evaluative stance is crucial, for there is much of the self that one may wish to abandon. There is also much that one may wish to maintain as integral to the continued growth of a self one hopes to become.

Without an evaluative calculus, how is one to decide which aspects of the self and of one's past to repudiate and which to maintain? Freeman's text identifies in the life of Augustine the ways in which the rewriting of self, coupled with the conceptual triad of history, memory, and narrative, serves as a central pivot around which to think about human lives and development.[23]

In responding to the question in the preceding paragraph, I shall ponder some of the questions posed by Freeman and then consider some of the tools he provides by way of a narrative approach to the self and self-identity. He wonders whether narratives, by virtue of being told or written at a significant remove from the flux of immediate experience, inevitably falsify life. He concludes that "even if we do not live narratives of the same nature and scope as those we tell when we pause to reflect comprehensively on the past, the very act of existing meaningfully in time, I will argue, the very act of making sense of ourselves and others, is only possible in and through the fabric of narrative itself."[24] And it is through narration that we will come to entertain the possibility of the new and innovative; to become conscious of the "discursive order of [our] culture," which will make transgression possible.[25] A narrative approach to self-construction and analysis and evaluation of the narrativity of one's bequeathed self-identity involves in part the ability to scrutinize those narratives treated as givens—provided, of course, that one has the requisite autonomy competency skills.

Since my project is to describe how an aspiring cosmopolitan would go about rewriting the self, there is a way in which Freeman's interpretation of Augustine's life of becoming can be useful. His interpretation, I hope, will flesh out some of my notions of moral imagination and moral thematization as viable options that any would-be cosmopolitan might wish to pursue in his or her narrative quest and ordered moral becoming.

The *Confessions,* Augustine's autobiographical account of his life of becoming and eventual conversion, is often a retrospective evaluation of his life from the position of one who was in darkness but now is enlightened, one who can interpret the (unseen at the time) orchestrated forces that governed his life. Augustine's description of his boyhood as a normal one in which he went along with the currents of the time and the normal demands that were made of a boy of his age is, according to Freeman, an admission that he had been constructed strictly in accordance with the expectations of others with no other possible mode of existence.[26] He was living a narrative others had written. Augustine traveled an interesting journey. He lived a lustfully hedonistic and libidinally driven life, experimented with the theater, lived with a woman, taught rhetoric, came under the spell of Manichean religion, and in general wrestled with spiritual malaise and restlessness. It appears that while Augustine did not yet know what specific direction his life should take, he was becoming more and more aware of the direction that it should not take. He writes of a new will that he was beginning to have, a will that was approved of by his moral consciousness but was nevertheless in conflict with other parts of his moral character, or as Augustine would put it, his old will. Augustine writes:

> So my two wills, one old, one new, one carnal, one spiritual, were in conflict, and they wasted my soul by their discord.
>
> In this way my personal experience enabled me to understand what I had read—that *the flesh lusteth against the spirit and the spirit against the flesh.* I, no doubt, was on both sides, but I was more myself when I was on the side of which I approved of for myself than when I was on the side of which I disapproved.[27]

I take this to be a crucial normative stance on Augustine's part. We can see how moral imagination and the moral thematization of one's life are aided by this elusive and yet invigorating normative suggestive quality that says, "Not this way but that." Such a quality precedes the discovery of any full-blown moral vision that one can hold before one's life and figuratively point to and say: "That is the way I ought to follow." But the suggestion of where one ought not to go is clear and distinct. I regard this as a crucial stance because what is involved in the recognition of the directions one ought to avoid is an abandonment of certain aspects of one's identity and a curtailment of specific psychological traits one might be dependent on. I am speaking of the massive clearing that has to occur before the realization and manifestation of any vision can take place. This may be referred to as *psychic distanciation;* that is, a distanciation between the outlived and worn-out paradigms from which one constructed a life as well as the yet-to-be realized state that one envisions as a future possibility. Augustine described this in-between state and the recognition of the path he ought not to follow as a work of God's providence. God was using his stubborn perversity and dissoluteness in order to clear a space for the possibility of his finding a path that would eventually get him somewhere real. Augustine describes himself as existing in a state of what Freeman calls spiritual anoxia that heightened the unstable and dizzying sense of his divided existence. Through Catholicism Augustine began to find some measure of hope. His confused conception of God, which he had understood as a body with limbs like our own, began to grow clearer. Freeman writes:

> He had thus moved on to a second moment of the developmental process, one which might be referred to as 'distanciation' (see Ricoeur 1981), which we can think of simply in terms of the need for divesting oneself of these modes of experience that, by virtue of their inadequacy, have prevented one from moving forward as readily as one might. To realize what one is not, while surely being a step in the right direction, is of course only a part of the developmental process. The far more arduous task of realizing what one is still remained.[28]

The challenge that Augustine faced, the obstacle that initially obstructed his attempts at moral thematization and a life of ordered moral becoming, was breaking from the habits that held him to a self that neither satisfied nor fit him. While the will desperately willed the birth of a new moral self, the will and the desperate urge for a new moral self were struggling to come into existence, Augustine was weighed down by habit. His conversion came unexpectedly and quite dramatically. He writes of the great storm rising within him and the wrenching of his heart and a downpour of tears. He heard the words of a child saying: "Take it and read it. Take it and read it."[29] Interpreting this as a divine command, Augustine read the first passage of Scripture that his eyes fell on. He interpreted it as a command to change his profligate ways and dedicate his life to God. But the knowledge of what to do with his life was insufficient. His ideated conception of what his new self would be like had to be wedded to a life of action. The discovered truth had to be instantiated by living according to its ideals.

I would issue one caveat for living a morally thematized life: Ideals should remain open-ended. Since the self exists in a state of becoming and remains potentially open to revision and modification because of its varied experiences, a critical-minded and autonomous self that judiciously inspects its interactions and responses to life experiences should be ready to abandon ideals it might have outgrown. A first-person narrative, as we have seen, is both selective and interpretive. It cannot be impartial. As Ricoeur notes, a person understood as a character in a story is not an entity distinct from his or her experiences. In fact, it is the person who shares the condition of dynamic identity peculiar to the story recounted. Ricoeur writes: "The narrative constructs the identity of the character, what can be called his or her narrative identity, in constructing that of the story told. It is the identity of the story that makes the identity of the character."[30]

If the identity of the story is characterized as the striving toward an ideal, then the development of the moral character in question exists on the horizon of the future, which calls us forward toward the self-to be, or as I would say, the visionary self. The ontological predicates of this self consist in a series of stories that have yet to be told and are not fully formed. The novelist who has a vague idea of the type of character she would like to write into existence realizes that the character will be dependent on the story she executes, and vice versa. The story idea rumbling inside her head will determine to a significant extent the type of character she writes about. If she is planning a Harlequin Romance novel, then the lead character (to the extent that she remains faithful to the genre of the story and the formulaic motifs that preserve its authenticity) cannot be a middle-aged, alcoholic cross-dresser. One of the essential constitutive features of the genre is that the male hero must fall within a specific character range replete with certain traits. These include his unambiguous masculinity and heterosexuality. Likewise, the moral visionary who is motivated by the ideal of a different type of self is impassioned by the possibility of a different set of stories that she might one day write with the actions of her life, stories that will be representative of a different type of self, and stories that will shape a different type of self.

How is this type of moral personality possible? In other words, what sort of psychological machinery am I going to need so that the cosmopolitan personality may flourish? Bear in mind what is at issue. To the extent that we are speaking of persons with the requisite autonomy competency skills and of ontological rebels who have evaluated the narratives that formed the basis of their lives, they must simultaneously find a way of writing those narratives out of their moral psyche while also attempting to write a different self into existence. Ontological rebelliousness at best reflects an attitude adopted to psychically divest one of the seriousness of the values, mores, and edicts of tribal ontology. But the stance or attitude is not sufficient. In other words, rebelliousness as an attitude and as an activity must be accompanied and defined by certain types of actions.

As a plausible psychological architectonics to equip the would-be cosmo-politan to write a new self into existence, I propose a dialectical interplay of *masking* and *forgetting*. A transition from one identity state to the next must be supported by some psychomoral transmutation. If, as I suggest, self-transfor-mation is crucial to any meaningful philosophical life, then part of what is involved in living the moral philosophical life is finding a way of plausibly effecting this transformation. Short of this, those of us attempting such an undertaking succeed only in bandying about words, phrases, heavy concepts, "deep thoughts," and moral musings. Our visions and words are left suspend-ed in midair while we watch perhaps a few who might have been inspired by our words jumping, some groping frantically and some not so frantically to catch the words and visions.

MASKING: MORAL PERSONAE AND THE CONSTRUCTION OF NEW IDENTITIES

Moral masking, far from being a bad thing, is the projection of a type of self one wishes to be and a self one wishes to grow into. Instead of an entire con-cealing, can we not say that masking is a transitional state one occupies while on the way to a place of which one wishes to be the architect? Wearing a moral persona is not necessarily a pretense. Christians, when asked how it is that one can love one's neighbor as one loves oneself, often reply that love consists in a series of acts. If you repeat the "acts of love" enough times, you will come to love your neighbor, since on this account love is not mere sentimental feeling. The comparison is apt because a projection of the self one wishes to be comes also with a set of imperatives. To reach the state where one need no longer project that type of self, to reach the state where the desired self has been earned, entails commitment to a set of behaviors that completes this meta-morphosis.

Masking is intimately linked to the concept of person. The word *person* derives from the Latin *persona,* which is the ancient word for the mask used by actors in Greek and then Roman theater. The masks had a double role, both hid-ing and revealing. Aldo Tassi writes: "Moreover, the theater is a place in which a world of masks is created by the deliberate and conscious manipulation of a hid-ing/revealing dialectic: the same dialectic that the human self exhibits."[31] From the theatrical standpoint, the actor in a theater who assumes a mask by means of a character type, voice patterns, and physical alterations establishes a new identity. The persona that the actor creates has its own reality. It is its own right, and it consists in projecting a sense of self. The self that is projected is the self in the play. There are three distinctions among the various types of masking. The actor in the play withdraws behind the mask and hides his/her personal identity. The hiding of the actor stands in contrast to that of the gunman who robs a bank. There is no pretense here at being someone else. The gunman does not conceal the fact that he is a gunman. What he conceals is his identity. The woman who masks herself at the masquerade is situated somewhere between the actor and the gunman. Like the gunman, she wishes to hide her proper identity, yet she does this by pretending to be someone else. If she gets caught up in the identity of the pretended person, then she is closer in status to the actor in a play. In the drama, masking is used to project to the audience a convincing reality of the identity of the person who is undergoing the events on the stage. Tassi writes: "Although he retains his personal identity, in assuming the mask the actor becomes the person in the play. In contrast to the masquerade, where the woman's partner may seek to know her true identity, in the theater the mark of a successful performance is the fact that the audience is not aware of anyone else on-stage."[32]

The object of acting, then, is to bring about a metamorphosis, to produce a "from beyond," a transcendent reality that is the character in the play. The actor transforms himself into someone else. The metamorphosis is achieved by the actor's "withdrawing," but not in the way that the gunman or the woman at the masquerade withdraws. His withdrawal is an effacement that seeks to establish a "place" from which there can arise the projection of a new sense of self. It means to be a withdrawal that reveals. And the actor accomplishes this by "wearing a mask." He hides "behind" the mask in such a way that it releases a "revelation." There is a "coming forth" that is the essence of the mask: it is a projection that reveals.[33]

Tassi's notion of masking as a coming forth is useful in terms of our project. A self that is committed to moral thematization and that has sufficient moral imagination to aid this thematization does not merely pretend through the use of persona to be something that it is not: It acts in a committed manner to be the type of person it is consciously attempting to become. The moral mask one wears as a persona is part of the process of becoming that type of person. Since we are describing how to become a cosmopolitan person, the mask is a space in which cosmopolitan values, ideas, and principles can be projected as moral ideals until the individual has fully, or at least substantially, grown into the mask's projected ideals: the moral cosmopolitan. In certain types of devotional exercises and religious training, this is not unusual. The would-be priest, though he participates in the same activities and pledges allegiance to the same set of values as his superiors (bishops, cardinals, and second- and fourth-year seminarians), is immeasurably lower in spiritual rank than his superiors. Yet he behaves and projects the reality of one who is the type of person he is being molded to become. The projection is a part of the moral and psychological machinery that will allow for this transformation. Any type of moral training (consider the inculcation of values in children and the entire socialization process) involves some sort of masking and moral projection. At some level in the moral development of the child, the parent will begin to act as if the child's moral and mental developments are at a sufficient level for the child to make crucial distinctions between right and wrong. This apparent assumption on the part of the parent is not really an assumption at all. The parent knows that the child is lagging behind in his moral development but acts deliberately as if the child, who is required now to behave as if he is the type of person for whom this moral program is designed, is capable of making the necessary leaps to reach the desired moral state. The punishment is designed to act as a catalyst to spur the child's growth because such growth ought to be forthcoming. The child often acts as if he is that type of individual. A moral persona is a training mechanism. One of the disorienting factors that many actors face has to do with the character roles they portray. The actor begins to feel that he is losing his personal identity and begins to really feel, think, and act like the pretended characters. Most actors—I think of Robert DeNiro, for example—will do almost anything that is required of them to prepare for a role. DeNiro has in the past gained as much as sixty pounds to realistically portray a character. Besides that, he does an extraordinary amount of research on the emotional state of the characters, their childhood, speech patterns, conceptual mode of functioning, hobbies, personal tastes, and sexual proclivities. Several actors speak of losing themselves in their characters and find it excruciatingly difficult to "get out of character" even months after the filming or performance is complete.

According to Tassi, when the actor assumes the mask, he is like his antecedents in the Dionysian rites celebrating the effacement of reality for the benefit of a vaster reality. It should be obvious that this approach is helpful in transcending the problematic aspects of the Natural Attitude. To efface present reality for the sake of a vaster one indicates that the present ground has to be cleared and sometimes demolished in favor of a new one. And this is just the ethos and mind-set of any aspiring cosmopolitan. An ethos that one is striving to adopt that stands in sharp contrast morally and psychologically to the one in which one is presently situated cannot come into existence without a repudiation, many cancellations, and a willingness to abandon much of what has been sacrosanct. Masking, we can see,

> becomes a creative undertaking that is aware of itself and its ground. The consciousness of the self involves an awareness of a surpassing reality and value and consequently an awareness of the pretension in all other value schemes. It yields then a detachment that carries along with it the recognition of the illusory character of all that is not, or is taken to be in some way independent of, the self.[34]

The theatrical mask, whether it is achieved through an artificial device or through the actor's body, is not meant as an escape from reality but as a way "to establish a place that is able to facilitate the journey from one reality to another."[35] The mask assists in the goal of any drama, whether it is the dramaturgy of everyday life or a theatrical or cinematic event. To "undergo" in the theater refers to the fact that events that have a particular form in the real world take on a new form that enables them to constitute, or compose, the world of the play. When the actor seeks and expresses inner feelings, he is attempting to build and give shape to a character. We gauge the veracity of these inner feelings according to whether they reveal the new reality we call the character.[36]

Part of what is involved in a narrative approach to the self, we ought to remember, is that as one begins to morally thematize one's life (which, among other things, consists in deciding the type of life and the type of person one wishes to live and be), one evaluates the stories that have generated the moral themes of one's life. As one faces the ideal of one's thematized life, one decides which stories one will abandon because they are causally insignificant and do not contribute to the life and person one wishes to become. An ordered moral becoming, therefore, is analogous to the character in the theater who uses the mask for transformation to the extent that one willfully discounts certain stories, focuses on some, and deliberately chooses values and principles that will structure the current and future narratives of one's life. Like the actor who underwrites the metaphysical significance of his own personal background, his tastes, dislikes, and idiosyncratic makeup as causal inhibitors against effecting a real and plausible character, the aspiring moral cosmopolitan, in the spirit of an autonomous ontological rebel, discounts the particular former narratives of her existence as the unauthored and non-autonomously-chosen aspect of her identity that she now overthrows by the guidance of a spirit of moral creativity that is to be put in the service of a new and radically different person. The mask—the moral persona, the training place—is the provisional reality that permits this transition. And now for moral vision to flourish, for an authentic metamorphosis to take place, for one to really wean oneself from the unchosen identities, the bequeathed narratives foisted upon one, the inherited and internalized prejudices and pathologies and fears, one begins the process of *forgetting*.

4

FORGETTING WHERE WE CAME FROM:

THE MORAL IMPERATIVE OF EVERY COSMOPOLITAN

Memory of a certain type reinforces a nostalgia for the familiar. It can breed sentimentality that valorizes the traditional because it is comforting and because it is the traditional. Fixation to the inherited and the bequeathed prevents the innovative and the creative from coming into existence. Like the inheritor who spends a lifetime slavishly devoted to preserving her father's estate as it was, never considering effecting a change by applying her own style of management, the would-be cosmopolitan who fixates on the narratives and seductive myths spawned by the tribe stymies her potential for self-transformation. If the goal is to fight for a new self-interpretation, then one has to learn to forget the old and the familiar: the weight of ancestral values and of outdated tenets is too much for one to resist for oneself.

I recall another conversation with my friend Kevin, who came to the United States from South Africa at the age of fifteen. We met in college. He already had a degree in engineering and was taking classes in philosophy. We bonded immediately and often had long, candid conversations about our lives. He admitted to me that I was his first black friend and that he found the philosophical give-and-take fascinating, since the closest thing to a conversation he had ever had with a black person was to say, "Put the garden hose over there" to his gardener in South Africa. He once said to me that he wished he could forget everything about being South African and retain most things Jewish. We talked about this for a long time, and I came to understand the occasional embarrassment he felt over his socialization as a privileged Caucasian raised under apartheid. He regretted the way racist values had colored his view of people outside his racial category. I remember telling him that he had a right to forget where he came from, to forget the past that would prevent him from really seeing the world differently. In effect he was being held hostage by a set of values and a narrative paradigm that he had not chosen. I came to see that a moral forgetting would be necessary if he was to be successful in depathologizing crucial aspects of his self-image, at least those parts of his moral sensibilities that he came to accept as being morally questionable because they were mired in morally reprehensible beliefs and attitudes. If one were to speak in

Freudian terms, one could say that in this case the superego had to be revamped and provided a different set of postulates and value premises. Claudia Card writes that there is such a thing as justifiably disowning a heritage. Forgetting dispenses with the attachment that makes difficult the resocialization of self and values warranted by any attempt at radical self-transformation. The enemy fought by a commitment to self-transformation is overdetermination. Forgetting can vanquish this enemy. It is a self-inflicted type of death to one's past and the identities and the selves that were shaped to that past. The ontologically rebellious aspiring cosmopolitan has no automatic respect for such-and-such a memory. Forgetting is an act of moral defiance, because memory reinforces attachments an individual does not want to have. Forgetting is deliverance. It gives one permission to be what one wants to be—self-permission, that is, since one's desire for a new moral self is the major legitimate criterion for determining what to be.

Forgetting is a temporary form of dispensing with certain voices, slogans, and rules of the community. Indeed the would-be cosmopolitan wants to open the gates of community and let the radical Others in; she wants to hybridize the community and rid it of any form of purity that is associated with race, culture, tribe, or nation. The moral cosmopolitan, if necessary, will put the existence of every culture at risk, even her own. Like the foreigner who is free of ties with her own people, she feels completely free. It is in this respect that forgetting is an act of defiance. The ontologically rebellious person has no respect for *this* and *that* memory out of a sense of misguided nostalgia. Forgetting is a psychic deathblow in many respects to the troublesome aspects of the Natural Attitude and tribal ontology. We have seen that the latter is made up of a series of narratives, some with more binding power and seductive appeal than others. In the formation of national identity, for example, we see the narrative accretion of some myths and stories and the crucial omission of others. Some narratives become more genre specific than others. For example, black identity in North America seems more genre specific than white identity. Notice the ways in which the authenticity of black identity is closely measured by one's responses to particular issues that are said to be either black issues or issues directly affecting the black community. But this is not the case just with blacks. Identities of so-called marginalized peoples become like archetypal banners. They are specific and binding. The narrative genres in which our identities are encapsulated already delimit the ways in which our stories can be told. Let us recall the literary constraints of the romance writer. A heroine dying in childbirth shortly after finding out that her dashing hero is a hermaphrodite is a formulaic anomaly. No such novel written as a Harlequin Romance would find a publisher. The writer would have to forget the rules of that genre and devise a different type of novel. The story might be interesting, perhaps more so, once the author forgets the classic rules and becomes truly inventive. Moral *becomers* and would-be cosmopolitans will have to be concerned with inventive narratives whose function literary linguist Tzvetan Todorov describes as one of not only inventing new plots but also rendering previously familiar ones uncertain or problematical. The politics of forgetting is a way out of much of this.

Cosmopolitanism is against the idea that identity is nonnegotiable. David Hollinger states that cosmopolitanism is based on recognition, acceptance, and eager exploration of diversity. Cosmopolitanism urges each polity and each individual to absorb as much experience as it can while retaining its capacity to function as a unit. Cosmopolitanism is willing to assist in the creation of new affiliations and is more oriented toward the individual, whom it is likely to understand as a member of a number of different communities simultaneously. It is suspicious of the potential for conformist pressures within communities celebrated by pluralists.[1] Although pluralism might defend varied ways of life and an environment in which a multiplicity of cultural groups can coexist, it is still suspicious of the ways in which any cross-cultural value pollination may upset group identity. It is, above all, intent on preserving the demarcations of group identities. Timothy Earle and George Cvetkovich argue that pluralism stands in contrast to cosmopolitanism because pluralism favors the maintenance of rigid, tight group identities. It supports tight and separate communities and a unitary self within traditional cultural limits. Cosmopolitanism is risk taking and favors wide, loose, and overlapping communities, multiple selves, and fluidity within universal human limits. Cosmopolitan social trust is based on emergent group values; an understanding of this is the first step toward a better future. Earle and Cvetkovich write:

> To contribute usefully to the solution of social problems, however, we have to learn how to move from pluralistic social trust, with its rigid, defensive solitudes, toward cosmopolitan social trust, with its fluid, inclusive interweaving. *We have to learn how to move into futures that we can't describe because we have liberated them from their ties to our pasts.*[2]

I submit that this liberation, or what I shall term *psychic distanciation*, from the ties of our past carries a great deal of moral weight for the conversion and transformative praxis that I believe to be crucial for the cosmopolitan ethos of any individual. But let me hasten to add that the distance, and in some cases the downright disowning, will vary according to the moral nature of what is described in one's past. A former apologist for apartheid and Nazism who is reared under those cultural systems has a more morally compelling reason to distance herself from such a past than, say, someone in a cultural milieu in which any pernicious tenets might be operative but are not constitutive of the culture in the way that anti-Semitism is a crucial tenet of Nazi ideology.

Liberation from our past carries with it a twofold advantage. First, it allows for a radical resocialization of the self. This resocialization accommodates a self that is able to get beyond the markers of race, ethnicity, and national identity, markers that more often than not prevent us from getting to know other people and from being like other people in crucial ways. The second advantage of this liberation is that it completes the *weaning process*. Ethnic/racial and national fixations are transference of the infantile need for the parental figure. The weaning process that is necessary for maturity is sublimated and prolonged; hence our psychic immaturity and the neuroses that are expressed in ethnic and racial fixation. A cosmopolitan identity will be a weaned identity and therefore a moral identity. Agency begins with moral independence. But the true liberation that results from this approach occurs when one is capable of revising the narrative structure of one's life. One's ordered moral becoming, the process by which one is in charge of the narrative flow of one's life, becomes something inspiring and real. I will explicate these points with a bit of autobiographical information that will give examples of my own expanded identity and the genesis of what I hope will eventually become a full-fledged cosmopolitan identity.

In 1985, at the age of twenty, I, along with my mother, my grandmother, and brother emigrated to the United States. My primary purpose in coming to this country was first to establish myself as a novelist (this has yet to happen) and to get a college education. I hailed from a modest middle-class family with a strong tradition in politics, trade unionism, and intellectual pursuits. If I had to characterize my political orientation upon arrival in America, I would say that I was a strong individualist and a supporter of liberal values; that is, I supported a host of causes and freedoms consonant with the values of liberalism: freedom of speech, freedom of religion, a broad conception of the good, the right of persons to choose their own conceptions of the good, and the indisputable value of autonomy as a social good. My major ignorance in coming to America—and it was an ignorance, I must say, that I fought fiercely to maintain in order to protect my identity in several areas—was the failure to understand the more nuanced ways in which race defined much of the life and realities of its inhabitants. In other words, I was quite aware that racism existed in America, and I was aware of the pernicious one-drop rule, which identified anyone with any trace of African ancestry as black. All this I had learned in my twelfth year in high school in Jamaica when I studied American history.

On the whole, middle-class Jamaicans coming to America are a peculiar lot. Having been socialized without any formal notion of race, most Jamaicans, even those with the darkest of skin, do not consider themselves members of a race. There are brown people and red people and black people whose skin color literally is black. So in a way, upon arrival in America I and my family, along with a few other family friends who emigrated at the same time, properly considered ourselves a raceless people. There is also a really weird mentality among middle-class Caribbean people regarding black Americans. They view black Americans as a culturally bankrupt people, people with little class and social breeding. This mentality, of course, stems from the same very class-conscious group of individuals who distinguished themselves in their native lands from the lower classes of persons, often describing them as backward, peasants, and "butus," a pejorative term analogous to "white trash," "niggers," "spics," and "Chinks." Bourgeois Jamaicans and Caribbeans often see themselves as culturally sophisticated and possessing a lot of "class." This class consciousness and a life of manners and social protocol are expressions of English values and norms from both colonial and postcolonial socialization. The negative attitude implied by the Jamaican term "butu" is often carried over to refer to black Americans, whom many Caribbeans see as too hung up on race and too limited in their outlook on life.

The common criticism one hears frequently leveled against blacks by Caribbeans is that race consciousness dominates too much of their lives. It does not occur to many of them that race consciousness rules the lives of many whites and that it certainly dominates the institutions of which they are eager to prove themselves worthy. Many Caribbeans simply have not learned to read whites' subtle, usually unexpressed race consciousness. They have not calibrated the ways that positive discrimination pits them against American blacks by playing upon their own sense of pride and dignity. In an article "Black like Them," Malcolm Gladwell explores why West Indian and American blacks are perceived differently and cogently addresses this point. He reports that after dozens of interviews researchers uncovered a persistent pattern of what they called "positive discrimination." Employers had developed an elaborate system for determining "good" blacks from "bad" blacks and "good" Hispanics from "bad" Hispanics. Criteria for goodness included being an immigrant, since for employers that meant being industrious and loyal and not coming from an outside neighborhood. In the Red Hook area of Brooklyn, the good Hispanics are Mexicans and South Americans; Puerto Ricans are excluded from this category. Gladwell notes that the idea of the West Indian as a kind of superior black is not new. Upon arrival in New York and Boston in the early 1900s, those in the first wave of Caribbean immigrants were dubbed by other blacks as "Jew-maicans." They earned this nickname because of the emphasis they placed on hard work and education. In the 1920s the garment trade in New York was first integrated by West Indian women because when they saw the sign on the door saying No Blacks Need Apply, they simply walked on in.[3]

Often Jamaicans mistakenly believe that racism on the part of whites against blacks is a result of perceived behavioral traits. Many Jamaicans and Caribbeans are sure that they do not possess such traits. Along with a spirit of defiance and confidence (sometimes bordering on superiority) and a keen sense of determination and ambition, they are sure that they cannot be held back by problems of race and racism. They will often be the first persons of color to move into an all-white suburban neighborhood and will drive miles to find a Catholic church in which to worship. That it is an all-white church makes little difference. They don't want to be shut off from the world, to be limited and isolated by the restrictions of race. There is among Caribbean folks (and this is not perhaps unusual among other ethnic groups) a deep desire to hold on to their Caribbean identity, not to become polluted by race consciousness, to maintain Caribbean values and ways of life, and to return to the homeland as often as possible in order to remain close to their roots so that they do not become Americanized. To become Americanized is to culturally devalue oneself; hence many immigrants see America as a land of economic opportunity but not one that can bring them cultural enrichment.

When Jamaican and Caribbean folks cling to their national and ethnic identities, they are prevented from truly seeing the ways in which race has wreaked havoc with the lives, identities, and consciousness of many persons of color reared here. Many immigrants, however, are afraid of making political and deep social alliances with black Americans because they are afraid of acquiring a victim identity. Since they are American residents by choice—they asked to be here—the fear is that if they begin to see the diseased and pathological nature of some aspects of America, they will have to question the very root of their self-image and sense of place in the world. They will cease to romanticize their sense of otherness and foreign status and become simply a very real part of the despised landscape they inhabit. To be hated just "like them," the "other blacks," is a nightmare, a failure of their fundamental life plan, and an insulting slap in the face of their "exotic differences." Does the experience of racism affect the sociopolitical racial sensibilities of Jamaicans and Caribbeans? Sometimes, but in my estimation not profoundly enough. A very close friend with whom I attended high school in Jamaica and who has resided in the United States for over fifteen years told me the following story. He is impervious to racism in America because he does not know what it is like to sit in the back of a bus, and he does not know what it feels like to be socialized as an inferior creature. Since he considered himself brighter than his graduate peers at Harvard Business School, he had no idea what it felt like to be less intelligent than white people. Over the years we have had many arguments over his obsession in clinging to stale cultural ways of interpreting his world. I once asked him if he feels angry when he goes back to Jamaica and observes the ways in which the treatment of the poor people there is analogous to the treatment of blacks in America. "No," he answered. "In fact I make the transition easily when I go home. Whereas in America I can sometimes identify with black causes, once I get to Jamaica, all I think about is the meal my mother's maid is going to cook. It's a different culture," he explains. "Poor people know their place. Who am I to take that away from them?" When I accuse him of not growing morally and politically, he asks: "What should I do?" I answer, *"Forget where you came from."*

To forget in this instance is to cease attaching metaphysical importance to the contingency of your identity: the set of customs, traditions, and myths that have formed you.

Forgetting is a form of death. To turn your back on memories, on the past, and on previous pleasures of the basic stuff that you think has formed you is unimaginable to many. In the service of a moral ideal it is an indispensable imperative. Radical moral transformation demands it. Or to put it another way, a particular kind of living—let us call it moral excellence—demands a form of dying, and it is this dying that is terrifying. Indian philosopher Judi Krishna-murti advises: "To live completely wholly, every day as if it were a new loveli-ness, there must be dying to everything of yesterday, otherwise you live mechanically, and a mechanical mind can never know what love is or what freedom is."[4] Krishnamurti is radical in his articulation of the necessity of dying and of forgetting in the psychological sense as means to achieving evolved living in the present. One dies to everything one knows, including one's family, memory, and all that one has felt. To die a kind of psychological death, to die to one's pleasures, is a way to freedom. Regardless of what one makes of this type of philosophy, it speaks to a deep belief in the individual's capacity for becoming. It acknowledges a self that is capable of robust retrain-ing. To forget is to start anew, to forge something sui generis into existence. It is a moral loneliness that one must be prepared to face.

In the racial constellation of the United States, the need to forget is also offered as a moral invitation to whites. What does it mean to forget that one is white? What does it mean to be white? What is purchased with one's whiteness? If we accept that whiteness or the status of being white is not an ethnic identi-ty but a social badge of privilege—a badge that ceases to be socially functional in this privileged way in the absence of distinct Others (Chicanos, Latinos, blacks, whose social and formal identities are defined by whites), and if we ask what being white in America would mean if there were no one-drop rule by which to define black people and thus an artificial superstructure against which to create institutions that practice structural exclusions of those persons defined as black, we might see a world in which whiteness was either absent or where its procedural jurisdiction over the lives of nonwhites was seriously threatened. To forget that one is white, to forget whiteness, is not a fight against racism. It is a fight against a pernicious form of tribalism that is rampant in our culture: white supremacy. There is much inspiration to be gained in this area from the depth and breadth of Cornel West's moral vision. A progressive thinker whose broad moral appeal cuts across class, racial/ethnic, and national lines by appealing directly to the moral spirit and highest possible good in all persons, West articulates the need for soul transformation in the lives of white persons. While not at all ignorant of the political machinery necessary to institutionalize the best moral visions, West, like John Stuart Mill, Søren Kierkegaard, and other moralists, realizes that morality has to come from within, that it cannot be coerced and forced into the hearts of those who are not willing to yield to its grandeur, its humbling presence. Asked in an interview what his response is to whites who ask him what they can do about racism, he replied: "First, that you need to look deep down within your own soul and recognize what kind of human being you are. Who do you see in the mirror in the morning? What do you see in your face? What's in your soul? Ask yourself, 'what makes me a moral person and a politically committed person?' And if you're serious about combating evil and suffering, then the vicious legacy of white supremacy is something you take a stand against."[5]

The ability to forget that one is white springs from the recognition and then admission of what it takes for whiteness to function as an oppressive social standard. One looks within oneself and sees the extent to which one's life in some way functions like a mini-institution. What exactly is it like to be a social standard that perpetuates injustice, shame, degradation, and automatic privilege?

In the fall of 1997, while teaching an introductory philosophy course at Purdue University, I devoted a few weeks to a the philosophical foundations of racism. This was a welcome relief to most of my students, who were burned out on Descartes's epistemology. Much of the section focused on Naomi Zack's deconstruction of the concept of race by pointing to the biological absence of any racial chromosomal marker analogous to those that objectively and clearly identify gender. On the day that we looked at philosopher Anthony Appiah's piece dealing with the physiological distinctions between race and sex, the class discussion focused on the power dynamic of sex versus race. I asked my students, most of whom were white males, whether they would prefer to have a sex change or a race change. Answers from my female students were nuanced and varied. Some spoke of the uniqueness they felt in being female; others called attention to the gains in social power that might result from a sex change. Surprisingly, most of the males said that they would opt for a race change over a sex change. They thought that being a black man was still more socially empowering than being a white female. When I asked them about the decline in social power that would certainly result from becoming black, most of them asked me to give them examples. I did and also recounted a story of a Jamaican family friend. She had married a German man, and they both emigrated to

America. At the time, he was not a legal immigrant. Both were professional chefs and were looking for employment. Without exception he was offered jobs at all the hotels he applied to. Not one of the human resources personnel requested any proof of legal residency. His wife, identified as black, was immediately asked for papers. I asked my students, What would it be like to give up that automatic badge of legitimacy that comes from being white in America? What would it mean to no longer be the normalized standard? And even if in one's race change one had the good fortune of being transformed into an educated black man—say, a black philosopher like their professor—what would it mean to all those who knew your status? What would it mean to go from being a racial stereotype to one who is exoticized? Would you be able to cull some semblance of autonomous agency? But this is the best-case scenario. What would it mean to live a life in which one's pigmentation became not only one's single most unavoidably distinguishing attribute but also an attribute that carried with it a host of very problematic and dehumanizing connotations? What would it mean to go from being perceived as the embodiment of agency to having an identity that was suspect until proven otherwise? When you think of a black man, I asked them, what would your biofeedback register if you were hooked up to the corresponding machine? And then I became very intimate. If you opted for the race change and became, let us say, a black philosopher and you retained a remnant of the consciousness you inhabited as a white socialized in a racist society, how would you feel knowing that your very presence is an offense because you are offering conceptual and moral instruction to those who are seen as your superiors?

The students looked thoughtful. Most said nothing. Some nodded. I said no more on the topic, allowing the reflection and dialogue that are part and parcel of philosophical elucidation to take their roots in the hearts and souls of my students. But the underlying idea must have been quite clear. Every point raised had little to do with being black. It had everything to do with being white.

Naomi Zack articulates three aspects of what she terms "white normativity": the normalness of whiteness to American whites; the goodness of whiteness to American whites; and the imposition of this normal and good whiteness on nonwhites and its use as a standard for evaluating them. Normativity results from the existential effects of a culture that is still largely segregated by race. If you are a white person who interacts with other whites in all the important aspects of your life—your friends are white, the person you marry is white, the leaders of your society and professional life are white, most of your teachers have been white—then two things happen. Zack writes:

> First, you are not aware of your whiteness and the whiteness of those around you during most of your daily activities. And second, whiteness is the accepted and expected

racial condition for you, and nonwhiteness and nonwhite people seem to be unusual. The result of taking whiteness for granted and reacting to nonwhiteness as an exception is that in the minds of white people, persons, those beings who can take effective action and are worthy of respect, are white."[6]

One of my students concurs. "The only time I really feel like a white person is when I am the only white person in a crowd, or when I am around another nonwhite person." He agreed that because for most of the day he was usually around white people, he did not feel like a white person. In other words, the burden of race was not always on his shoulders. This, however, is not a luxury that blacks have, since even when they are mainly around black people (a rarity in a culture in which whites are the majority), their lives in many respects are institutionally regulated by whites.

Forgetting that you are white is not to forget the rights and entitlements and other privileges that are due you as a person. It is to morally disown and disassociate yourself from the constitutive features of a sociocultural identity that relies for its existence on racial and ethnic exclusion; it is to disown those features of a social identity that feed on the denigration of nonwhites. When your particular social identity functions like a prism that does not enhance understanding but clouds judgments, reinforces unexamined assumptions about the natural worth and value of others, and actually depends on the murky portrait of others that it has created, your identity has become parasitic. To live from the standpoint of moral health requires that you cease to be complicitous in the construction of such portraits.

There is then a dialectic of remembering and forgetting that is vital for our goal. Much of our national debate about racial problems has centered around what it means to be a black person in this country and in those white worlds in which moral, civic, economic, and social lordship is exercised over nonwhites. Civil rights, liberties, and basic decencies accorded to nonwhites have been evaluated against the backdrop of unfair, unjust, and often evil acts committed by whites against nonwhites. But whites have engaged in very little moral introspection. Analyses of what it means to be black have, in some peculiar way, prevented a moral examination of the preconditions, the superstructures, and the white standpoints that created the conditions that made blackness possible. In other words, many whites have never made the connection between the physical world of blackness and their own whiteness. Since it has never been incumbent upon them to question the legitimacy of their whiteness, only the external conditions of blackness, they have never come to morally grapple with the socially constitutive features of their white identity: exclusion of those who are nonwhites, moral superiority in being white, and moral superiority over those who are not white. I am not suggesting that all dialogue about what it means to be black in America and in the world in general should cease. I am suggesting that new moral attention should be given to radically questioning what it means to be white and that the bulk of answers should not come from nonwhites but from whites themselves. Moral lessons cannot be drawn by shoving interpretations in the faces of those whom we are inviting to engage in moral introspection. The initiative has to be voluntary and the answers uncoerced. Morality has never worked in any other way, nor can it.

All the indictments leveled against whites who oppress nonwhites may be applied to all cases of tribalism. Some of the least-discussed forms of tribalism today are the ethnic persecutions of one group of ethnic Caucasians by Caucasians of another ethnic group and tribal persecutions of Africans by other Africans. I follow Charles Mills's line, however, that white global domination in the world over nonwhites remains central.[7]

THE ETHICS OF FORGETTING

A right to forget is not a right to moral amnesia. Identity is not possible with amnesia. Some forgetting breeds moral irresponsibility. There is a good case for not forgetting the Holocaust and the horrors of chattel slavery. The need not to forget is reinforced by the moral immaturity displayed by many who still practice, albeit in highly nuanced and often sublimated forms, the ethos that generated the Holocaust and the philosophy that legitimized slavery. It is also reinforced by the blatant and outright barbaric practice of ethnic cleansing that is still going on today. It is reinforced as well by the complicity of many of us who permit such atrocities to continue by failing to register our moral protest out of a basic love for humanity and pain at the sight of human destruction, by failure to revive our moral imaginations, which ought to echo in our hearts the reminder, "There but for the grace of God go I." Here memory serves to remind some of us how far we have to advance in basic civil decency. We certainly can keep alive the memory of historical atrocities, however, without requiring members of the relevant groups to adhere to a specific historical identity when they may have personally gone beyond what they started out with at birth. We need not behave like slaves, think like slaves, and wear slave identities to keep alive memories of the institution that subjugated us. In fact, the moral imperative to keep alive certain historical memories applies to everyone on the grounds of a common humanity and out of a spirit of moral decency. Our moral commitments need not stem from shared historical burdens or from membership in the group of those who may have been wronged. The beauty of the cosmopolitan morality and identity is precisely its capacity to garner moral commitments by appealing to broader sensibilities than those found within specific groups. Expanded moral consciousness and commitment are the goals of cosmopolitanism. Nowhere are such goals more clearly exemplified than in the capacity of those who have never experienced a particular moral infringement to be as morally committed to the causes of those who have suffered that infringement as they would be to their own kind had they been in the same situation.

Let me try to deepen the central point here by referencing one particular aspect of Carl Jung's analytic psychology. Jung adheres to the basic idea that the deepest level we humans can reach in our exploration of the unconscious is the layer where the individual is no longer distinct but where the mind widens and merges into the unconscious mind of humankind "where we are all the same." Just as the body has its anatomical conformity in its two eyes and two ears and one heart with only slight individual differences, so the mind also has its basic conformity. On this collective level we are all one. Jung defends his theory by studying what he calls the psychological structure of primitives, which he believes expresses the basic, universal structure of mind. Primitive mentality expresses the psychological layer that he identifies as the collective unconscious, or the underlying level that is the same in all. He writes:

> You are human, and wherever you are in the world you can defend yourself only by restricting your consciousness and making yourself as empty, as soulless as possible. Then you lose your soul because you are only a speck of consciousness floating on a sea of life in which you do not participate. But if you remain yourself you will notice that the collective atmosphere gets under your skin. You cannot live in Africa or anywhere else without having that country under your skin. If you live with the yellow man you will get yellow under your skin. You cannot prevent it because somewhere you are the same as the Negro or Chinese or whoever you live with, you are all just human beings. In the collective unconscious you are the same as a man of another race, you have the same archetypes, just as you have, like him, eyes, a heart, a liver, and so on. It does not matter that his skin is black. It matters to a certain extent, sure enough—he has probably a whole historical layer less than you. The different strata of the mind correspond to the history of the races.[8]

Jung's position is interesting from several points of view. First, it has a cosmopolitan sensibility of its own. I also find the idea of identifying historical layers as the substrata that form the basis of racial markers relevant from a cosmopolitan point of view. Part of the problem of the Natural Attitude—and certainly one of the big problems with tribalism and seeing the world and persons predominantly through tribal lenses—is precisely that we mistake the historical layer for the essence of persons. But historical layers are not irretrievably lodged within the psychic landscape of persons. Institutionally consecrated, reified, and taken as the badge of humanity, these layers instill in most of us not only the sense that they really are who we are but also that they are who we will always have to be. The truth is, however, that we overcome historical layers and limitations in our day-to-day lives, and we attempt all the time to morally overturn and subvert historical structures that have governed for generations. Those of us who revisit our family history without undergoing psychoanalysis often liberate ourselves from the patterns we formerly repeated. A moral society, to the extent that it is moral, questions and tries to remedy its proclivities for perpetuating such patterns.

Here is another way of looking at the ethics of forgetting. Let us take the phenomenon of dreaming. It is said that in deep sleep one does not dream. In subtle sleep the soul is said to stir. We dream. We awake. We forget. Most of us forget most of what we have dreamed. On waking, everything that we experience in the waking world we regard as reality. The requirements of our waking state, which include the various demands of living in the physical world, necessitate this forgetting that is accomplished upon waking. To vividly recall every dream and to experience the keenness of all the dreams we have had the night before (as opposed to the hazy, unfocused, and vague recollection most of us have of dreams) would jeopardize our perceptions as we navigate in the physical world. Many of us would mistake our dream world for the actual day-to-day world, as happens occasionally when we are unable to figure out whether we truly had a conversation with our mother yesterday or whether we just dreamed the whole thing.

Forgetting most of what we dream might not be a good thing if you believe our dream lives are keys to our ability to live successful, fully knowledgeable, and meaningful lives, that they teach us something about our deepest desires and fears, and that to forget all dreams is to render ourselves unable to form an appropriate relationship between our internal and external life. I certainly share such concerns. But here is another way of looking at the issue: Forgetting the majority of our dreams seems to be nature's way of freeing us psychically from the altered world of our dream life so that we may function successfully in our waking state. This is the state in which most of the things that we consider meaningful in our lives are executed: we have sex, we form attachments to persons, we love, we pursue our dreams, we plan long range, we live short range, we smoke our cigarettes and gossip endlessly with friends. To have our waking hours inundated with imagery from the dream world would require us to navigate between the two worlds in a manner that would surely compromise efficiency in at least one of them. Imagine the unsteady hand of the physician performing heart surgery whose vivid dream the night before of performing a vasectomy on a four-headed bull is as real, that is, as deeply perceived, as the actual surgery he is about to perform.

Somewhat analogously, I argue that a precondition for creating a new, morally successful self from which a certain type of life is lived is a good dose of moral forgetting. To live in the universe of this newly created and awakened self is to forget the habits of heart, rules, ways of seeing, and spurious paradigms of the world in which the old tribalist self resided. The analogy does not hold, though, in that nature does not provide us with a way of naturally forgetting the questionable vestiges of one world as we make the moral transition to another the way it does for the dreamer who leaves the dream world for the waking world. The impetus for this moral forgetting will come from both a moral wisdom and a moral utility. One comes to know that to execute a new self, one must die to the old. And the old self dies partly by forgetting those resources on which its survival depends.

On a personal note, I must say that my own growth, commitments, and cosmopolitan spirit have been honed to the extent that I have refrained from reifying and deifying my own culture. For someone now to accuse me of being an inauthentic Jamaican or betraying much of my cultural heritage I regard as a very crucial compliment. It means to some extent that I am finally weaned. I am somewhat grown. Julia Kristeva writes: "Free of ties with his own people, the foreigner feels 'completely free.' . . . [A]vailable, freed of everything, the foreigner has nothing, he is nothing. But he is ready for the absolute, if an absolute could choose him."[9] In a flattering way the foreigner, the self-exiled, and the wanderer are somewhat valorized for their psychic disposition, which orients them toward a cosmopolitan identity. The foreigner, like the philosopher at work, does not give the same weight to origins that common sense does. The foreigner has fled from origins, family, blood, and soil, and "even though it keeps pestering, enriching, hindering, exciting him, or giving him pain, and often all of it at once, the foreigner is its courageous and melancholy betrayer."[10] He is indeed haunted by his origins. However, it is elsewhere that he sets his hopes and that his struggles take place.[11]

A criterion of moral maturity and moral autonomy is that persons must be capable of cultivating identities separate and apart from the ones they inherit from their parents and/or their immediate socialization spheres.

To begin morally thematizing one's life, one has to reflect on the seemingly disparate elements of one's life and begin the process of disowning that which is not conducive to the thematized identity one wishes to construct. Although they may genuinely desire to change, people who are heavily compartmentalized do not have a foundation from which to begin to unify their lives. To morally thematize one's life, to invoke the moral imagination and then live according to self-created moral narrative, is a way of not living the lies of one's immediate culture and socialization. The lies we live, of course, are often the dictates or legacies of a heritage we have not overcome. Lewis Mumford notes that the grandeur of the axial prophet—who, in the sixth century B.C., was dedicated to bringing about profound changes in human values—consisted in his taking wing instead of trudging along the paved road of civilization. He seems to leap over centuries of collective effort in a single generation. Individual man, once deeply stirred, might bring about a complete self-transformation.

Does all this mean that one must abandon everything? This would be almost impossible psychologically. When I speak of forgetting, I am speaking both metaphorically and literally. The mechanism of moral forgetting is a willed, intentional stance, a way of psychically distancing oneself and effecting a moral cancellation of the often dated and bland schemata of bequeathed value systems. The mechanism of forgetting is not a veil of ignorance. An ethical theory epistemically based on ignorance is highly problematic. The forgetter knows. She knows that her identity is enslaved to narrative paradigms she has outgrown. She knows that they lack the design of her vision, style, and deepest way of really existing in the world.

The cosmopolitan in the making, one who at the end of her life would like above all to say, "I am a cosmopolitan," with the full knowledge of all that has gone into the making of that identity, thinks that such an identity has been achieved by wringing from her soul those values that superficially bind her to others and prevent her from knowing them.

One forgets and then one becomes. One becomes surprising things that one would not have become had one remained nursing at the breast of the culture that one thinks is the best on earth only because one was born into it. Isn't that the way children feel about their parents? That their mother is the most beautiful woman in the world, their dad the strongest man?

Ethnic/racial tribalism is pernicious. It is infantile. It is at base perhaps, as Freud suggests, an instinct in humans but at the same time the most limited and ghettoized way of living. Tribalism, along with its variants, nationalism and racial/ethnic pride or glorification, is *psychic infantilism*. In Freudian terms they represent a sublimated process of transferring the infantile need for parental protection on to the ethnos, the nation, the *Volk*. The entire weaning process—which is a precondition for maturity—is prolonged and then sublimated; hence our psychic immaturity, which plays itself out in tribal squabbles. Those who place an inordinate pride in the race, the ethnos, and the tribe are displaying the psychic sensibilities of children who deify their parents in a way that is integral to their identity. Observe that at thirty-five you still love your parent, but your relationship to your parent is not as integral to your identity as it was when you needed that relationship for your very sustenance. Fierce national identity, for example, which I think is analogous to clinging to the parent long after weaning should have occurred, is maintained only to the extent that those who fall outside that identity are denigrated. Like infants competing for the love, protection, and sanction of the parent because on some level they perceive that the parent's resources are limited, and like children who fight to protect the identity of the parent in order to protect and develop their own, the nationalist must keep the Other at a distance. One of the worst ways in which one child can insult another is to insult his mother to his face—the infamous "yo' mama" epithet. It wreaks psychic havoc on the child because to the extent that his mother's reputation and identity are sullied, then his own precarious and emerging identity is also called into question.

Sublimation occurs when one displaces the need for acceptance, approval, validation, and authentication onto the tribe, with one crucial factor that augments and reinforces its codification as part of tribal ontology: it is granted societal approval. But the analogous relationship between parent and child would not be granted approval, it would be frowned upon. A fifty-year-old who still needed the same approval, authentication, and love from her parent would be seen as something of an anomaly, a neurotic perhaps. But societal approval on the sublimated level makes this psychic infantilism almost a matter of policy: It is respected and taken as the mark of an authentic type of person. One keeps oneself real by staying close to the tribe.

CULTURALISM AND OPPRESSIVE CULTURES: DO WE OBLITERATE THEM?

David Bromwich makes a compelling argument against those he labels as culturalists. He defines culturalism as

> the thesis that there is a universal need to belong to a culture—to belong, that is, to a self-conscious group with a known history, a group that by preserving and transmitting its customs, memories, and common practices confers the primary pigment of individual identity on the persons it comprehends. This need, culturalism says, is on par with the need to be loved by a father and a mother, and with the need for a life of friendship and associates.[12]

He thinks that in the trivial sense that claim is correct but that in the strong sense in which it is worth discussing, the claim is false. Why, he asks, should each of us be more than matter-of-fact in committing our lives to our history and cultural identity? A culture may indeed be like a family, but are we to presume it a happy family? We owe nothing to any object or condition as a mere forced consequence of its permanence.

He invokes the Blakean characterization of the artist as the exemplar of a highly evolved agent. The artist is any person whose highly particular material is sufficient for reflection. Bromwich writes: "We had better admit from the first that we are touched by individuals, and by the idea of their lives, and that by association with these alone do we ever come close to imagining a race or its way of life."[13]

What emerges from Bromwich's article are the ways in which the culturalist, like the pluralist, must be committed to ways of preserving cultural identity by filtering out those values, beliefs, and practices that can cause the particular culture to become extinct. He locates this thesis by analyzing the arguments of Charles Taylor, Michael Walzer, and Joseph Raz. Taylor, for example, worries that if cultures are assimilated by a liberal society, they will suffer extinction and each member will suffer a loss of integrity. Raz fears that a loss of cultural identity will result in a loss of some sense of the meaning of life. He advocates the education of the young of all cultures in the culture of their own groups. Bromwich sees evidence in Raz's argument for the idea that the state should bear the costs of this education. Cultures that are undereducated should be educated; cultural support must be found for "autonomous cultural institutions" such as museums and charities. What is done for artistic and community activities should extend to "public space (as well as air space on television)." Bromwich sees many problems with implementing these recommendations on the culturalist agenda. He writes:

> A liberal society has a commitment not to infringe the rights of unaffiliated talent. A thinker may chose, as Spinoza once did, or an artist may choose, as Naipaul and Rushdie have, to cease to belong as reclaimable property to the culture that "constitutes" them. They are doing what Walzer, Taylor, and Raz agree is epistemologically impossible. Nevertheless, they are doing it.[14]

The suggestion of culturalism, he argues, is that tribal cultures will abate not a jot of their property in each member whom they own and that they are sufficiently flexible proprietors to allow us a spotless conscience as we commit to their care individuals of the many nations-within-nations tending toward dissolution.

I find Bromwich's position interesting, for I think it complements my notion that tribalism (of which culturalism, along with racial, ethnic, and national identities, is a variation) is a form of psychic infantilism that delays weaning and therefore stymies moral maturity. What he describes as culturalism is described by others as a form of *liberal nationalism* that puts great weight on the distinction between insiders and outsiders, members and nonmembers.[15]

Another criterion for moral maturity is the ability to make judgments based on some decreed rational standard. The judgments rendered ought to be binding on the commitments one makes, the values one holds, and one's emotional responses in any given situation governed or influenced by one's decisions.

Now, here is where the culturalists and other tribalists fail: In personifying culture (a move that fails all sorts of conceptual, logical, and psychological standards), they often exempt it from the very standards that they would insist that individuals meet. They treat culture as if it is something worthy of love in the same way that human beings are. And whereas to retract one's love or modify it when dealing with an undeserving agent is regarded as praiseworthy, to treat one's culture in a similar manner is seen by too many of the tribalists as a mark of inauthenticity. I shall call this the *clinging syndrome*. The clinging syndrome is a way of preventing individuation, autonomy, moral responsibility, and becoming in any meaningful manner. One's life remains thematized by the tribe, and one therefore has no way of redressing, challenging, or circumventing those aspects of the tribe that are deserving of reproach. In this way one cannot assume narrative control of one's life and thematize one's ordered moral becoming. It is for this reason that cosmopolitans are no respecters of culture qua culture, although they recognize that it is in culture that one develops, learns, and morally matures. Cosmopolitans, however, do not validate a particular culture because it is the culture of specific groups of people. In the words of Jeremy Waldron:

> The cosmopolitan may live all his life in one city and maintain the same citizenship throughout. But he refuses to think of himself as defined by his location or his ancestry or his citizenship or his language. Though he may live in San Francisco and be of Irish ancestry, he does not take his identity to be compromised when he learns Spanish, eats Chinese, wears clothes made in Korea, listens to arias by Verdi sung by a Maori princess on Japanese equipment.... He is a creature of modernity, conscious of living in a mixed-up world and having a mixed-up self.[16]

Regardless of how Waldron might feel about the cosmopolitan self, the notion of a mixed-up self is not to be regarded as conceptually anomalous nor as confused and chaotic. A mixed-up self is a self that is a compound or mixture of ingredients.

If the culture is bankrupt, then the moral cosmopolitan in good faith will condemn it as such, refraining from the sentimental temptation to honor and protect it because it is of value to some people and because some people cannot conceive of a way of life without that particular culture. Cosmopolitans would not hesitate to deliver a judgment of cultural inferiority to cultures that deserve that label, nor would they refrain from encouraging persons to render that verdict with respect to their own cultures. In this instance I concur with Anthony Appiah that although cosmopolitans value variety, there are other social goods of a liberal society that they value more. Such social goods would include a basic respect for human rights, the dignity of all persons, and the autonomy of persons. As Wilfrid Desan points out, belonging to the human totality transcends all belonging to nations and races and supersedes all local convention. This implies that *simply to be* is prior to *being such-and-such.*[17]

Let me flesh out what I mean when I say that the moral cosmopolitan ought not to be deterred from making definite moral judgments about morally bankrupt cultures. The notion that a cosmopolitan is someone who grants equal importance to all cultures and honors cultures because they are cultures is conceptually misguided. I am arguing for a more radical position. If we define a culture as a set of codified and practiced values, norms, customs, traditions, and lifestyles, then there could be cultures that the cosmopolitan thinks ought to be annihilated. The world would be better off without certain cultures. This does not mean that the individual members of the culture ought to be annihilated; rather, the customs, practices, and traditions that are constitutive of the culture ought to be abolished. In a rather illuminating essay regarding human rights in the Muslim world, Azizah Al-Hibri, a professor of law and founder of Karma: Muslim Woman Lawyers for Human Rights, notes numerous problems in many Muslim countries. These problems range from a denial of democratic rights to restrictions on speech, movement, and education. She cites a rather severe example from Afghanistan, where the Taliban have exiled women from public life. This stems from their desire to achieve the perfect Muslim state. Relying on an eyewitness report, she recounts from Kabul the following story:

> Recently, a man was arrested for not growing a beard. His wife and infant child were left unattended at home. The woman finally had to leave her house, with the infant in her arms, to purchase a loaf of bread. She was detected by the Talibans and was beaten mercilessly because her flowery skirt showed accidentally from under her chador. The woman lost her sanity. She ran home, where she was boiling meat, and splashed hot water on her assailants. They killed her on the spot, in front of her child.[18]

This, I submit, is an example of moral perniciousness carried to its extreme. If such are the requirements of a perfect Islamic state, then such a state would be a moral atrocity that no person with a shred of moral decency would defend. On cosmopolitan grounds, any attempt to do so is a sure sign of moral degeneracy. To grant such behavior any form of moral legitimacy is tantamount to sanctioning the atrocities. As a person of color I would find equally pernicious any equivalent attempt to justify slavery by explaining the sociocultural and economic realities from which the institution emerged. Part of my response would be: But the Quakers and other conscientious moral objectors did not own slaves, and they were also individuals of the times. Numerous cases of Talibanism have come to light. Women are absolutely restricted from working outside the home and in many cases are routinely prohibited from receiving medical treatment. Women who have no male supporters have been forced to live by begging. Working women have been forced to resign from their jobs.

Regardless of the fact that Muslims take spirituality seriously, as Al-Hibri counsels, and regardless of the fact that any attempt to secularize laws in Muslim countries will have to be based on a "proper understanding of the nature of the problem and the people involved," a moral commitment to the destruction of such practices is the responsibility of all ethical cosmopolitans. This commitment is reinforced by the understanding that valorizing cultural practices because they are traditional and because they are the properties of particular groups of people is to treat culture with false reverence or artistic mystification of the sort evinced by mindless suckers baffled by nonrepresentational art who still treat it with reverence, using both their ignorance and their inability to comprehend as proof of the depth and sacrosanct nature of the phenomenon with which they are faced. This places culture outside the province of critical rationality and moral scrutiny. But cultural practices, unlike nonrepresentational art, are representative. They are representative of how institutional practices are codified and regulative of human beings in a way that denies them the right to their dignity and ownership of their lives. Similarly, the American cultural practice—and, yes, it is a cultural practice—of classifying people into racial categories according to a dubious and scientifically specious one-drop rule must be abolished. Why do I classify it as a cultural practice? It is certainly a custom. It is part of American tradition. It regulates the lives of the nation's inhabitants, and, more important, it is the organizing principle of much of civic and institutional life. It affects the ways in which resources are made available and distributed to certain people. It is a decisive factor, in fact, in determining whether and how people are allowed to pursue the acquisition of resources required to maintain human existence: health care, jobs, wealth, property, and retirement benefits, to name just a few. Since naming power in America is the privilege—legally, socially, and, more important, institutionally—of persons who are white, the question to ask is, What would it mean in the long run—and here I mean in the very, very long run—for such persons to lack this particular form of institutionalized and political power over the lives of other people? It would certainly mean a great many things. Would we ultimately see the dismantling of a kind of reality in which persons who are white are deeply enmeshed? Resoundingly, yes. Ought moral cosmopolitans to be concerned with the discomfort and dislocations of such morally questionable realities? In this case, let the voice of your own moral consciousness answer. The very same appeal to cultural integrity, however, was used as an argument not only to justify chattel slavery but also to uphold the racial apartheid that existed in the South and elsewhere only a few decades ago. Should moral cosmopolitans be upset because the dismantling of segregation in the South or the abolition of plantation slavery resulted in the destruction of centuries of traditions and meaningful lifestyles for the beneficiaries of those cultures? The very same relativism that sanctions cultural atrocities is part of the reason that a terrorist organization such as the Ku Klux Klan is allowed to thrive in this culture without being outlawed. It constitutes a culture—indeed, children are raised by its values, communities are formed and fostered around its ethos, and an enduring tradition is passed on to new generations. If we adhere to the definition of culture I have advanced, what would be wrong with annihilating such a culture? The same, of course, would hold true of similar cultures built on hatred, whether in Africa, the Orient, Europe, or right here in America. If part of what it means to be a cosmopolitan is to advance and live the idea of love of humankind, then the moral cosmopolitan in good faith cannot sanction any culture that is destructive of human dignity, life, value, and flourishing. If moral-minded persons were not committed to the total destruction of those social realities and the pernicious cultural practices that upheld them, I would not have had the freedom and the opportunity to sit here as I do and write these pages. I would not have had the freedom to become the person I have become. Since in a profound way I see the act of writing as a crucial tool in moral becoming—that is, as a way of achieving the identity imagined in one's moral vision—it ought to be clear why I regard this issue as critically important. Philosophical writing, the preservation of the identity that makes such writing possible, and the possibility of forging a new identity through the act of writing are matters of life and death.

If cosmopolitans refrain from moral judgments for fear of disrupting the sovereignty of particular cultures or undermining the value of pluralism—that is, undermining the procedures, criteria, and standards that are used to maintain and nurture distinct cultural identities—then people who regard themselves as cosmopolitans are complicitous not only in fostering the worst forms of tribalism but also in allowing the unchecked growth of the precondition for cultural, racial, ethnic, and national tribalism: psychic infantilism.

I have suggested that societally sanctioned and fostered psychic infantilism is best overcome via distanciation, forgetting, and embracing cosmopolitanism. Cosmopolitanism completes the weaning process on two levels. First, it entreats us to embrace the Other, not in the spirit of exoticism or shallow sentimentality, but simply as a creature who on a real and fundamental level is the same basic type of creature as we are. If this seems an obvious point, then the mentality and actions of tribalists and cultural nationalists certainly obfuscate it. When people cling to beliefs about cultural authenticity as a legitimate moral marker of what they take to be real kinds of persons, we are, it seems to me, treating the issue of cultural, national, and racial identity with too much metaphysical seriousness.

The second way that cosmopolitanism completes the weaning process is that it invites an introspection and subsequent examination of our sense of the real markers that be believe properly distinguish us from those we designate as strangers and as Others. In this respect, Julia Kristeva's contribution to the literature on cosmopolitanism directly strengthens much of what I am trying to accomplish. Kristeva identifies herself as a cosmopolitan, which for her "means that I have, against origins and starting from them, chosen a transnational or international position situated at the crossing of boundaries."[19] In *Strangers to Ourselves*, she creatively carves out a space that could be filled by a real cosmopolitan ethos by examining the reality of the stranger and the foreigner as well as the concept of otherness in Western civilization. She encourages readers to look into their own otherness. We are all really strangers to ourselves, Kristeva argues. If we accept this and simultaneously accept the foreignness that lives within, then the geographical foreigner becomes less abhorrent and less of a threat. In fact, we might learn to embrace the foreigner and the radical Other as complements to ourselves. Kristeva's delineation of this idea is inspired by Freud's approach to the Unconscious. The Unconscious indicates the existence of the *strange* in the psyche. The strange loses its pathological aspect and integrates within the assumed unity "of human beings an *otherness* that is both biological *and* symbolic and becomes an integral part of the same."[20] The foreigner for Kristeva is neither glorified as a secret *Volksgeist* nor banished as a disruptive presence. Foreignness is within us, as we are our own foreigners. We are divided. There are discontents one feels when living in the midst of the other: the discomfort of one's own strangeness, which makes one feel like an Other to oneself and the actual strangeness of the other person. These discontents rest on a quirky logic that governs the way the Unconscious deals with symbols, languages, and gestures. All these are already shaped by the Other. Kristeva writes:

> It is through unraveling transference—the major dynamics of otherness, of love/hatred for the other, of the foreign component of our psyche—that, on the basis of the other, I become reconciled with my own otherness-foreignness, that I play on it and live by it. Psychoanalysis is then experienced as a journey into the strangeness of the other and of oneself, toward an ethics of respect for the irreconcilable. How could one tolerate a foreigner if one did not know one was a stranger to oneself?[21]

For Kristeva the encounter with the other and the identification of the self with that good or bad other that transgresses the precarious boundaries of the uncertain self are the source of an uncanny strangeness. To flee from or struggle against the other is a form of escapism, for we are fighting our unconscious. Kristeva writes: "To worry or to smile, such is the choice when we are assailed by the strange; our decision depends on how familiar we are with our own ghosts."[22]

To discover one's disturbing otherness and foreignness and to accept it in others is to obliterate the concept of foreignness: If I am a foreigner, there are no foreigners. The politics implied by the ethics of psychoanalysis would "involve a cosmopolitanism of a new sort that, cutting across governments, economics and markets, might work for a mankind whose solidarity is founded on the consciousness of its unconscious—desiring, destructive, fearful, empty, impossible."[23]

Kristeva's invitation to explore our own otherness is a high-minded one that rests on a benevolent and optimistic reading of human maturity, or at least individuals' potential willingness to entertain a level of psychic introspection that can lift them from the familiarity of their ordinary self-images. Moral entreaties are, for the most part, by nature difficult to grapple with. But to the extent that her invitation can be accepted by any number of willing and able individuals, it stands as a very plausible mechanism that can play a healthy role in fostering the sort of mind-set that is necessary for a cosmopolitan ethos. To admit that we ourselves are strangers is at best to admit that *strangeness* is not a criterion for exclusion from the human community. Locating the stranger in ourselves obliterates the notion of a radical Other. If the other as stranger is crude, exotic, and primitive, then so am I, so are all of us. Few like to be offensive to themselves for very long. The strangeness of the other at best complements the stranger that one is to oneself.

There is a way in which the dialectical interplay of masking and forgetting and then seeing the strangeness of oneself is crucial in fostering the cosmopolitan ethos. Masking involves the projection of the morally ordered self one wants to be and provides a transitional reality that can accommodate this new self. Moral forgetting provides the freshness and clears the space for a newly constructed identity. In fiction writing the device known as the *what if* premise is used by many a writer in the development of plot structure and story line. The writer asks herself, "What if?" accompanied by a series of scenarios ranging from the fantastical to the mundane. The use of the "what if?" though, is meant to entertain the notion of expanded possibilities. It is a way of introducing a sort of paradigm shift from one context to another. An analog to this would involve asking yourself, "What if?" with the range of possible answers serving as a catalyst to your moral imagination, and then moving on to a plan of action (similar to the plot structure of the writer's story) that leads to the emergence of a different type of self by way of a transformative praxis. Forgetting allows the "what if?" premise to rear its curious head. This technique—if one may refer to it as such—is exactly what masking permits. The suggestion of forgetting, of real psychic distanciation between what you are trying to forge and what you are attempting to overcome, is valid as a psychological tool. Freeman writes that "for every instance of self-gain, of moving forward into a new and superior region of existence, there is also inevitably self-loss: we must distance ourselves from that dimension of our lives that has been found wanting and see if there is a better way."[24]

The question that must be asked at this stage, though, is: Can the weaning process ever be complete? Can humans live without the sublimated parent? And further: What of those cultures whose individuals need the affirmative nurturing of the tribe? I am, for example, speaking of marginalized cultures within a larger cultural sphere, such as Brazilian or American blacks, ethnic Albanians living under Serb rule, the Gypsies of Romania, ethnic Tibetans. I am speaking about cultural affiliations that offer respite and support in ways that are not provided by the dominant culture, where the dominant culture has been destructive of the dignity and well-being of its inhabitants. I shall answer by saying again that I regard tribalism as an unweaned state. However, it seems to me that the question can be posed another way: At what stage might members of marginalized groups be encouraged to shed tribal loyalties and rigid tribal affiliations? The answer is perhaps that such an answer can never be collectively made. The answer will be given by individual men and women, and their responses will be determined largely by their perception of the ways their life plans and flourishing can be achieved. One by one they may opt to answer the challenge by seeking other affiliations and by underemphasizing their attachments to their roots. This is precisely the issue in today's discussions about the alleged crises of identity and community in the "postmodern" world generally and among black people in particular. The point, therefore, is that no one can adopt a noncontextual position and say that such-and-such a time is right. Persons will make such decisions as they see fit. It very well could be that persons from marginalized groups as a whole may not be ready in large numbers to dispense with tribal loyalties because the larger culture has not made it entirely clear that it will provide the support structures and resources that are conducive to their well-being. I think that overall the time for moral growth and weaning, and thus the time for a true cosmopolitan morality for all people, has come. But there is also a way in which the question as posed sets up a dilemma for which there might be no resolution. That is, there might never really be an ideal time for any of the ideals as I have described them. If one were to wait for the right time before deciding to embrace a particular morality, then one might indeed wait for a very long time. A radical cosmopolitan ethos is one for courageous individuals wherever they may live. All the risks undertaken in adopting such an ethos and embracing its ethical corollary, letting go of tribal affiliations, will be borne by individuals alone. To the extent that their lives may be worthy of emulation, then their examples might inspire others to test the waters, so to speak. Historically those who have decided to take moral charge of their lives have generally not waited for the right sociopolitical time or for the approval of others. They have done so alone and because they were compelled by the demands of their own souls.

I could also answer the question in another way. I could say that the degree of forgetting and the extent to which one distances oneself from the tribe will depend on the type of cosmopolitan one wishes to be. In the next chapter, I sketch two plausible types of cosmopolitanism: *radical cosmopolitanism,* which is the type I have been delineating, and *moderate cosmopolitanism.*

5

RADICAL AND MODERATE

MORAL COSMOPOLITANISM

RADICAL COSMOPOLITANISM

Moral Identity

A radical cosmopolitan is one who refrains from fixating on tribal (racial/ethnic/national) loyalties and is especially suspicious of employing such loyalties as criteria in moral deliberations. Such an individual would not attach any sense of superior value to his cultural, ethnic, or racial identity but would instead see himself as a compound of several contingencies that make up the identity he has.

A radical cosmopolitan feels no compulsion to be loyal to his "roots." He harbors a love of the distant. He is future oriented, especially with regard to the ways in which his identity is open to moral modification and reconstitution. Such an individual is always receptive to new experiences that will orient him toward expunging from his frame of reference specific values, value commitments, and group identifications.

Such a person does not feel a need to authenticate himself in terms of the sodality of his origin. Human culture, according to the radical cosmopolitan, is properly the property of all humans in the world. Cultural appropriation, therefore, to the extent that it enhances moral identity, is an ideal that ought to be embraced. Far from believing that he is betraying his cultural identity, the radical cosmopolitan knows that he is enriching his human identity and is thoroughly individualistic in his approach to others. He regards other types of personal self-identities as more crucial and morally relevant to persons. That is, valuing autonomy as an indispensable social good, the first-order cosmopolitan regards identities that are consciously chosen as superior to those one uncritically accepts. The cosmopolitan validates consciously crafted identities according to the standards evoked by his ideated self and the morally thematized ways he wishes to order his life. We may call this *self-ownership*. Such a life is committed to actions, projects, and moral commitments. It is a morally evaluated life and is therefore more compatible with the conceptual aspect of the human condition, which sees human beings as self-made creatures who have to construct their own humanity. The cosmopolitan attempts to construct a humanity that is imbued with features that are morally relevant to, and indicative of, the person constructing it. Whereas the tribalist self grants moral legitimacy to accidental features of a person's makeup, the cosmopolitan self grants legitimacy to features of the self that are laden with specific attributes (moral cosmopolitan attributes) that specify the moral status of the individual. Since human beings are primarily conceptual creatures, the cosmopolitan life of continued moral construction and evaluation is representative of the species in its highest form.

The radical cosmopolitan cannot accept racial, national, or ethnic identities as compelling indicators of a person's moral worth. Therefore anyone, for example, who claims to be a cosmopolitan but is against nontribal marriages (marriages where the parties do not share the same ethnic, national, or racial background) on purely tribal grounds—on the premise that failure to oppose such marriages undermines the existence of the tribe—cannot be a radical cosmopolitan. A radical cosmopolitan, furthermore, to the extent that he recognizes that physical phenotypes are, indeed, merely physical and not racial, would not be inclined to believe in the biological existence of races. This is a crucial aspect of cosmopolitanism, since the particular brand I am constructing is one that opposes all aspects of racial and ethnic tribalism. Since the radical cosmopolitan considers himself a member of many groups and subcultures, he is less likely to valorize any particular one on the basis of its being his roots or birthright. Rather, a radical cosmopolitan may valorize his membership in, or his attraction to, one group over another to the extent that he can rationally and objectively demonstrate that the values, ethos, and principles advanced and practiced by that group or culture achieve values to which his moral consciousness commits him: a life that respects the dignity, autonomy, and individuality of each person; a life that, therefore, allows independence of mind and independence of vision to flourish; a life that honors the creative impulse of persons to fashion themselves according to the highest (and, perhaps regrettably, even the lowest, although this would not be encouraged by the cosmopolitan) standards conceivable. It is, therefore, obvious that racial or ethnic affiliations are not powerful affinities for the cosmopolitan. Nevertheless, a radical cosmopolitan is a human being, albeit of a morally different type. He will not automatically discount the cultural familiarity felt by members of the same ethnos along with the concomitant psychological accouterments of such a familiarity: feelings of comfort and security, empathy and deep understanding of the lived contexts of those who have shared experiences. The radical cosmopolitan, however, to the extent that he is morally committed to a nontribal approach to human living, would not attach moral or deep ontological significance to such affiliations.

A committed radical cosmopolitan would react with as much vehemence and moral indignation to injustices perpetrated against someone from another ethnicity or race as he would to those against his own. True, to the extent that he still has attachments of some kind to his roots, he may feel more acutely the emotional pain caused by injustice to that group. But an ethical cosmopolitan is committed to principles, values, and specific social and ethical goals and not merely to subjective, sentimental feelings associated with his kin group.

The value of this cannot be discounted. If one looks at the emotional vibrations emitted by several alleged human rights activists, one sees that very often when they make charges of violations, there are often questionable self-serving criteria involved. Quite often some tribal affiliation is used as a standard. A radical cosmopolitan who happens to be of Croatian origin would reject on principle the violation of the rights of a Serb. Some would say that, carried to extremes, that sort of ethos is political suicide. Part of what separates a radical cosmopolitan, however, from others is the unwillingness to allow sociopolitical considerations to interfere with the operation of his moral consciousness. In other words, the cosmopolitan morality is not dependent on the social or political convenience of the moment, although the manner in which the expressed ethos can navigate its way throughout the culture is quite dependent on the culture's sociopolitical climate. An analogy may help clarify this point. One cannot claim to be an advocate of nonviolent resistance but, when challenged, respond violently on the ground that one lives in a violent culture. Although existential factors (the hostility of others) tempt one to violate one's commitment to nonviolence, one could not use sociocultural factors (the violent tendencies of others) as a reason for violating one's position since that position is actually validated on the premise that one is or could be the recipient of others' aggression.

I do not want to claim that radical cosmopolitanism blurs the distinction between the public and the private self or that to be a radical cosmopolitan means that persons cannot hold moral principles distinct from a host of private interests, concerns, and preferences that are not linked to a cosmopolitan index. It is quite possible and permissible for individuals to like a certain form of music, a certain type of food, and certain genres of literature without filtering these styles through a cosmopolitan prism. But radical cosmopolitans blur the distinction between any real and robust notion of the public and private self by undermining the distinction between *personal identity* and *moral identity.* Their personal identity is thickly infused with a set of moral ideals. Those ideals limit what is permitted within the personal sphere. Hence, moral and conceptual vigilance demands that we cultivate a set of criteria to determine what is worthy of being admitted into the personal sphere. Persons do this to some extent and with varying degrees of consistency. Most of us do not befriend serial killers, known rapists, neo-Nazis, or persons who would seek to rob women of their legal rights. Most of us would properly find the admittance of such persons into our personal universe abhorrent.

Anne Colby and William Damon observe in their study of moral exemplars that the unity or conflict between personal and moral goals is central to a discussion of morality and the self because goals are an important component of one's identity or self-concept. Several individuals in their study state quite emphatically that there is a very close relation between their sense of personal identity and their moral goals. Their study indicates that goals are a very central component of any moral self. When moral and personal goals are unified, moral goals are central to the self. Individuals who define their self in terms of their moral goals will more likely interpret events as moral problems and see themselves implicated in the solution of these problems.[1]

This is not unique to cosmopolitanism. Christianity, besides being a religion that predicates a particular moral system and a type of moral self, functions in a similar way. The type of self predicated by the system will rule out specific goals, attitudes, and values within the personal identity sphere; the precise goals will depend on how rigorous the concept of the Christian self turns out to be. Could a Christian self remain Christian while professing a disbelief in the divinity of Jesus Christ? Absolutely not. Belief in the divinity of Jesus Christ is a constitutive feature of Christianity. Can one disavow some of the commandments and remain a Christian? Perhaps. All of them? Unlikely. Again, it all depends on how strong the concept is and, to some extent, on how it expresses itself in the empirical world.

Can one be a Christian and a racist? Empirically, yes, this certainly has been the case. Ku Klux Klan members are just that. Is racial discrimination a violation of a constitutive feature of Christianity? Strictly speaking, the answer has to be no, which perhaps accounts for the existence of many racist Christians. Being a racist might violate other key features of Christianity or, at best, of a Christian ethos: namely, acknowledging the brotherhood of humankind, loving one's neighbor as oneself, and being the keeper of one's fellow human. One can violate these ideals without ultimately perverting the concept itself. One can hold on to minimal Christianity by being a racist and failing to love one's neighbor as oneself. The violations are not sufficient to render the concept void.

I point this out to show that if cosmopolitanism is going to function as a moral system and as a conception of the self as well, then its conceptual base has to be established firmly. Cosmopolitanism must be committed to this goal so that ultimately cultural nationalists, racists, ethnic particularists, and mindless patriots—that is, uncritical and unreflective patriots who pledge allegiance without examining at each juncture the values and contexts to which they are pledging loyalty—cannot claim these identities and call themselves cosmopolitans. On moral cosmopolitan grounds they would be deemed conceptually out of order. Radical cosmopolitanism and its corollary self will delineate the concept in its most rigorous form.

I have argued that a moral identity that is volitionally owned is chosen from among competing moral options out of a moral sense of life. To be a cosmopolitan is to practice cosmopolitanism. Radical moral cosmopolitanism requires more than saying, "I am a cosmopolitan because I believe such-and-such." A practicing moral cosmopolitan gives the identity what I shall term its *moral efficacy*. This means that individuals who practice cosmopolitanism are morally efficacious persons.

To say that a cosmopolitan identity is morally efficacious is to specify another key feature of the concept, namely, that it is an active identity. Its constitutive features are connected with the practices and actions in the world that give the identity its character. This distinguishes it from those sorts of identities whose formal content has to do with an intentional stance, a passional stance, or a set of beliefs and attitudes all of which can be disconnected from behaviors that foundationalize them. Thus a Kantian philosopher may be someone who reconstructs Immanuel Kant's arguments in the *Critique of Pure Reason*, who believes that Kant's philosophy is conceptually valid and his arguments correct, but who may not live according to Kantian principles. I recall a conversation with a philosopher who did work in theistic philosophy and who identified himself as a theistic philosopher but who in life was an atheist. I suggest that in these cases, the two identities cannot be called *active identities*. In fact, they may be properly referred to as *passive identities*, because the possession of the identity commits their claimants only partially to a set of practices, behaviors, and actions that the identity in its widest and fullest scope demands.

Radical moral cosmopolitanism actually stands in correction of racial and ethnic identities, which are passive identities with little or no causal moral potency. Unlike racial and ethnic identities, cosmopolitanism, besides being a morality and a conception of self, is a form of practice. If we examine racial and ethnic identities, we see that those who cling to them as formal and strong concepts do so without strengthening or adding anything substantive to the concept; that is, they fail to delimit it by subsuming under it features that pertain only to the concept; they fail to make it distinguishable in a rigorous and binding way from other concepts. One who clings to a racial and ethnic identity attempts quite often to wring a great deal of virtue out of it without adding anything, such as, say, moral behavior of a certain type, to make the concept content specific. A white person or an Indian or a Caribbean person may take pride in his racial or ethnic ancestry; but because the identity is so fluid and open-ended and its bearers so diverse morally and also in terms of character, styles, tastes, occupations, and life plans, the particular white, Indian, or

Caribbean person contributes nothing constitutively to the identity in question. For example, if we look at Dr. Martin Luther King Jr.'s moral heroism, we will see that it contributes nothing to the concept of blackness, because that concept may refer to or cover the actions of those who are the antithesis of Dr. King's moral heroism. The term *blackness* can refer to people whose behaviors are morally deplorable. Dr. King's moral heroism contributes a great deal to concepts like martyrdom, selflessness, and courage because those concepts rule out individuals who display antithetical behaviors.

Cosmopolitanism is not passively worn; it is actively practiced. Hence announcing oneself as a cosmopolitan is less important than living like one. The life the cosmopolitan lives is determined by the requirements of moral cosmopolitanism. Unlike those who cling to racial and ethnic identities, cosmopolitans see their identity as constantly being shaped by the future. This forward-looking quality of cosmopolitanism means in part that identity is negotiable. Racial, ethnic, and national identities are not inherently deterministic, but the view of the self on which they are predicated treats them as though they were. Any privileging of roots is dependent on a view of the self as linked in some nonmodifiable way to its past. Psychologically we know that this is not the case. People need not be chained to states that characterized their pasts. If this were the case, psychiatrists' couches would be empty and individuals would not be able to free themselves from a plethora of psychological disorders from anorexia to obsessive-compulsive disorder. Tribal affiliations are no more central to a person's identity than are such psychological disturbances that people are eager to rid themselves of.

Tribal Idolatry, Tribal Psychological Cloning, Homoraciality, and Homoethnicity

Two crucial aspects are at issue here in relation to the idolatry of tribal identity. One is a deep form of narcissism that is born out of seeing oneself as a special type of self because of one's particular racial, ethnic, or national identity. The reason many of us prefer to be around others of "our kind" is not simply because of the opportunity to express common values but because others reinforce the infantile narcissism typical of young children as they are developing a sense of themselves as separate entities. As an infant begins to make a distinction between herself and the objects around her, as she realizes that she is not just an extension of the objects in her immediate environment but a separate, independent entity, other human beings reinforce this cognitive advancement on her part.[2] It is the birth of any real notion of an "I" within the child's emerging sense of self. This realization is a necessity for any sense of future relationship with herself. The recognition of the other reinforces her separateness and paradoxically will be instrumental in any sense of self-love she may later acquire. The instrumentality of the other lies in her ability to act as a mirror to the individual. To the extent that you can mirror my sense of life, my sense of values, to the extent that through you I gain some semblance of psychological visibility, then I need you in order to have a relationship with the world. You are integral to my emerging sense of efficacy in that you are the first sign that the world is pulsating and alive and responsive to the unique creature that I am. To the extent that you respond to the gyrations of my psyche, you are also the first sign that the world is malleable, that it can be remade in the image of that which the "I" begins to stand for. To the extent that you are that sign, I find ways of producing an army such as you: markers that resemble me. And so we begin to look alike and to feel alike. We become interchangeable members in a pristine universe; and when we look at each other, we each are in some way looking at ourselves.

In tribal idolatry, this sense of uniqueness and holding on to an indubitable "I" whose precarious existence is threatened by the ego strengths of others is preserved by a process of *tribal psychological cloning*. The concern today about genetic cloning is patently sad in its myopic, one-sided focus. The same phenomenon on the tribal psychic level has been going on in the souls of humans for thousands of years and, perversely, has been morally sanctioned as a good thing. Tribal idolatry is an attempt to clone the individual "I" en masse. Whether it is cultural authenticity, racial solidarity, or ethnic or national particularism, the phenomenon at work reveals itself in *tribal psychic militarism*. The manifestation of racial/ethnic and national tribalism is the spiritual tattooing that is tantamount to dirtying one's moral consciousness. To the extent that these tattoos are replicated generationally, we are literally instantiating the notion of original sin. Individuals thus marked are trapped in psychic ghettoes and cannot achieve any breakthrough in history, culture, and profound moral maturity. To the extent that human beings reproduce their balkanized states of moral immaturity by continuing to demarcate themselves tribally, radically new selves cannot be created. If radically new selves are not created, then there is no hope for a radical moral revolution in human existence.

To replicate one's racial or ethnic caste by a set of systematic and institutional procedures with formal criteria that operate against the backdrop of racial/ethnic purity on one side and impurity on the other is not just a form of institutionalizing narcissism; it is also a way of inescapably pathologizing identity. I think of a group of little goons who decide amongst themselves to make up a ghastly game replete with all sorts of perversions, arbitrary rules, and self-centered goals. They then invite and ultimately force other children into the game. After a while, the game takes on the appearance of normality.

Refusing to play that game in the neighborhood not only makes one a bad team player, it also makes one seem less human. To try to point out what is wrong with the game is to act like a madman, since over time the universe of that game comes to seem natural. The game and its dark pathology become inscribed not just in physical reality but also indelibly in the minds of the participants, who take it as their birthright to decree arbitrarily that their universe is the natural order of things. Tribal identities are instantiations of such perversions. Tribal idolatry is the reification and deification of one's immediate environment and of people in that environment who look similar to one. It is the attempt to attach moral and social significance to a set of culturally decreed markers that in essence are morally neutral and irrelevant to human agency. To go through a sex change is one thing. But the response to those who go through what may be termed a race or ethnic or national identity change is on the order of, "You are not just betraying your own kind. You are betraying, violating, and perverting a crucial part of your personhood." But as we have already seen, to hold persons slaves to their roots is to take a social fact, an artificially created feature of the human condition, as an immutable metaphysical brute fact. Race, ethnic, and national identities are not descriptive laws of nature. They are always negotiable. When their predications are morally problematic and seriously threaten a life of decency, dignity, and psychic maturity, then the time for serious moral evaluation is at hand. It is my contention and moral conviction that deep and honest evaluation will suggest the annihilation of all racial and ethnic tribal identities.

The second point to be made regarding those who are reluctant to abandon racial identities has to do with the sense of dread that people feel in relation to giving up their racial and ethnic tribal identities. Kierkegaard makes a distinction between dread and fear. Fear is the feeling that accompanies something that is definite, regardless of whether it is real or imagined: the menacing dog in the neighbor's yard, or the boogie monster that haunts the child in his dreams, or the snake under the bed. Dread, however, is concerned with the unknown, the indefinite, and the mysterious. The child who is attracted to a secret fantasy is both repelled and attracted at the same time. Dread is a mixture of excitement and repulsion.[3]

How is this related to relinquishing racial and tribal identity? It would not be an exaggeration to assume that many feel a mischievous sense of power and excitement that accompanies the violation of some taboo. One senses that something is opening up, something that was not there before. One has discovered something new, but what is it? It is here that dread opens up, for here the explorer has entered uncharted territory and faces, not scary demons and barbarians, but an unknown future. Dread is the contemplation of life without an anchor, without a foundation. It is the inability to contemplate the possibility of such a life. To take away one's language is in a sense to take away one's capacity to be. To take away one's racial and ethnic tribal identity is for many, perhaps most, to take away what they perceive to be their very being. Dread is the feeling that such a possibility is tantamount to a type of incomprehensible death. Death, as we perceive and experience it through the loss of others and through knowledge of our own inevitable demise, still makes sense because it calls upon resources and features that not only are familiar to us but also form the stuff of who we are. Race and ethnicity are so interwoven in the essence of who people take themselves to be that even to begin the process of contemplating life in the name of something else, something higher, is, according to most, to invoke a form of madness in the place of sanity (albeit a troublesome sanity, many will admit) that has reigned for a very long time.

It is here that profound lessons can be drawn from some of the spiritual and philosophical heroes of our past. Those of us who are hero worshipers, who honor the best in humankind and believe in the realization of life's better possibilities, will understand why the existential dread that is bound to accompany the voluntary and moral weaning away from ethnic/racial and national tribal identification cannot deter one from doing what is ultimately essential for preserving one's humanity and realizing one's highest moral achievement. This weaning process is the antidote to the spiritual malaise and suffocation that accompany *homoraciality, homoethnicity,* and *homonationality.* And it is a spiritual malaise indeed. We feel a soul starvation from the gorgings on tribal diets we have been fed. The starvation occurs because the possibility for fulfillment in the form of grandeur, bravery, and generosity of personality demanded by extending ourselves radically to the world is denied. Like a primitive habituated creature the tribal self grows, unable to imagine a world without its immediate local thickness, while the future self, the larger moral self, the universal self, is starved and acknowledged at times with a faint sense of embarrassment. Its heroic and herculean demands are suppressed all too often in the name of practicality.

In this moment of existential dread when one is called on to dispense with troublesome and often very bad habits, when one is commanded in the name of moral and soul maturity to dispense with crutches that befit helpless invalids in favor of wings fit for the daring and the innovative, we can, above all, take the moral leap of faith that is the proper response of moral heroes. Consider the moral plight and existential dilemma of the biblical Abraham, in whom Kierkegaard finds the source of much inspiration as one who embodies life lived in the religious stage of existence. God summons Abraham and commands him:

Go from your country and your kindred and your father's house to the land that I will show you. I will make of you a great nation, and I will bless you, and make your name great, so that you will be a blessing. I will bless those who bless you, and the one who curses you I will curse; and in you all the families of the earth shall be blessed. (Gen. 12:1–3 NRSV)

The command was, in essence, *lech lekha:* Get up and go.[4] Abraham in effect was required to leave behind the consolations of familiarity and tradition. He had to give up his family, his homeland, and the old ways of worship. Noted Genesis interpreter Karen Armstrong argues that moral faith starts by demanding a radical break with the past and facing the terrors and enigmas of the unknown.[5] We have already noted that in some strains of Indian philosophical thought, a breaking of the past reads as freedom from the known, that is, freedom from the kind of familiarity and predictability that stymies growth and prevents the individual from existing as a tower of omnivorous moral possibilities. Abraham is a shining knight of faith who, while living in what Kierkegaard calls objective uncertainty—that is, in a universe in which all familiar moral signposts and ways of relating to the world are lost—still continues to affirm the world. The knight of faith lives the life of possibilities without being guaranteed the realization of any of them.

I am not suggesting, of course, that any modern-day moral knight of faith must follow the actual path of Abraham or Kierkegaard's leap into total objective uncertainty. I have argued for an ordered moral becoming because in our case there is a definite telos in mind. But the goal will require that we give up, out of moral necessity, some of the familiar and traditional crutches that we have relied upon as our essence, those things that we believe we cannot live without. In this sense, our existential plight mirrors somewhat the life of uncertainty because we realize that the goal of becoming a moral cosmopolitan cannot be mapped out all the way. The ideal can be conceptually delineated, and there are things we must refrain from doing in order to become a moral cosmopolitan, things that are totally contrary to the spirit of moral cosmopolitanism. But there are also unknown paths, new encounters with others, and new life experiences that will shape our souls. We may put these experiences in the service of the moral ideal we wish to attain, or we may refrain from doing so. The openness to it all exists. But short of the gift of clairvoyance, we have no way of knowing exactly what will happen after the radical break with the past has occurred. We sense, however, those of us with a vision of humankind's moral grandeur, those of us who realize that tribalism has shackled our souls and moral consciousness, that tribalism has to go. One is glad to be rid of it, as though it were a cancerous tumor that is eating away at one's life, but not quickly enough to eradicate one's capacity for all enjoyment.

MODERATE COSMOPOLITANISM

Local and Particular

If radical cosmopolitanism is an ethos that rejects the metaphysical importance of any one specific culture or ethnicity to the humanity of the individual and does not rely on the moral climate of the community to instantiate its value, then one may describe moderate cosmopolitanism as less visionary, idealistic, and transcendent in nature and more likely to regard sociopolitical factors as reliable gauges when determining the desired degree of the cosmopolitan spirit. Moderate cosmopolitanism places less emphasis on the weaning process I have described. It expends more effort in cultivating cultural resources associated with specific ethnic groups, not on cultural, ethnic, or nationalistic grounds, but on the premise that such measures are provisionally necessary until the moral climate of the particular culture has changed enough to accommodate a more full-fledged cosmopolitanism that would demand that persons refrain from substantively identifying themselves in tribalistic ways. This is perhaps what Alain Locke had in mind in honoring both cosmopolitanism/culture citizenship and communal identities such as African American cultural identity. Alain Locke believes that persons should be cosmopolitan rather than partisan, that they should embrace "culture citizenship rather than parochial citizenship." He argues that persons should aspire to be citizens of the world and cosmopolitans so that they can appreciate both the complexity and the similarity of the human community. The appreciation of cultural goods across partisan lines is entailed by culture citizenship. Leonard Harris finds in Locke a deep commitment to both partisan causes and cosmopolitanism. I would place Locke within the category of a moderate cosmopolitan with a tentative radical vision. Although he defends the right of African Americans to their culture, he is not at heart a culturalist who feels that there is a one-to-one connection between persons and their roots. Rather, as Harris notes, Locke sees such cultural affiliations as necessary because they act as sources of advocacy against oppression and because they offer universalizable cultural goods.[6]

Another contemporary thinker who may be classified as a second-order cosmopolitan is Kwame Anthony Appiah. In his article "Cosmopolitan Patriots" he attempts to reconcile cosmopolitanism, which he argues is more of a sentiment than an ideology, with a certain strain of patriotism. The branch of patriotism that is compatible with cosmopolitanism celebrates the institutions of the state or states within which one lives. The sharing of a political culture, however, is dependent upon the degree to which it honors certain social goods and principles. For example, Appiah thinks that one can be a certain type of

American patriot and remain cosmopolitan. Many have loved America because it has enabled them to choose who they are and to decide how central America is in their chosen identities.[7] Patriotism predicated on such liberties granted by the state is important because ultimately cosmopolitanism values human variety for what it makes possible for free individuals. The cosmopolitan does not value all types of variety, for some types of cultural variety constrain more than they enable. Appiah writes, "Cosmopolitans value cultural variety, but we do not ask other people to maintain the diversity of the species at the price of their own autonomy."[8]

Martha Nussbaum and Her Critics

Perhaps the most committed advocate of what I would term moderate cosmopolitanism is philosopher Martha Nussbaum. In two books, *For Love of Country* and *Cultivating Humanity: A Classical Defense of Reform in Liberal Education,* she lays the foundation for what a liberal cosmopolitan education would look like in American schools. Nussbaum's cosmopolitanism is indeed a clarion call for us to resist seeing ourselves wholly in terms of our local affiliations and to join the ancient Stoics in realizing that we share a core common human identity. Her cosmopolitanism is also motivated by the indisputable fact that the continued habitability of the earth will depend on the capacity and willingness of its inhabitants to live together cooperatively. An identity built on world citizenship and an educational ethos that fosters and reinforces such an identity are, in Nussbaum's estimation, the best means to accomplish global cohabitation. Nussbaum, however, is not motivated only by prudential concerns. Her writings and commitment to world citizenship stem from a deep moral source. Her moral sensibilities are undoubtedly drawn from the best of the ancient Greek tradition. Acknowledging that cosmopolitanism is a lonely business and a kind of exile in which the comfort of local truths, warm feelings of patriotism, and the specialness of one's own kind are absent, she states quite simply that the only refuges offered by cosmopolitanism are reason and the love of humanity.[9]

Nussbaum offers two versions of the classical ideal of world citizenship. The primary loyalty of the first type is to human beings the world over. One's national and local identities are secondary. The second is what Nussbaum calls a more relaxed version and what I would refer to as moderate cosmopolitanism, which allows a variety of views about what our priorities should be. To be sure, this more relaxed version would allow persons to place primary emphasis on their local identities drawn from the ethnic and cultural spheres. This more relaxed version, however, still emphasizes a continued respect for the value of all human life and entreats us to see ourselves as bound by common human abilities and problems to people who live both geographically and culturally at a great distance from us.[10]

In defending the more relaxed version of cosmopolitanism, Nussbaum outlines three capacities that are essential to the cultivation of humanity. The first is an elaboration of the Socratic exhortation to develop oneself through critical self-examination and by questioning one's culture and traditions. This involves refusing to take for granted the authority of appeals to tradition since the belief system generated though one's immediate environment is never sacrosanct. Challenges to tradition enable one to be fit for citizenship; they are also vital for the existence of democracy itself. This capacity is best developed by honing the ability to reason logically and to examine all knowledge claims for consistency and correctness of fact.

The second capacity involves seeing ourselves along the lines that the ancient Stoics addressed. They presented an image of a series of concentric circles. The first circle is drawn around the self, while the next surrounds one's immediate family. Next would be one's neighbor, local groups, city dwellers, countrymen, and so on. Beyond all the circles is the largest one, which is humanity as a whole. Our task as citizens of the world will be to draw the circles somehow to the center. Like the Stoics, Nussbaum does not think that we need to give up our local identities to become citizens of the world. Local identities can be a source of richness in life. She writes:

> We need not give up our special affections and identifications, whether ethnic or gender-based or religious. We need not think of them as superficial, and we may think of our identity as constituted partly by them. We may and should devote special attention to them in education. But we should also work to make all human beings part of our community of dialogue and concern, base our political deliberations on that interlocking commonality, and give the circle that defines our humanity special attention and respect.
>
> In educational terms, this means that students in the United States, for example, may continue to regard themselves as defined partly by their particular loves—their families, their religious, ethnic, or racial communities, or even their country. But they must also, and centrally, learn to recognize humanity wherever they encounter it, undeterred by traits that are strange to them, and be eager to understand humanity in all its strange guises.[11]

This second capacity involves cultivating the part of our moral machinery that enables us to get outside our local and parochial identity markers. Nussbaum writes:

> Cultivating our humanity in a complex, interlocking world involves understanding the ways in which common needs and aims are differently realized in different circumstances. This requires a great deal of knowledge that American college students

rarely got in previous eras, knowledge of non-Western cultures, of minorities within their own, of differences of gender and sexuality.[12]

The third capacity is what Nussbaum calls the narrative imagination, which gives one the ability to think what it might be like to be in the shoes of a person different from oneself. It enables one to be an intelligent participant in the life drama of others different from oneself and to understand the emotions, wishes, and desires of such persons.[13]

Nussbaum's *Cultivating Humanity* is a defense of broadening the narrative imagination of individuals by studying non-Western cultures, women's studies, human sexuality, and African American studies. This new liberal education is to be the basis for the cultivation of an ethos that can equip all of us for world citizenship.

Nussbaum has been taken to task by some of America's most formidable intellectuals for her defense of cosmopolitanism. I will reconstruct some of these criticisms against Nussbaum and then respond to them.

In *Must We Choose between Patriotism and Universal Reason?* philosopher Hilary Putnam writes that like most of his contemporaries, he has inherited or acquired more than one identity—Jew, philosopher, American, and so on—but that it would never have occurred to him to say that he is a citizen of the world. If he were asked why discrimination is wrong, he would not respond by saying, "Because we are all citizens of the world." That someone is a fellow human being, a fellow passenger to the grave, has moral weight for him, while "citizen of the world" does not. Putnam's explanation is interesting. He writes:

> And that has to do, I think, with the fact that appeals to the notion that we are made in the image of God, or to sympathy with all other human beings, while they appeal to potentials, which are indeed universal, also have a long history in the traditions to which I belong, traditions we inherit. It may be that "citizen of the world" will one day have that kind of moral weight and that Martha Nussbaum will have been the prophet of a new moral vision. But it doesn't today.[14]

This argument is not convincing. Imagine slaveholders saying to the abolitionist: "Slaves may one day be seen as creatures equal to the rest of humanity. They are not today." Or, imagine the British colonialist attempting to convince Gandhi that "India may one day be allowed to rule itself and recapture the glories of its past traditions. Not today." My point is that moral strides are not made by allowing our moral imaginations to be shackled by current realities. New realities are formed when brave new souls dare to dream and dare to inspire a change by the strength of their visions. The fact that "fellow passenger to the grave" has moral weight for some but "fellow citizen of the world" does not is more indicative of the meagerness of the moral imagination of some than an inherent emptiness in the notion of citizen of the world.

Putnam offers as a viable alternative to cosmopolitanism a brand of patriotism that takes the form of loyalty to what is best in the tradition one has inherited. That just does not seem to be the way that patriotism plays itself out in mass culture, where it takes the form of unearned and often mindless pride, a fierce and unexamined attachment to country that is often accompanied by an equally fierce suspicion of foreigners. One of the most frightening television experiences of my life came, not from any horror flick or seventh-rate daytime talk show, but from a brief experience I had while channel surfing one evening during the 1996 presidential campaigns. There amidst a throng of men was ultraconservative and unabashed nationalist, presidential hopeful Pat Buchanan shouting to the cheers of admirers, "White males! White males! White males!" Loyalty to the best of our traditions is not patriotism; it is precisely what Martha Nussbaum and cosmopolitanism in general are trying to cultivate in all persons: moral common sense and critical rationality.

But Putnam's response raises a crucial problem that comes up whenever discussions of patriotism arise. It has to do with identifying the real markers of gestures in the world that may be plausibly interpreted as patriotism or adherence to principles that are being practiced by the institutions of one's country. Some would describe these judicious and principled standards as bloodless, abstract, and devoid of the passional features of authentic existence. Such seems to be the moral attitude of Robert Pinsky. He describes Nussbaum's formulations as arid and says that her sentences present a view of the world that would be true only if people were not driven by emotions. He accuses Nussbaum of lecturing about jingoism, which he describes as another form of provinciality, and identifies all attachments to homeland or groups as forms of love. He writes: "The utopianism of her formulations is so bloodless that I would sooner stick with what is: with the varying feeble mixture of vague 'basics' and half-hearted, constantly changing special area 'studies' that the young get from— well, the marketplace."[15] He identifies certain features of regionalism and ethnic pride and "even outright patriotism" as cosmopolitan because

> I grew up when many immigrant families routinely flew the flag on national holidays, with no meaning of self-righteousness or reactionary politics. Even the very flag itself: This summer, in the hilly farm country around Saratoga, New York, near the Erie Canal, I saw a line of laundry hung between a telephone pole and the window of a tidy-looking apartment over a grocery store—the classic procession of clean clothes in the sun, and pinned at the end nearest the window an American flag. The informality and idiosyncrasy of this gesture—practical, intuitive, inventive, and resourceful in the ways of Odysseus—seemed in the spirit of cosmopolitanism to me, as patriotic gestures go, because it put the flag into the world of daily life, flapping above the market downstairs.[16]

I submit that the willingness to take such cosmetic gestures as markers of a real cosmopolitanism is not only the reason for the continued careless use of that term but also the reason that moral excavationism into the heart of tribalism in America remains unsatisfying. Pinsky interprets the presence of the American flag at the end of a clothesline in an immigrant family as evidence that cosmopolitanism coexists with ethnic pride and patriotism and that all is just fine and dandy in America. Part of the uniqueness of America is precisely its ability to allow tribal impulses to be grafted onto a society regulated by constitutional edicts that theoretically champion the preeminent rights of the individual above the tyranny of any group. This is the great liberal principle around which America has tried to organize civic life. It was and remains a titanic effort. But the old cliché that America has yet to rise to a full embracing of this principle is true. What prevents America from fully realizing the ideal is a problem inherent in liberalism itself: an unwillingness to valorize any particular conception of the good that members of a civil society ought to adopt. Moral cosmopolitanism, however, has no such tension, since it sees itself as the most moral way of interacting with others in the world.

There are those, and perhaps Pinsky is one of them, who worry that moral cosmopolitanism lacks the visceral and emotionally charged features of the best that may be found in nationalism, patriotism, and love of the racial or ethnic group. I argue most emphatically that this worry is shortsighted and one-sided. It is shortsighted because the worriers fail to recognize that the alleged bloodless, arid, and unemotional features of moral cosmopolitanism are inherent in any set of principles, edicts, rules, and laws. Moral instruction simply works that way. The child who gets a good feeling from simply jabbing his pencil in his mother's furniture, the adolescent who feels good about getting high today at the cost of her future tomorrow, the rogue who gets a good feeling from playing his music as loudly as he wishes in the train station while hurling disparaging remarks at every insulted onlooker must all be taught virtues like respect for other people's property, delayed gratification, the ability to think long range about one's life as a whole, and sensitivity to the feelings of others. These are arid, unemotional, and moralizing features that all civilized persons must incorporate into their moral consciousness. Whether they are validated on utilitarian, deontological, or Christian grounds, civil society is dependent on them. They function as self-policing devices in any society. Moral cosmopolitanism is such a moralizing tool, only it emphasizes one condition not stressed in any of the other institutional edicts of our age: that one must divest oneself of racial, ethnic, and national forms of self-identification, because if we fail to do so, we end up falling short of the best of the ideals we have embraced as well-meaning persons. To be a new type of person, a radically different type of person, demands this self-policing.

There is a smugness and a tacit willingness in Pinsky's criticism to take the cosmetic features of patriotism at face value. For example, exactly what is symbolized by the flag? Well, a lot of things, both good and bad. The flag has been flown in the name of several morally questionable enterprises, including territorial occupations of various kinds and unreflective patriotism. Many in the world see it as the symbol of a bully, some see it iconically as benevolence incarnate. The flag has also stood for positive values such as freedom and tolerance. It is not a definitive symbol. It is ambiguous and, like a complex work of art, open to many interpretations. Pinsky should realize, as does superstar actress and singer Madonna, that humans can and do appropriate symbols and remake them in the image of their own fantasies, desires, and passional sensibilities. That a thinker at the dawn of the new millennium should interpret this cosmetic gesture as an irrefutable sign of healthy patriotism and cosmopolitanism is one-sided because it again fails to take seriously the voices of those who have been hurt, those who have received tribal blows in the midst of those neighborhoods in which the flag flies proudly at full staff: Do we need to revisit those scenarios, those voices? Nonblacks are beaten and thrown out of black neighborhoods; blacks are ridiculed and thrown out of Irish neighborhoods; Italians, Latinos, and Poles are persecuted and ridiculed, and they in turn do the same. And these indignities are often done in the name of many things deemed positive, such as honor, authenticity, and solidarity. They are also done in the name of values not as nice: the denigration of others and the insistence on their ethnic and racial inferiority. But all of these turn on something quite nasty, something deeply pernicious, and something that, if we do not correct it, will rip the humanity out of every human being and make the new millennium a continuation of the old. That thing is tribalism.

The move to reject cosmopolitanism on the grounds that it is not grounded in the passional paradigms under which people house their values is again expressed in *Neglecting History* by Leo Marx. He accuses Nussbaum of situating her cosmopolitanism in the realm of affectless rationality and argues that she dismisses the importance of most people's place of birth and their national identities as accidental and unnecessary. He argues that to disregard the role of the contingent and the irrational in human experience is to risk "adopting merely visionary, hence unfeasible programs of action."[17] Marx brands Nussbaum's version of cosmopolitanism as abstract with a hothouse character that is distant from the actual record of cosmopolitanism and nationalism. He writes:

> If cosmopolitanism is as superior among conceivable views of the world as she persuasively demonstrates, why has it so rarely been adopted? Why has its appeal been so largely restricted to small, eccentric, avant-garde, or elite groups? Why have institutions

like the League of Nations or the United Nations, or movements like the World Federalist failed to elicit widespread support? Why do more parochial—nationalistic—creeds usually carry the day?[18]

One is tempted to answer his question of why it is that cosmopolitanism has so rarely been adopted by saying, "For the same reason that consistent good manners are harder to practice if one has a gruff temperament, or bad eating habits are easier to acquire than good ones." The vices are easier to indulge in and the virtues harder to acquire because they require, as Aristotle recognized, a great deal of moral habituation, discipline, and courage. Who in today's culture is likely to get a good dose of moral cosmopolitanism and all that is entailed in that doctrine as part of his or her daily spiritual diet? But the point is very clear. If bad habits are deeply ingrained, the exercise of good ones becomes an arduous, "unfeasible," and "impractical" undertaking. If the appeal of cosmopolitanism has been restricted to small eccentric or elite groups, it is because it is far easier to satisfy the great appetite of tribalism, which, arguably, might be an innate impulse. But then so might be the urge to rape, to murder, or to slap the face of someone with whom you disagree. It is precisely because tribalism appeals to the crude, the primitive, and the undisciplined in humans—traits that are far easier to express than their antitheses, whose formal application demands moral inculcation and a view of human beings as malleable and receptive—that in its various instantiations such as cultural nationalism and racial/ethnic pride, it is for the majority of people more acceptable and easier to practice. This in no way commits me to an uncharitable view of human beings as we find them in the empirical world. Children who have not yet learned how to behave properly would not necessarily provoke negative feelings in me. The comparison is meant to be taken quite seriously. Human beings qua tribal beings are as morally immature as children who can mimic moral gestures but who have yet to reach their highest moral potential.

There is, however, another way in which I find problematic Marx's proclivity for dismissing cosmopolitanism on the grounds that it remains largely unadopted by the majority of people. If cosmopolitanism as a moral ideal is not so superior after all since most people do not accept it, then the ideals or principles that are most popular and that are the antithesis of it must be correct. Does the fact that millions of South Africans were complicitous in racial apartheid and rejected the ideas of integration and equality prove that apartheid was correct or that integration, because it was so rarely adopted, was not such a superior ideal after all? One can imagine a logical continuation of Marx's argument wielded by a racist on the order of: "If freedom of association and intermarriage between blacks and whites and people from different cultural backgrounds in general who truly love each other are such great ideals, why are they not popular among people in general?"

The truth is that a moral doctrine cannot be measured by its popularity. If that were the case, slavery would still exist and women would still be regarded as the property of their husbands (as they certainly are in many countries outside the West).

Marx, like many of the respondents to Nussbaum's version of cosmopolitanism, argues that what makes the American Republic so distinctive is that its citizens are not asked to pay their primary allegiance to any one group of people. Instead they are required to declare their allegiance to a particular kind of multicultural polity dedicated to a distinct set of moral and political ideals to which the country remains committed in principle. I argue that this is true but that there are features in people's ethnic, racial, and national tribal identities that prevent them from attaining this ideal. We can continue to pay a great deal of lip service to what America remains committed to in principle without attempting to get rid of those features that will ensure that the ideal will forever remain theoretical. Cosmopolitanism is a way of ridding the individual of these tribal problematics. If in principle what makes the American Republic ideal is that it asks that its citizens not pledge allegiance to any one group of people, a race-obsessed society such as ours overturns the principle and invites this sort of allegiance, albeit often in subtle ways. Any moral enticement must be addressed to the potential goodness, rationality, and humanity in all persons regardless of whether these ideals are dominant features in our world today, and regardless of whether the majority of persons care to honor them.

I find this very same shortcoming in Benjamin Barber's "Constitutional Faith." He argues that in an overly tribalized world cosmopolitanism might be a useful counterpoint. He asserts that American national identity has from the start been "a remarkable mixture of cosmopolitanism and parochialism" and says that the colonists and founders were engaged in uprooting and rerooting. The new American patriotism was all about combating religious parochialism and persecution. It brought about the creation of a new man, new laws, new modes of living, and a new social system. He characterizes Americanism by suggesting that, from the beginning, to be an American was to be encapsulated within a unique story of freedom, to be free (or to be enslaved) in a new sense that was more existential than political or legal. In colonial times the New World offered a fresh start and freedom from rigid and heavily freighted traditional cultures. Deracination was the universal experience. To be an American "was not to acquire a new race or a new religion or a new culture, it was to possess a new set of political ideas."[19] He identifies the "tribal" sources that form the basis of our national identity as the Declaration of Independence, the Constitution, the Bill of Rights, the inaugural addresses of our presidents, Lincoln's

Gettysburg Address, and Martin Luther King's "Free at Last" sermon at the 1963 March on Washington.

I do not know what Barber hopes to accomplish by identifying as our tribal identity a range of moral, conceptual, political, and legalistic tropes, sermons, and preambles. It would indeed be a glorious world if our tribal identities were centered around the ideals embodied in some of those inspiring monuments. But to look in the face of a tribalistic society such as America, with its obsession with race and ethnicity, a society that organizes civic life around its capacity to categorize persons primarily as racial and ethnic constructs, and then assert that any tribal identity we have comes from Martin Luther King's "Free at Last" sermon or the inaugural addresses of our presidents—addresses whose content ranges from conceptually vacuous to morally inspiring—is to suffer from a very serious form of epistemological blindness.

In *The Racial Contract*, philosopher Charles Mills argues that as a general rule, white misunderstanding, misrepresentation, evasion, and self-deception on matters related to race are among the most pervasive mental phenomena of the past few hundred years.[20] The more I read the respondents to Nussbaum's essay, the more I believe that most of them are involved in gross conceptual hallucinations that lead them to deny the existential reality that thrives in their faces while granting legitimacy to principles, documents, speeches, and sermons. That is, they treat the texts to which they refer as the living reality and regard the features of the world that do not match those texts as exceptional, anomalous, aberrant, and therefore not deserving of very much attention. To pay attention would upset the theoretical bodies that they are forced to see as the real thing.

Barber, however, is correct when he writes that to be an American was to acquire not a new race, a new religion, or a new culture but rather a new set of political ideas. In other words, being an American had nothing to do with becoming a new type of moral person, which is why mass exploitation, extermination, and enslavement of others were possible and quite compatible with being an American. In fact, the entire enterprise of founding the United States was legalized by this selective application of the new political ideals. Old selves were simply grafted onto new landscapes. The tribalist ethos gained a new respectability and sanction. To be an American did not mean subjecting oneself to moral scrutiny and giving up pernicious, questionable aspects of oneself; it did not force one to see oneself as a negotiable entity in relation to one's deepest sense of oneself as a moral agent. Rather, it engineered innovative ways of chartering a political system that would standardize, routinize, and normalize the self one carried over from the Old World.

To be a moral cosmopolitan, as I have argued, is to become a radically different type of person. Old selves cannot be grafted onto new landscapes, since the moral cosmopolitan euthanizes much of the old self in order to create a new moral self. And since moral cosmopolitanism is the antithesis of tribalism, mere lip service to bromides and sermons cannot be the basis for organizing one's inner life or the institutions of society. There is a popular saying that gasoline and alcohol just don't mix. Racial and ethnic tribalism is an unmixable element in the soul of a moral cosmopolitan. To outgrow the need for tribal affiliation is not a sacrifice but the precondition for a higher self.

Although I have identified Nussbaum as a moderate cosmopolitan and although this section is intended to explicate the temperament of the moderate cosmopolitan, I am guilty in my defense of her honorable moderate cosmopolitanism of arguing like a radical cosmopolitan. Be that as it may, the moderate cosmopolitan does not differ in principle from the radical cosmopolitan. The difference between the two lies only in the degree to which the psychic crutches that a culture has become used to relying on to maintain ossified ways of seeing itself and the world ought to be jettisoned. The moderate cosmopolitan dreams of radical cosmopolitanism but realizes that the dream may have to be delayed until certain aspects of a liberal democratic society are accessible to a great many persons.

I have, of course, been describing a rather idealistic state of affairs that may undoubtedly be interpreted as naïve and imprudent. The desire to attain an ideal, however, does not preclude other projects and commitments from coexisting and working toward their goals. I am well aware that the most moral and exalted vision and conceptualized project by itself can never be a panacea. While it is obvious that, almost by definition, cosmopolitanism can find no friend in cultural nationalism and cannot encourage a nationalist ethos, it can coexist with other projects that have as their goals feasible antidotes to parochialism, tribalism, and stringent racial and ethnic categorization. In a liberal democratic society, numerous projects can play themselves out that, while different from cosmopolitanism, are not entirely inimical to the goals of the cosmopolitan spirit. My main concern, however, has not been to describe the ways in which a certain type of cosmopolitanism may be compatible with other feasible antidotes. I am at this point interested in laying down the theoretical requirements and a minimal psychomoral machinery for developing a moral cosmopolitan personality.

I say this to indicate that at the moment I am situated somewhere between the two types of cosmopolitanism. Existentially, I have not yet grown into a full-fledged radical cosmopolitan, although I remain one in principle. I write, however, in order to become the person I would like to be. The radical cosmopolitan represents an ideal. Its ethos is the one I would most like to see saturate the culture in which I live because it is predicated on and attempts to capture crucially salient (but infrequently exercised) features of the human condition: becoming and moral maturity.

6

LIBERALISM, COSMOPOLITANISM, COMMUNITARIANISM:

FRIENDS OR ADVERSARIES?

I like to think of myself as a philosopher who is an eclectic and a freethinker in the best sense of those terms. We rarely credit those we designate as villains or adversaries with any truths at all. In our obsessions we often fail to appropriate the kernels of wisdom contained in the confused premises of those with whose cherished standpoints we differ.

It is this with this caveat in mind that I explore the possibility of reexamining some of the tenets of an ideology I find problematic from the point of view of the moral cosmopolitan: communitarianism.

I also explore the tensions in liberalism's reluctance to endorse any particular conception of the good and its insistence that the state refrain from determining which moral judgments are true or not true. As a liberal who espouses a moral cosmopolitan ethos and who believes with all his heart and soul that this ethos is the best and the most exalted and heroic way of existing in the world—a liberal who would like to see this conception of the good not only accepted as the standard of moral health and the prevailing doctrine of all citizens but also encouraged by the state—I find myself at odds with the mandates of much that is today understood as constitutive of political liberalism. Nevertheless, some form of political discernment informs me that any conception of the good that hopes to win pride of place in the hearts of people is best realized within the sort of society championed by the best within the liberal tradition. Since the conception of the good that I most favor—moral cosmopolitanism—affirms the autonomy, dignity, and equal value of all persons, it seems quite unlikely that it could find a home in despotic totalitarian regimes or political environments that do not treat citizens as ends in themselves who, as rational and spiritual beings, can be touched by the best within any moral system. This is a crucial feature of liberal theory. As holders of liberty of conscience, persons must be free to determine how, for example, values within their political domain are connected to those values in their own conceptions of the good, their own comprehensive doctrines.[1]

LIBERALISM AND THE MYTH OF NEUTRALITY

The most honorable spokesman of political liberalism of the past twenty-five years is indisputably John Rawls. His *Political Liberalism* is an attempt to reconcile the difficulties inherent in a heterogeneous society in which different conceptions of the good life and varied value systems, beliefs, and principles can coexist and yet affirm the political conception of a constitutional regime. How can a nation entreat its inhabitants to carve out their conception of the good life and their own value systems and yet achieve agreement on a set of principles that all citizens may abide by? The basic problem of political liberalism evinced by Rawls is: How is it possible for there to exist over time a stable and just society of free and equal citizens profoundly divided by reasonable religious, philosophical, and moral doctrines?[2] He sets out to provide the fair terms of social cooperation in such circumstances. In such a society reasonable and rational persons organize their multifaceted selves around a fundamental idea that systematically connects and relates their diverse ideas, values, and principles. In this way, persons are free to exercise their judgments, which is the right of all citizens, and yet also relinquish their particular preferences in times of conflict. They are able to do so because they agree to adhere to principles of fairness and are willing to propose and abide by fair terms of cooperation, provided that others do so as well. This last point is important. It is part of the moral psychology that Rawls assumes for each citizen: when persons believe that social arrangements are just, they are willing to play their part.

Even though citizens share a common reason, disputes will still arise between reasonable persons over specific causes. Rational human beings, however, are supposed to recognize that in a pluralistic environment, some permissible ways of life, conceptions, and values will conflict with others. Persons therefore affirm only comprehensive doctrines or conceptions.[3] A conception is comprehensive if it covers all recognized values and virtues within a carefully delineated system. Since citizens cannot universalize their own subjective and personal conceptions, rational citizens who hope to live peacefully within a pluralistic society advance a political conception, which attempts to elaborate a reasonable conception for the basic structures of society alone. It does not involve any wider commitment to any other doctrine.[4] Rawls realizes that in a pluralistic society there are no philosophical, religious, or moral doctrines that are affirmed by all citizens. He limits the conception of justice that is affirmed in an ordered democratic society to what he calls "the domain of the political." Rational citizens come to realize that the values of the special domain of the political—which makes possible the realization of all other, nonpolitical values and protects them—must outweigh those that conflict with them. Another way of putting it is this: You and I may differ on any number of issues. We must, however, agree on the particular principles that allow us to disagree and cohab-it in a civilized manner.

Do I believe that Rawls's notion of a reasonable and comprehensive doctrine allows persons to override their personal interests and strive for principles of justice within the context of a racially and ethnically tribalistic society? From an empirical standpoint, we certainly are still struggling with this issue despite the fact that one of the great accomplishments of this century, civil rights for blacks, was achieved within the liberal state. Liberalism's reluctance to make moral judgments leaves intact the problematic features of a weighty tribalistic society. The problem with this from the moral cosmopolitan's point of view is that in a pluralistic and politically liberal society individuals can still maintain the primacy of their ethnic, racial, and national identities and continue to engage in racist and ethnocentric behaviors. Ultimately this is the way racist and other tribalistic institutions are fostered and maintained.

The political problems spawned by this tension are still obvious within the historical consciousness of most Americans. Racial segregation, denial of the right to vote for blacks and women, the prohibition of equal treatment of racial and ethnic minorities and women, the denigration of human life, the ascrip-tion of worth and intrinsic value on the basis of race have all been upheld with-in a society governed by the cherished principles of political liberalism. Fortu-nately, those problems have also been redressed by appealing to the best within the liberal tradition. I would like to suggest, however, that the best within lib-eralism, the part that is alleged to appeal to the most rational, reasonable, and therefore (in my estimation) the best within all persons, falls short because the poisonous, demoralizing features of tribalism ultimately interfere. The analogy I like to think of is one of a cancer-riddled body that is being pumped full of drugs that allow it, miraculously, to function normally. The body, however, can never reach its optimal potential, never realize the wonders it was intended to perform, so long as the cancer remains. If the analogy seems hyperbolic, it should leave the reader with little doubt of my emotional and moral distaste for racial, ethnic, and national tribalism.

Liberalism does not explicitly require that persons filter out racial/ethnic/national markers when relating to others at the most basic and deepest level. Here I am not talking about the unconscionable lip service we pay to the idea of a color-blind society while still living according to a racial and ethnic ethos. Quite the contrary. Tribal identities heavily influence conceptions of the good; for many, they are actual constitutive features of the good. Those conceptions of the good cultivated by most people—marriages, friendships, professional associations—are organized around racial/ethnic and national boundaries. We think that is simply a natural part of the human condition. Many of these con-ceptions carry with them the moral connotation of goodness that comes from the inclusion of the word "good," as in "the conception of the good each person chooses for him- or herself." The contemporary self, which is encapsulated within racial and ethnic paradigms, is defined almost exclusively in such terms. I have argued that this view of the self is predicated on the false assumptions that racial/ethnic concepts of the self are stable, objective, and closed. Liberalism, in hesitating to make judgments about the moral value of certain conceptions of the good life, by default grants philosophical legitimacy to the racial/ethnic constructs of the self.

This problem is compounded by the fact that the liberalism articulated and defended by Rawls does not allow for sufficient critiques of social relations and forms of power as they relate to gender, race, and ethnicity. Rawls admits in *Political Liberalism* that race, ethnicity, and gender are some of our most basic problems and that they are of a different character that calls for principles of justice that he does not address. This omission, while it should not detract from the integrity of Rawls's work, is quite serious, and it points the way to understanding why American liberalism is unable to deal adequately with racial problems. There is no sustained, systematic critique of persons' proclivity for carving out for themselves conceptions of the good along deeply demarcated racial/ethnic lines. A liberalism that addresses this is said to be guilty of tampering with the autonomy of persons and is accused of moral proselytizing and, like a lord of the manor, trying to build the lives of persons around some high-minded notion of the good, betraying in the process its commitment to the right.

In this respect moral cosmopolitanism has much to contribute to the development of a higher self. Philosophical analysis finds the assumptions on which racial/ethnic constructs of the self are predicated to be wrong. Cosmopolitanism entreats the self to aspire to a new vision and the creation of a new self. This new type of self, the cosmopolitan self, is also shaped by an ethos or, loosely speaking, a cosmopolitan morality. Whereas liberalism sets as its goal the task of organizing civic life around differences and crafts constitutional edicts that allow persons to get along with such differences, moral cosmopolitanism exhorts us to cease attaching importance to those differences in any serious sense. The goal is to transcend those differences, attaching to them no more moral importance than one would to one's body size or (and here I know I am being extreme) the inconsequential mole on the tip of one's nose. This is not to say that the weaning process will not be difficult. But cosmopolitanism, as a future-oriented ethos and conception of the self, cannot encourage persons to be mired in the shallow present. Because it advocates a radically different type of life, its practitioners properly understand the reluctance of many to disassociate themselves from the ways of life that have always made them feel good about themselves and their lives while refraining from seeing how those conceptions and feelings spawn ways of life for others and in general generate an ethos that diminishes the prospects for human thriving.

A central tenet of political liberalism turns out to be either empirically ambiguous or false; that is, that political liberalism has no business endorsing any conception of the good. It seems unlikely that any civic life is possible without state endorsement of particular conceptions of the good outside the domain of the political. The state grants certain tax exemptions to churches and refrains from treating them as equal to other voluntary associations. In Germany, the state finances the church by levying a tax on its members. In various liberal societies including the United States, the state grants tax breaks to married couples, thus, of course, promoting the idea that marriage is a good in which it is in persons' best interest to partake. Might compulsory education be regarded as a conception of the good imposed upon persons? Yes. A precondition for good citizenship within a democracy is that persons have a minimum of skills to carry out specific requirements of citizenship.

There are countless other examples that would show that many of the conceptions of the good are either encouraged or explicitly mandated by the state as reasonable and necessary for a civic life that permits human beings to flourish. Political liberalism as expressed through the state has gone beyond imposing its conception of the political and has imposed conceptions that fall into the domains of the personal and private, domains that are common to the great majority of persons: family, religious, and moral life. In doing things such as providing federal subsidies to help save farms, the government transmits the message that this way of life ought to be preserved.

A strong case can be made that no liberal and democratic state in which civic life is conducive to some modicum of human flourishing and prosperity is possible without state imposition of some form of comprehensive good. The state also goes beyond encouraging conceptions of the good that reasonable persons might in some sense endorse though not participate in. The state formally discourages its citizens from organizing their lives around particular conceptions of the good that they create for themselves, conceptions that are not all self-evidently unreasonable and detrimental to human flourishing and moral efficacy. Persons, for example, are not free to practice polygamy or polyandry, although the state has not demonstrated why a consensus about the virtues of a monogamous marriage partnership means that partnerships of a different kind are unreasonable. In this case the state not only dissuades persons from forming lives around such a conception but also actually outlaws it. The Mormons in Utah were forced to abandon the practice of polygamy as a condition for membership in the Union. The most the liberal philosopher John Stuart Mill could say for Mormonism's sanction of polygamy was that it was an infraction of the principle of liberty and a "mere riveting of the chains of one-half of the community, and an emancipation of the other from reciprocity of obligation toward them."[5] Mill gives no substantial argument for why the practice of polygamy endorsed by Muslims, Chinese, and Hindus warrants the moral opprobrium of English-speakers. He suggests that the arrangements are voluntary and that the women who are most harmed by it are complicitous in the enterprise. He locates its legitimacy in the stock of common ideas pertaining to woman's need for a husband. Many women, he argues, would prefer to be one of several wives rather than not being a wife at all. This does not mean, however, that other countries should be released from their laws and customs on the basis of what he calls "Mormonite" opinions.[6]

State prohibition of nonheterosexual couplings through virulent antisodomy laws is also a state mandate of a specific conception of the good. This area is of crucial importance. The sexual domain is an area around which a host of other goods and life affirmations are centered and expressed. One's capacity to love and to express that love, to form unions that enhance the quality of one's life and one's capacity to experience one's body most intensely, are all features of the sexual domain. Through its power to legislate consensual human sexuality that does not threaten public welfare, the state exercises jurisdiction over the essence of one's core as well as the goods needed to flourish in areas such as friends, work life, pensions, living wills, assets, and property, to name but a few. In saying that the sexual domain is an area that represents one's core I am not endorsing the view that sexual activity represents the core of one's life, only that the sexual domain is the vehicle responsible for generating much that is meaningful and valued in life. The liberal state's intrusion into the lives of nonheterosexuals ought to strike persons as more unreasonable than any conception of same-sex unions.

The liberal state's imposition of various conceptions of the good violates the notion of public reason, or the reason that any reasonable person would accept regardless of his or her particular system of values and principles. Indeed, under a veil of ignorance (that is, under an assumed condition in which one did not know relevant features of one's life such as gender, nationality, and social class), one would be denied knowledge of one's sexual orientation and would therefore opt for a society in which differences in sexual orientation ought not to figure greatly in determining which conceptions of the good are acceptable. Similarly, because one would have no knowledge of one's tribal affiliation, reasonable persons ought to opt for a nontribal society, since anyone could have the misfortune of belonging to the tribal category whose members had the least chance of organizing a meaningful life. We have seen that along racial and ethnic lines, the liberal state has not refrained from mandating conceptions of the good. How could one explain antimiscegenation laws except as a way for the state to keep its epidermal landscape predominantly a certain color? In this way the codified and institutionalized power structures are protected and tribally maintained. One could discuss not only the ways in which a state-racialized society has mandated certain conceptions of the good but also the ways in which members of certain groups are unable to cultivate their own conceptions of the good. In certain cases, particular conceptions of the good have been deemed societally out of order, as in the case of any black who might have dared dream of becoming a doctor or a philosopher at specific moments in our nation's history. The liberal state has gone even further in its endorsement of a racialized society by making it illegal to dissent from structural exclusion along racial lines. Consider the laws that made it illegal to rent or sell property to blacks or to grant employment to them in certain fields.

I point to these examples to debunk the myth that political liberalism and the agencies that apply its theories have refrained from imposing comprehensive doctrines on its citizens outside the domain of the political. The race-based ethos that dominates the consciousness of Americans and affects all of their activities and personal relations, ranging from what is seen on television to who is placed on the cover of a magazine or who becomes chief executive officer of a multinational corporation, is the most comprehensive doctrine ever imposed upon a people. It is for this reason that the state has a moral obligation to promote another doctrine, a conception of the good that is the antithesis of a race-based tribal society: a cosmopolitan morality and code of ethics whose explicit goal is to foster the growth of a profoundly nontribalist society. How such a society would be organized and structured is a task for the future and for all who care enough to challenge the dominant trends of our culture. Theory and action go hand-in-hand. Lip service to multiculturalism, pluralism, and diversity is not sufficient, and in fact such efforts are often specious. Homage to multiculturalism and pluralism requires that we still carve up the world into neat little tribal areas. It requires that we see individuals first and foremost as ethnics, as races, albeit ones that are to be protected. The fault lies not so much with the intentions but with the optical illusions that cloud our capacity to perceive, judge, and understand. Those optical illusions betray our true capacity to determine the markers that determine who people at their core really, really are.

Liberalism and cosmopolitanism may ultimately make a wonderful alliance when liberalism takes up the cosmopolitan challenge to disengage itself from tribal ways of identifying people. Some critics of liberalism doubtless will gasp at what I am suggesting and say that liberalism has in fact refrained from seeing people as ethnics, as races, and merely regarded them as rights-bearing entities. They will say that the demands I am placing on liberalism are excessive since liberalism already invites persons to revise their life plans, their conceptions of the good, and the values of the larger society from which such conceptions are drawn. Liberalism, we will be reminded, has a built-in revisability clause that allows people to detach themselves from any communal practice they deem morally pernicious. Liberalism will allow for this and the possible moral conversion that could result without an attendant loss in people's institutional or public identity, which means that the state will not view them as radically different sorts of persons vis-à-vis their capacity as rights bearers. I am suggesting, however, that a society saturated with race and ethnic consciousness does not invite this sort of communal detachment. And, further, a society that organizes public conceptions of the good around racial lines cannot plausibly expect its citizens to distance themselves from this prevailing public ethos, especially when doing so would result in a loss in their capacity to enjoy social goods that make their conception of the good more robust and meaningful.

When liberalism graduates from its tribal encapsulations and yields to the cosmopolitan demand for a weaned and complete moral identity, then it will have realized a noble potential, that of creating a new universal humanist ethics.

COSMOPOLITANISM AND CULTURAL HEGEMONY

Communitarianism's emphasis on the ends of the community and their constitutive role in forming the identity of persons is problematic when viewed against the backdrop of the communitarian definition of community. Communitarians are so deeply divided on so many of the issues in the communitarian ideology that it is difficult to pin them down to specific conceptual markers that delineate the parameters of the term. One could classify communitarians along a soft core/hard core index, with thinkers such as Alasdair MacIntyre, Michael Sandel, Michael Walzer, and Charles Taylor bearing the former label and Robert Bellah, Richard Madsen, and Amitai Etzioni bearing the latter.[7] Derek Phillips defines community according to communitarian standards as "a group of people who live in a common territory, have a common history and shared values, participate together in various activities, and have a high degree of solidarity."[8] In line with this working definition of community, communitarians articulate and advocate a communitarian ideal. In the modern world there are several actual referents indicated by the term *community*. Rigid tribal societies in Africa and homogeneous societies like Japan and Iceland may well closely fit the definitional standards. But in pluralistic and multiethnic societies in which ethnicity and national identities rip human associations and civil society to shreds, as in Yugoslavia, the Middle East, and parts of sub-Saharan Africa, Phillips's definition seems like a term totally divorced from reality. Lack of shared values, quarrels over who has a right to territory and who does not, and divides along lines of activities and commitments that prevent solidarity are a more accurate picture of much of the modern world.

But the communitarian ideal follows closely the definition offered by Phillips. Communitarians place the aims and values of the community in the service of what they claim to be one's real and most pervasive identity. All of us are implicated in social practices, customs, and interpretive ways of viewing the world and our places in it. Some of us, however, do not see ourselves as permanently bound to such communal features. We embrace the aspect of our civilization that allows us to revise our conceptions of the good and our judgments about our world and ourselves. We realize that we are not infallible and that we need to embrace the competing options that not only reveal our errors but also allow us to change radically and opt for membership in communities or associations whose values modify our values and in some cases pit us against the communities to which we currently belong. Conversion, then, can be a virtue if it leads to a better and more moral way of life.

Communitarians cannot endorse such a move. Not only are the ends and values of one's communities constitutive features of one's identity, but also one's embeddedness in a *particular* community with its values and customs provides the indisputable resources for one's sense of self. Communal values are, according to one of communitarianism's leading spokesmen, Charles Taylor, authoritative horizons that set goals for us.[9] Liberalism need not deny that claim. Liberals can acknowledge that "we have an ability to detach ourselves from any particular communal practice. No particular task is set for us by society, and no particular cultural practice has authority that is beyond individual judgment and possible rejection."[10] Communitarians reject this possibility. One's membership in a community and one's communal role are treated as givens. Will Kymlicka points out that communitarians such as Sandel and MacIntyre maintain that the self is under no obligation to accept the moral limitations of the communal roles and values that it discovers as its own. But they fail to explain how such a position is distinguishable from the individualism of liberalism, which communitarians reject.

The truth is that communitarians can provide us with no mechanisms for performing such moral feats since this would jeopardize precisely the logical features of the self on their account. Unlike the liberal self, which exists prior to its ends—which means that it has a discerning capacity that enables it to judge and then modify or reject the values, principles, and roles from which it derives its identity—the communitarian self is constituted by its ends, roles, and communal affiliations. If it extricates itself from such roles and ends by morally evaluating them and then judges that they are morally incorrect, then by the logic of the communitarian calculus it cancels itself out.

The ideal of this sort of self is certainly not reflective of a diverse society.

When I say diverse, I am referring primarily to diversity among value conceptions, including those conceptions that vary among cultures. The ideal communitarian self would have to view as a threat any feature or possibility that challenges the orthodoxy of the sacrosanct community. What happens, therefore, to the immigrant, the foreigner with her alien worldview and "quirky" values? What happens to the traditional Christian heterosexual who has never taken a job outside the home who meets a militant lesbian feminist who invites her to rethink her place in an institution that does not permit her to test her many potential ways of being in the world? What happens when she realizes that her becoming has been stymied, not because she now necessarily sees her life up to the moment as immoral or even damaging, but because it has placed particular parameters that make any modification in her way of life conceptually out of order? Can she decide to become a political lesbian? Liberalism grants her the right to devise such a life plan (at least theoretically; i.e., if she decides to become such a person, she will not lose her public or institutional identity, to use Rawls's phrase, although she might lose custody of her children and she could be fired from her job and ostracized by her community).

A defining feature of communitarianism is the centrality of the values, precepts, and customs held by the majority within a particular community. In communities where the values of an oppressive minority rule, there is still an appeal to majoritarian consensus: procedures are devised to ensure that those falling within the numerical majority do not count as valid members of the community. They cannot vote, they cannot endorse principles because they are deemed intellectually incompetent to do so.

Majoritarian endorsement of a community's values says nothing about the moral correctness of those values. Valorizing majoritarian consensus, the community stands immune to the moral remonstrance of outside value inspections. Since communitarians have not fully given us ways to separate ourselves from our communities and to remove ourselves from certain ends, the doctrine clearly reinforces those tendencies inimical to human growth, autonomy, and the moral revisionism that is crucial to any progressive society.

Communitarianism also imposes a false condition of preservation on its signatories or its involuntary practitioners. Why do I say so? In the contemporary world, at least in the Western industrialized democracies, our moral sensibilities are constantly challenged by the values of morally and politically competing communities. To treat the majoritarian endorsement of one's values in one's immediate community as a sign of their moral correctness betrays a predilection for certain types of epistemological errors that are bound to occur in one's moral reasoning. The idea rings true that the popularity of an idea or its numerical endorsement is never a sign of its infallibility, nor is its unpopularity a sign of its immutability. But if communitarian ideology is to prosper, its vanguards must maintain a somewhat ambivalent relationship to those attitudes, values, and ethos that would challenge its ruling principles, which constitute the very identities of its practitioners. Feminist ethics, emerging from the community of feminist thinkers, challenge the codified norms of communities ruled by principles and attitudes that fail to acknowledge females as ends in themselves and full-fledged moral agents. Principles of fairness and equality for all, values emerging from the community of liberal thinkers and activists, challenge communities in which ossified class systems prevent social mobility. Would any Western morally minded liberal shed a tear if the Hindu caste system modified itself beyond recognition by admitting untouchables into the larger community of human beings, complete with all the primary social goods, dignities, and plain decencies accorded the Brahmins?

Similarly, cosmopolitanism is a challenge to societies arranged along racial, ethnic, and nationalistic lines. Communitarianism spawns several satellites, chief among them homogeneous societies that would seek to advance an ethnic and racial ethos. Jeremy Waldron writes: "The communitarianism that can sound cozy and attractive in a book by Robert Bellah or Michael Sandel can be blinding, dangerous, and disruptive in the real world, where communities do not come ready-packaged and where communal allegiances are as much ancient hatred of one's neighbor as immemorial traditions of culture."[11]

Communitarian majoritarian conceptions of the common good have proven morally detrimental to peripheral conceptions of the good. Since they cannot allow persons to critique their ends and roles in a robustly repudiative manner and then remove themselves from such ends and roles (at least without obliterating their identities, on the communitarian view), they force individuals whose inner moral sensibilities are at odds with the dominant community to uphold, at least tacitly, values that their moral consciousness cannot defend and their judgments cannot corroborate. Without the power to radically alter the majority's conceptions, principles, and values, individuals who are ensnared within a communitarian ideology are forced to live dual lives. A huge dichotomy opens in their souls: their moral judgments and evaluations lead them to conclusions that they cannot uphold or express. The chasm between their inner moral consciousness and their lived day-to-day existence grows. The mechanisms for adapting, changing, and morally challenging communal traits they know to be morally suspect are not permitted to operate. This point rises above any discussion of the value of dissent and radical disengagement. It points to a feature of the human condition that moral cosmopolitanism stands against: tribal idolatry and deification of communal values, norms, and principles. The ideal community that must be preferred by communitarianism, given the logic of its ruling ethos, is homogeneous and nonpluralistic. John Danley notes that the push toward community on the communitarian model means not only that the group takes precedence over the good of individual group members but also that pluralism and cultural diversity are threats to the homogeneity implicit in the communitarian ideal.[12]

In its strongest version cosmopolitanism can find no ally in communitarianism. The communitarian ideal as embodied in majoritarian conceptions of the common good has taken too many pernicious forms that its theoretical system cannot adequately address. Unlike political liberalism, communitarianism is hard-pressed to demand that its practitioners and devotees repudiate the constitutive features of their communal lives. How then would moral conversion be possible? How could a communitarian justify the conduct of a moral exemplar such as Martin Luther King Jr., who rejected some of the roles and ends imposed upon him by his moral (some may say immoral) community, repudiated many of its traditions, and invited moral shame upon its members by using his life and the lives of black persons as objects of moral meditation and mediation?

If, as I have demonstrated, cosmopolitanism can justifiably call for the obliteration of cultures that are inimical to human dignity and moral autonomy, then moral cosmopolitanism and communitarianism will come to blows somewhere on the world's moral stage. The communitarian ideal will ultimately find expression in all sorts of morally questionable sociopolitical arrangements, whether it be the tribalism of ethnic cleansing in Yugoslavia, the often forgotten disgraceful expulsion of Asians from Uganda, the systems of racial apartheid that still reign throughout the world, or the myriad forms of cultural nationalism that abound in the name of freedom, progress, and national sovereignty. Cosmopolitanism will, and ought to, declare moral war on all such movements.

The idea that the individual need gain his moral sustenance from any one community or even that the communal life of an individual need in all cases divide neatly into pristine zones is false. I submit that modern nationalism is a satellite, or at best an unruly stepchild, of the communitarian ideal. One of its staple claims—that persons have always belonged to specific, well-defined, and culturally homogeneous peoples—is, as Jeremy Waldron points out, to be treated with caution. Furthermore, the idea that everyone needs a single dominant entity to give shape and meaning to life is also to be challenged.[13]

Cosmopolitanism would not deny the importance of culture in human life. But as I have argued, it rejects the idea that persons need one particular type of culture, one that is specially suited to their constitution, within which to matriculate socially. As we are hardwired to communicate in language, but not one specific language, so culture is the place in which we realize our full humanity. But whatever culture it may be, it will have to be one that is not immune to critical rationality, repudiation, and eventual overthrow if, in our moral judgment, we deem it unworthy of human habitation, a place that is inhospitable to the moral gestation of persons.

A moral cosmopolitan such as myself will have to reiterate this point, for ultimately it is my hope that persons will come to realize that the best culture, the most exalted and heroic one, the culture that spawns the most honorable ethos toward other humans, is a cosmopolitan culture. It is my hope then, that many who classify themselves as communitarians, nationalists, radical patriots, racialists, and ethnocentrics will reach the point when they can repudiate the traditions from which they emerged and opt for the cosmopolitan universe.

I agree with Charles Taylor and communitarians in general that a good society is one that is organized around a common cultural conception of the good. I would be a tad ambivalent about arguing the extent to which this conception should be mandated as a moral ideal, although my evolving thought on this issue could commit me to such a claim. My hesitation stems less from any liberal concern about imposing one's conception of the good on anyone and more from the intuition that such a strategy might not be conducive to moral reflection and moral modification. The conception of the good qua moral ideal, however, should be aspired to as a principle around which people can organize their ethical lives, believing that they become better persons in doing so.

One of my reasons for fervently believing that such a culture ought to be cultivated is that it is one in which I think moral exemplars can come into existence and flourish. Moral exemplars are free to encourage and inspire a culture as well as the ethos held by those in the culture. Because they embody and practice values at a consistently high level, they inspire us to cultivate those values that inform an ethos designed to bring further advances in the evolution of human ethical consciousness. I am inspired by some of the last interviews of Jean-Paul Sartre shortly before his death. Speaking to his assistant, Benny Levy, Sartre shares his thoughts on what a realized humanism in human existence would mean. A truly ethical humanism can be realized only in the ongoing process of humanity's moral evolution. Sartre, who does not believe that people have yet attained full humanity, says that even so, "these submen have in them principles that are human—which is to say that basically they have certain seeds in them that tend toward human and that are in advance of the very being that is the subman" that each person might be at the moment. He writes:

> Humanism can only be achieved, lived, by human beings; and we who are in a previous period, who are pushing toward being the humans we should be or that those following us will be, we experience humanism only as what is best in us, in other words, our striving to live beyond ourselves in the society of human beings. People we can prefigure in that way through our best acts.[14]

The need for moral exemplars to provide correctives for a society that is deeply morally disturbing is one reason that I find problematic the communitarian tendency of justifying notions of the common good according to majoritarian consensus. On the one hand, we know that moral exemplars such as Martin Luther King Jr. and Oskar Schindler and the several Europeans who, against German orders, rescued Jews from Nazi persecution existed; we know that they existed in spite of the varied conceptions of the good that basically outlawed their humanitarian, and in some cases morally heroic, efforts. Communitarians cannot deny that the validation of the common good according to majoritarian ideals has in effect been a defense of some of the worst atrocities ever visited upon humankind. Kymlicka argues that eighteenth-century New England town governments probably had a great deal of legitimacy among their members because of the success of their shared ends. These ends, however, prevailed because atheists, women, and Indians were excluded from membership. If they had been allowed membership, they would probably not have been impressed by the pursuits of what could be termed racist and sexist common goods.[15]

Communitarians tell us that shared ends are to be located within a certain sociohistorical set of practices and roles. But as Kymlicka argues, "They do not mention that those practices and roles were defined by a small portion of the society—propertied, white men—to serve the interests of propertied, white men. These practices remain gender-coded, race-coded, and class-coded, even when women, blacks and workers are legally allowed to participate in them."[16] This is an example of how roles determined by a particular segment can achieve majoritarian consensus—the majority in any given context is simply those whose voices hold power over others and those who have the particular brand of power to make those roles, ends, and interests stick. Legitimacy is achieved by excluding some people from membership.

Because I intend the thrust of my work to be internationalist, I do not mean to say that a particular example of how a communitarian ideal has played itself out is the only existentially real one. Majoritarian conceptions of the common good find haven in all sociopolitical and cultural contexts.

A cosmopolitan identity is empowering if one embraces all that comes with the discovery and practice of that identity. Communitarians will find problematic that the creation of a cosmopolitan self can provide a recourse for those who have been marginalized and excluded from the community. Further, it gives such persons a license to explicitly reject and morally repudiate the roles and identities that others have defined for them. The cosmopolitan self, in recognizing that appeals to tradition and "community sentiment" have often been made in the name of some good that excluded the participation of certain persons, rejects and challenges the morality of such roles and sentiments. To the truly hard-core communitarian, the cosmopolitan is a carrier of the dreaded viruses that have threatened all cultures that aim at some form of cultural, eth-nic, racial, or sentimental purity: miscegenation and hybridization. Hybridiza-tion carries with it a set of features that subvert the neatness of an illusion. In the modern world those illusions are wearing thin. Zones of purity—that is, the purity that would have to exist for the ideal communitarian culture—fall away because the real complexities and overlapping boundaries, perspectives, and values of human existence are struggling in various ways to reveal them-selves. If one looks at the attempts of many nationalist movements today, one will see that a compulsion to preserve these illusions of purity lies at the heart of their attempts at legitimacy. Old ancestral stories of the past that no longer bear any discernible relation to any living member of the tribe are retold in a way that is meant to make disappear the centuries of reconstruction, modifica-tion, and mutation that have disrupted their neatness, The forced memories they are meant to evoke actually evoke nothing real. Fantasy runs wild, and conceptual distortions become the norm.

But the music plays on, missing all the cadences of modern life, imposing a false superstructure that is as morally deadening as it is existentially false. To the extent that communitarian ideology shares a common beat with such forms of tribalism, to the extent that its ethos guides and maintains such forms of trib-alism, it in no way can find a friend in moral cosmopolitanism, a morality that above all is a direct repudiation of all forms of tribalism.

EPILOGUE: COMING OUT

AS A MORAL COSMOPOLITAN

It has often been written by sundry intellectuals of varied ideological and academic persuasions that the enterprise of philosophy as a discipline capable of changing the world is an illusion that, if indulged in, at worst bespeaks contemptible hubris and at best, a naïve and self-indulgent form of therapy.

Philosophy, of course, if conceived of as a narrow and specialized discipline, might grant legitimacy to that indictment. It should be clear from my writing, both in content and in style, that I am a hopeless romantic who is truly unable to capitulate to the idea that ideas are impotent and have no redemptive qualities. It should also be obvious that my deepest commitment to, and love of, philosophy stem from a conception of it not as a primarily academic enterprise but as a way of life that is at best realized and articulated in academic formalisms.

With that preamble, I end this book with a somewhat old-fashioned call to those who I suspect might be living as closeted moral cosmopolitans. This epilogue is addressed to the best within you and the ethos that lies buried beneath the racialized, ethnicized, and nationalized self that your culture has given to you. This ending is an appeal to the best within you that precariously exists as a possibility but has yet to be realized. It is the continued process of moral becoming in you that I seek to address.

Many of us have been living as closeted cosmopolitans. That is, we have been living under the aegis of racism, racialism, nationalism, and excessive and bloated patriotism. Rigid tribal arrangements that even in their informal stances still dominate our conscious lives have acted as formal mores that regulate our civic alliances. Many of us, sometimes for inexplicable reasons, have felt a deep dissatisfaction in our souls and have sensed the existence of a deeper and more fulfilling way of being and living in the world. We have sensed that the excesses associated with the bloated tribalisms that have regulated our ethical lives have missed the mark entirely and have failed to satisfy our craving for an ideal that we sense we can achieve but for which we lack the requisite social moral goods.

Many of us have longed to live postethnic, postracial, and postnational lives, but fear of losing the security that accompanies group solidarity (delayed weaning) prevents the willed weaning that is a prerequisite for that type of "lifestyle." Whether we know it or not, our lives have been mandated according to a *cosmophobic* ethos; that is, an ethos that organizes much of civic and social life around racial, ethnic, and national tribal lines. We have lived morally dichotomized lives. We have sensed an inner reality to which the outer and formally legislated world is unsympathetic.

To come out as a moral cosmopolitan is first of all to declare the mental pathologies on which racial and ethnic tribalism is founded. It is to declare such pathologies nonconducive to moral health. Coming out, therefore, is not just a way of morally building a self that is radically different from the environmental self crafted by one's local and parochial milieu; it is also a declaration that the presuppositions, values, and qualifying methodologies of one's environment spurious and deeply morally flawed. The attendant self, then, the cosmophobic self that has been created, is genuinely not one's own. To come out as a moral cosmopolitan means that one has no truck with this milieu. One may need to continue living in it and grafting one's immediate life plans onto its surface structure, but one in no way treats its value premises, presuppositions, and so-called objective view of people and the world as valid and beyond modification.

To come out as a moral cosmopolitan, then, means that one ceases to be complicitous in the perpetuation of such pathologies. To come out in this context is to see that *moral* rehabilitation requires a total moral and conceptual break with the world of one's past. It is to face a paradox and yet remain undaunted by it. The paradox lies in the fact that to reject the familiar and embrace the distant and the unknown is an act of faith that nevertheless requires that one act with a kind of uncertainty. There is no moral universe at large that would be hospitable to such an ethos. Yet one must dare to consciously craft a new type of self and reject the old culturally determined self. To change the self is also to change the world. Despite the fact that there might be no political legislative and procedural mechanism to sanction such a change, one self that dares to effect such a change leaves the world, in the deepest existential sense, radically altered. It is not the same. A solitary effrontery does leave the world changed.

In this call, an aristocracy of the soul is being summoned. To come out is to point the way to a possibility that is unfathomable to perhaps the majority of persons. Dedication to that which is right is infectious. Many are struggling to repress or forestall their heroism. They do this not from a sense of cynicism or moral agnosticism but because they fear that there is no world hospitable to their deepest moral sensibilities. The aristocrat, in the noblest sense of the term, is one whose regal bearing and nobility of character have never depended on the recognition and sanction of those less than he, nor has he required that his values and integrity conform to current trends. The soul aristocracy of you, the moral cosmopolitan, resides in the fact that the moral vision that guides your life paves the way for the moral rehabilitation of others and of your society and culture at large. Rather than waiting for others to create a world that you yearn for, a world that must be in place for your so-called true self to emerge, you imbue the world with the noblest of values wrought from the depths of a dissatisfied spirit whose hunger only you can sate. Moral creativity satisfies this hunger, and in the process it provides the world with a new model, a new paradigm of existing and of dealing with your fellow human beings. In your efforts, you are in effect forging the honorable traditions of tomorrow. On examining your struggles and the values spawned by your moral consciousness, old men and women reflecting on their lives in the middle of the first century of the new millennium will say that at last our moral abilities and dispositions have caught up with our scientific and technological achievements. No longer will this dichotomy exist within the human soul: the chasm between the stupendous accomplishments of humankind's intellect and the stodgy, slothful, and primitive advance of its moral conscience. The dilemma has always lain in the fact that humankind for so long has been able to manipulate the universe, to ward off the threats of nature, to battle plagues, and to protect itself from invaders.

The greatest battle, however, the battle that is waged within the soul of each person and that has been responsible for the majority of atrocities that continue to plague us today, remains unwon. The battle I am referring to, of course, is the battle against tribalism. Let those who doubt the truth of this read the history of the world very judiciously. Tribal conflicts have been, and still are, the source of most of the world's carnage. To come out as a moral cosmopolitan is in effect to say, "No more. The time has come. Civilization requires that we annihilate entirely the problematic features of our natures that prevent our moral progress as a species." Those who do not believe that moral progress is a possibility do not matter in this issue. Their very survival and their capacity to provide a future for their children depend on this notion. Civilization requires this capacity on our part. Morality provides us with the means for doing so. History (along with current reality) demonstrates that we have yet to find an effective way of dealing with our tribal impulses. It is quite obvious that all of the moral configurations that we have devised and inherited have proved unsuccessful in vanquishing tribalism. It is obvious that our moral configurations have not been demanding enough of us. They have given us the capacity to have our cake and eat it too. That honorable and heroic Trappist monk Thomas Merton writes: "Human nature has a way of making very specious arguments to suit its own cowardice and lack of generosity."

To come out as a radical cosmopolitan is to align oneself once and for all with the will that follows the moral intellect that knows the good. It means refusing to have your conception of the good tarnished by the false beliefs of tribal morality: the belief that our chances for a good life (which includes a morally and spiritually healthy life) ought to be determined by morally irrelevant features such as one's racial, ethnic, and national designations. But because a morally constructed self is also a self that has been radically realigned—one that is positioned differently in the world and is a self with new interests, new values, and new moral and political dispositions—it could find its past associations an affront to what one has either now become or is in the process of becoming.

To come out as a moral cosmopolitan might mean breaking with those with whom you were close while you lived either as a rabid tribalist or as a closeted moral cosmopolitan. Deciding which of your past associations to break and which to keep is up to you. The determining factors are personal and individual. Some breaks will have to be made since there are alignments with your past that make it all but impossible to be a moral cosmopolitan. But the extent to which you might be able to still align yourself with those merely problematic features of your past that make the transition difficult but not impossible is left to your discretion. Moral evolution is above all a voluntary undertaking. The edification of your consciousness has to be your decision, one in whose execution you are a direct and constant participant.

To come out is to halt the habituated practice of capitulating to the arbitrary, glib, and specious ends of the labelers and categorizers—vanguards of our sociocultural and sociopolitical culture. Your interior life ought not be regulated anymore by such practices. To come out is to cease pretending that your moral inferiors who have the political and cultural means of constructing your identities hold a moral good over your head; a good you cannot fully comprehend, a good that fails to satisfy your highest moral callings but that you will one day, if you just try hard enough, come to grasp and accept. It will never happen. The edification of your interior moral consciousness has been hijacked by tribalism. The eyes of the tribalist remain too focused on the ground, like the foraging animal that, guided by scent and keen eyesight, never lifts its eyes to the sky for the possibility of glimpsing in the heavens another sense, another model of radically existing in the world. It cannot and will never happen. The tribalist is to behave so. But your constitution is an upright one. It is a constitution that permits you all sorts of creative ontological leverages from which to devise limitless possibilities outside the world of your immediate senses. You have not exhausted the range of moral progress. Recommence the journey of our moral evolution and realize that we have only barely begun. History has not come to an end.

Remember, a single solitary effrontery does leave the world changed.

APPENDIX: HISTORICAL PICTURES

OF COSMOPOLITANISM

CLASSICAL COSMOPOLITANISM

When Diogenes of Sinope, a contemporary of Aristotle whom Thomas Schlereth describes as antiquity's existentialist, proclaimed that he had no city and homeland and that in effect he considered himself a citizen of the world, or a *kosmopolite,* he may have been setting up one of the crucial paradoxes that civilized man would face and continues to face. If humankind's creation of the state and the concept of citizenry was a prerequisite for civilization and moral maturity, then Diogenes' proclamations are clearly problematic. Either his stance can potentially disrupt the desired existential neatness of the ordered state and the attendant conceptual clarity by negating the possibility of the individual as reclaimable community property and thus make her more difficult to train as a civilized unit within the environ; or, in widening the concept of citizenry, loyalty, and affiliation beyond specific geographical demarcations, he was enticing his fellow human beings to aspire to a higher level of moral maturity and civilization: to extend their moral inclinations and sensibilities beyond their tribe. In so doing, he was in essence calling into question the very means by which identities are formed and values lived by. Can we then say that Diogenes was also antiquity's gadfly who started the weaning process I have argued for? It is still not clear whether Diogenes, in widening the human community to include others, was advocating anything like what contemporary moral cosmopolitans such as myself have in mind. Derek Heater describes Diogenes and the ancient Cynics as intellectual hippies who wandered the world and sought wisdom "through a self-sufficient repudiation of the polis and its conventions."[1] An iconoclastic attitude toward the state and its values reminiscent of the ontological rebel is expressed by Diogenes' stance.

The Cynics were vehement social critics who, despite their inability to pass beyond their contempt for society, began the cosmopolitan tradition in Western thought and greatly influenced the Stoics. It was with the Cynics that a radical notion of cosmopolitanism emerged. Today, they might be labeled rugged individualists. They demanded total alienation from the racial exclusiveness of the polis. They sought identification with the cosmic universe and pledged allegiance only to other cosmopolitans.[2] Martha Nussbaum notes that the Cynics placed a great deal of emphasis on the worth of reason and moral purpose in defining humanity. Class rank and status, national origin, location, and even gender were treated by the Cynics as secondary and morally irrelevant. The form of moral affiliation that the Cynics sanctioned was the citizen's affiliation with his or her rational humanity.[3]

The concept of world citizenship in the sense of belonging to the whole of humankind emerged predominantly in the Greco-Roman era as an important component of Stoic thought. Stoicism, like its rival Epicureanism, became a response to an immense world in which the insulation of the small city-state was stripped away and individuals had to find a place in an expanding environment. Western cosmopolitan ideas originated in the polis and were best expressed in the notion that barbarians live in tribes and empires while Greeks live in city-states. This judgment was held with pride in classical Hellenistic Greece as proof of the superior and unusual sophistication of Greek civilization.[4] Heater attributes the receptiveness to the idea of a cosmopolis and a cosmopolitan frame of mind to the decline of the polis in the fourth century B.C. This decline was largely a result of the imposition on the Greeks of a monarchy, which failed to capture the former enthusiasm of the polis. A second factor is the lack of loyalty among colonists. Individual values replaced previous communitarian ones. The cosmopolis was not conceived as an organized political system. Rather, it was grounded in a belief that all social and cultural distinctions are superficial in comparison with the essential sameness of all members of the human race. The unquestionable factor that binds all to a world community is obedience to natural law. Indeed, as early as the eighth century B.C. both Homer and Hesiod attempted to articulate the view that there was a shared consciousness of persons as beings sharing attributes that differentiated them from the beasts. Hesiod contributed the idea that "men have a gift denied to beasts, namely a sense of justice and good order, which gives them the potential to live together in peace and unity."[5]

In the sixth century intellectual analysis in fields that today would be called geography, biology, and psychology attracted thought around the theme of human unity. Heater writes: "Travellers and cartographers considered mankind as a whole; biological and medical study led to the notion of the human race as a definable species; and emphasis on man's capacity for reasoned speech *(logos)* could be interpreted as a generalised function of humanity."[6] Consider, for example, Heraclitus's argument that the logos also embraced universal law: "Those who speak with understanding must rely on what is common to all, as a city relies on its law, and with far greater reliance. For all human laws are nourished by one law, the divine law, which has all the power it desires and is enough, and more than enough, for all."[7]

Human unity achieved by adherence to universals, though an ideal, was naturally constrained by the imperfectability of human nature. Human unity for Heraclitus was something that would be achieved only when wisdom was attained by more than just a minority of human beings.

The binding potential of universal moral laws and its clash with provinciality such as that embodied in state laws was also demonstrated by Sophocles in *Antigone*. Antigone defied King Creon's decree forbidding the burial of her brother Polynices. She announces to Creon:

> That order did not come from God. Justice,
> That dwells with the gods below, knows no such law.
> I did not think your edicts strong enough
> To overrule the unwritten unalterable laws
> Of God and heaven, you being only a man.[8]

Heater also points out the development of the Peripatetic teachings of the Sophists. He writes:

> Of most importance was Antiphon, who made the categorical statement, "by nature Greeks and barbarians are all alike, as a study of their essential attributes will show," Another, the well travelled Hippias, is portrayed in Plato's dialogue, the *Protagoras*. Here he addresses his fellow-guests in the following manner: "I count you all my kinsmen and family and fellow citizens—by nature, not by convention." A fair proportion of those engaged in this discussion were "foreigners—Protagoras draws them from every city that he passes through." They could probably, therefore, be considered "fellow-citizens" only by natural law, not by state-defined custom.[9]

The fourth century also saw a reaffirmation in traditional beliefs in the polis. Cosmopolitan values to some extent were practiced by Alexander the Great, who actually pursued a policy of ethnic integration between the Greeks/ Macedonians and the Persians and Medes. Armies were racially/ethnically mixed, as were Greeks and Persians in newly founded cities. Heater suggests that through a program of fusion and an attitude of racial and religious tolerance, Alexander showed himself more Macedonian than Greek.

Cosmopolitanism today perhaps has inherited much of its ethical and conceptual boundaries from Stoicism. Heater suggests that the admired *Republic* of Zeno, founder of the Stoic sect, may be summed up in one main principle:

that all the inhabitants of this world of ours should not live differentiated by their respective rules of justice in separate cities and communities, but that we should consider all men to be of one community and one polity, and that we should have a common life and an order common to us all, even as a herd that feeds together and shares the pasturage of a common field. This Zeno wrote, giving shape to a dream or, as it were, shadowy picture of a well-ordered and philosophic commonwealth.[10]

In writing about cosmopolitanism, Zeno did not mean something similar to an empire like that of Alexander the Great. Rather, the Stoics' cosmopolitanism was a matter of human relationships free of all political forms.[11]

Cicero, the next major Stoic figure, identified the common bond that existed between all human beings as reason and speech, which "by the process of teaching and learning, of communicating and discussing, and reasoning associate men together and unite them in a sort of natural fraternity."[12]

Seneca, tutor and confidant to Nero, also made a few references to a cosmopolitan doctrine: "'I shall know that the whole world is my country'; 'I am not born for any one corner of the universe; this whole world is my country'; 'the human race have certain rights in common.'"[13]

Seneca draws a distinction between the individual as citizen and the individual as human being and argues that if the performance of citizenly functions is denied to any human, he may still conscientiously perform the duties of a human being. He writes:

> The very reason for our magnanimity in not shutting ourselves up within the walls of one city, in going forth into intercourse with the whole earth, and in claiming the world as our country, was that we might have a wider field for our virtue. Is the tribunal closed to you, and are you barred from the rostrum and hustings? Look how many broad stretching countries lie open behind you, how many peoples?[14]

Heater argues that what makes this passage significant is its emphasis on service to people of another state, as opposed to the abstract notion of humankind as a whole. He argues that what Seneca is advocating is the translation of this sense of responsibility into practical political or community service in some specific locality other than one's own state. Seneca is speaking as an experienced politician in concrete terms.[15]

The entreaty is a step above the exalted vision of Diogenes and some of the more abstract and idealistic notions of unity proffered by the Cynics. If, as I have argued, we take the extension of our moral sensibilities to others as a sign of moral maturity, then Seneca's insistence on service in *other* communities is part of the concrete way those moral extensions are carried out. Those concrete acts may be viewed as examples of moral training that will eventually allow persons to make affiliations with first one community and then others as their capacity for cross-communal affiliation reaches an optimal level. It is the hope of the ultimate cosmopolitans as I have described them that with this capacity comes the concomitant decline in the significance of tribal fixation and its attendant overdetermination.

It was largely by organizing themselves into a philosophical and moral cadre and by acting as advisers to rulers and as men of letters against prejudices and provincialism that the Stoics widened the ethical concerns of cosmopolitanism and tried to make the ideal a reality.[16] Above all, the Stoic cosmopolitans held that persons should see their deliberations as primarily about the problems common to all human beings emerging in particular situations and not problems growing out of a local or national identity that would confine and limit their moral aspirations.[17]

Marcus Aurelius, who became Roman emperor in A.D. 161, is also regarded as a contributor to the Stoic creed. An advocate of world citizenship, he sought to validate the ideal by appealing to a holistic notion of the universe and of the individual's place in it. The Universe, God, Nature, Truth, Law, Reason, and human beings are intimately related in the cosmic order.[18] Attempting to prove this interrelationship, he writes:

> If the intellectual capacity is common to us all, common too is the reason, which makes us rational creatures. If so, that reason is common which tells us to do or not to do. If so, law is common. If so, we are citizens. If so, we are fellow members of an organized community. If so, the Universe is as it were a state—for of what other single polity can the whole race of mankind be said to be fellow members?—and from it, this common State, we get the intellectual, the rational, and the legal instinct, or whence do we get them?[19]

Aurelius regarded the place of one's birth as an accident, as any human being might have been born in any nation. According to him, it made little difference where persons lived provided that wherever they lived, they lived as a citizen of the world. Nussbaum writes: "Recognizing this, we should not allow differences of nationality or class or ethnic membership or even gender to erect barriers between us and our fellow human beings. We should recognize humanity wherever it occurs, and give its fundamental ingredients, reason and moral capacity, our first allegiance and respect."[20]

To obey the ethical dictates of nature-endowed reason is Aurelius's ideal. Admitting that world citizenship is extremely difficult, the emperor notes that it is crucial that wherever a man lives, he live as a citizen of the World-City.[21] Those who cannot abide by the dictates of universal reason are morally inferior. Persons are required to live a life not only of duty but also of true freedom and equality. Real freedom will consist in living in accordance with the laws of nature, laws that treat all persons equally.[22]

Stoic cosmopolitanism, regardless of its varied practitioners, was characterized by four primary features: (1) a disdain of patriotism; (2) a desire for harmonious international relations; (3) an emphasis on the primacy of the individual and the dignity of reason in each person; and (4) rule of positive and natural law. In one form or another it represents a major advancement over tribalism. Advancing the idea that our first moral allegiance is not to be given to any mere form of temporal power or any one locality but to the moral community made up of all human beings, one sees that the weaning process is encouraged by extending one's moral and even legal commitments to those outside one's immediate national, ethnic, or racial affiliation. Yet it is more than that. It involves refraining from the tribal urge to define oneself primarily in terms of one's parochial affiliation. One's standpoint in the world, or one's psychological frame of reference, which always starts with one's very intimate and immediate environment, is challenged and widened and ultimately becomes a compound of several orientations. To the extent that this phenomenon is not only interpreted as normal and appropriate but given much heuristic weight, one would see a significant decline in the metaphysical privilege granted to "roots," origins, and the traditions of one's own kind, which often characterizes the mind-set of tribalists, be they racists, nationalists, or ethnic chauvinists. As Nussbaum notes, no theme is deeper in Stoicism than the damage done to our political lives by faction and intense local loyalties.[23]

ENLIGHTENMENT COSMOPOLITANISM

In *The Cosmopolitan Ideal in Enlightenment Thought,* Thomas Schlereth notes that cosmopolitanism existed as an ideal and not in doctrinal purity.[24] It represented an attitude of mind that in its intellectual interests attempted to transcend chauvinistic national loyalties or parochial prejudices. Ideally, the "cosmopolites" or "citizens of the world" sought to be identified by an interest in, and a familiarity with or appreciation of, many parts and peoples of the world. They wished to be distinguished by a willingness to borrow from other lands or civilizations in the formation of their intellectual, cultural, and artistic patterns. Enlightenment cosmopolitanism was more symbolic and theoretical than actual and practical. It was often a highly subjective state of mind that sought to grasp the unity of mankind without attempting to solve the relation of the part to the whole. The Enlightenment cosmopolite maintained a belief in human solidarity and uniformity throughout the world.[25] Enlightenment cosmopolitanism was also a psychological construct that urged many philosophers to modify their attachment to their geographical region or sphere of activity with a more expansive, albeit abstract, attitude toward the world. David Hume has this to say of the cosmopolite:

> A creature, whose thoughts are not limited by any narrow bounds, either of place or time; who carries his researches into the most distant regions of this globe, and beyond this globe, to the planets and heavenly bodies; [who] looks backward to consider the first origin, at least, the history of the human race; casts his eye forward to see the influence of his actions on posterity, and the judgements which will be formed of his character a thousand years hence.[26]

By and large the Enlightenment cosmopolitan was someone who reacted against certain social, religious, economic, and political realities of the eighteenth century.

Perhaps no discussion of contemporary cosmopolitanism can be complete without some reference to Immanuel Kant's work on cosmopolitanism. His "Idea of History from a Cosmopolitan Point of View," along with his essay "What Is Enlightenment?" may be interpreted as a manifesto in moral training, a training intended to wrest the individual from his or her tribal tendencies into the sunlight world of universal reason. In that world, persons recognize that their shared common human identities reside in their crucial moral attribute of reason—not in racial, national, and ethnic affinities. I say that Kant provided this inspiration only potentially, for it is not at all clear that his work in cosmopolitanism prevented the old patriotism and ethnic tribalism it was intended to supplant. In fact, in certain parts of *Perpetual Peace,* Kant seems to recognize what he calls Nature's value in drawing lines of demarcation in the form of national barriers among human beings. It is arguable that Kant saw this merely as an empirical issue contingent upon mankind's moral graduation from barbarism and irrationality. One might say that he saw such demarcations and the right of the state to regulate the lives of its citizens around its edicts and values as part of the moral machinery to which humans had to be subjected before they could become entirely self-legislating. If, however, Kant wavers on this issue, much in his ethical system could normatively ground a spirit of cosmopolitanism that might be akin to radical cosmopolitanism. That is, there is much in Kant's ethics that, if articulated in a certain way, could sketch at least one of the very real precepts that any cosmopolitan must have: moral maturity, which in this case expresses itself as a weaned identity. Central to all of this is the ideal of universal reason and its communicability to those outside one's sociocultural milieu. Whether one holds to such commitments on rhetorical grounds—that is, as the best strategy from which to defend and realize particular goals—or on strong metaphysical and ontological grounds remains to be examined at another time. It seems to me, however, that short of some claim to universality and universal reason, my cosmopolitan project is compromised and becomes a potential host for all sorts of pernicious parasites: nationalism, strong patriotism, ethnic chauvinism, and even so-called objective racism.

In "Idea for a Universal History from a Cosmopolitan Point of View," Kant makes it clear that despite individuals' varied purposes and the varied ways they live their lives, they simultaneously all act (unknown to them) toward a common goal. All work "toward furthering it, even if they would set little store by it if they did know it."[27] As Kant sees it, humans exist somewhere between the state of animals and that of rational citizens. Their behavior is contradictory and often unsystematic. While there are rare displays of wisdom on the part of some persons, the behavior of most people appears quite idiotic. No great individual purpose among men can be presupposed by the philosopher. It is therefore incumbent upon him or her to discover what Kant calls a natural purpose in the "idiotic course of things human."[28] He writes:

> In keeping with this purpose, it might be possible to have a history with a definite plan for creatures who have no plan of their own.
>
> We wish to see if we can succeed in finding a clue to such a history; we leave it to Nature to produce men capable of composing it. Thus Nature produced Kepler, who subjected, in an unexpected way, the eccentric paths of the planets to definite laws; and she produced Newton, who explained these laws by a universal natural cause.[29]

Kant makes it clear that most human beings are not capable of the full and proper exercise of their reason. In "Idea for a Universal History from a Cosmopolitan Point of View," he describes a state in which the individual will be released from self-incurred tutelage. Until that period, however, a rational construct has to be imposed as the proper teleological end of humans. That is, given the fact that human behavior appears purposeless and without a telos, one has to be assumed and posited.

For Kant the crucial instrument needed to orient individuals toward a telos that is proper to the nature of who they are is reason. The latter he defines in *Idea* as a faculty capable of widening its rules and purposes beyond natural instinct. Besides having no limit to its conceived project, reason does not work instinctively but requires trial and error, practice and gradual instruction for progression from one level of insight to another.[30] It is obvious to Kant that moral maturity and rational sophistication are not automatically programmed into humans. Persons' status as rational beings is derived from their capacity to exercise their rational faculty and their capacity for making rational decisions in accordance with the dictates of morality.[31] Though persons are the source of the moral law and are capable of acting rationally, they do not always do what is right, since they are also creatures of emotions, desires, and weaknesses. This is all the more reason that for Kant the imposition of a telos is crucial. Humans need a positioned telos that will order the ways their reason is exercised in the phenomenal world. What is required to get to this telos? Enlightenment of a certain type. The moral instructions of reason are to be passed on through the human race as a whole and not in any one person. Passing on from person to person, moral maturity and sophistication in the exercise of reason would take a very long time and might be psychologically impossible. A single person, Kant admits, would have to live for a very long time in order to learn to make full use of this reason. Kant writes: "Since Nature has set only a short period for his life, she needs a perhaps unreckonable series of generations, each of which passes its own enlightenment to its successor in order finally to bring the seeds of enlightenment to that degree of development in our race which is completely suitable to Nature's purpose."[32] Kant argues that, short of this ideal, the natural capacities of humans would be vain and aimless.

The first three theses ground Kant's teleological agenda; the fourth and fifth lie at the heart of his brand of cosmopolitanism. Kant begins the fourth thesis by observing that nature achieves the development of the capacities of human beings through their antagonisms in society. This antagonism reads as the unsocial sociability of humans, or their proclivity to enter into society. This tendency for union in society is offset by oppositional forces in human beings that impel people to have things go the way they want them to. Humans expect opposition on all sides. This opposition forces people to conquer their avarice, because there is a simultaneous recognition that their wishes and desires cannot be met outside the context of a civil society. Individuals cannot tolerate each other, but they certainly have the wisdom to realize that they cannot do without each other. Describing the human endeavor at moral effort. Kant writes:

> Thus are taken the first true steps from barbarism to culture, which consists in the social worth of man; thence gradually develop all talents, and taste is refined; through continued enlightenment the beginnings are laid for a way of thought which can in time convert the coarse, natural disposition for moral discrimination into definite practical principles, and thereby change a society of men driven together by their natural feelings into a moral whole.[33]

The end to be achieved by humans is rational nature. Without their unsociable disposition, however, humans would not learn to aspire and achieve by degrees a high level of moral and rational maturity.

In the fifth thesis, Kant articulates the existential outcome of this reconciliation on the part of humans between their oppositional tendencies and their disposition for union in a society: the achievement of a universal civic society that administers law among humans. This in effect is Kant's cosmopolitan kingdom of ends. It is a logical extension of human rational nature.

The development of humankind's highest faculty as part of Nature's supposed purpose is achievable only in a society with the greatest freedom. This society is the repository of mutual opposition among its members. The society also exists along with the most exact definition of freedom and limits so that it may be consistent with the freedom of others. Kant writes: "Thus a society in which freedom under external laws is associated in the highest degree with irresistible power (i.e., a perfectly just civic constitution), is the highest problem Nature assigns to the human race; for Nature can achieve her other purposes for mankind only upon the solution and completion of this assignment."[34]

The challenge of establishing an ethical commonwealth among humans becomes the second task. Kant identifies this need by the logical deduction of an empirical observation regarding the state of humans within the same environment: The oppositional forces that exist among individuals toward one another will also extend transnationally. The antidote: the establishment of a league of nations in which even the smallest could expect security and justice from the league's combined power. The states give up just what is given up by savage man—brutish freedom—in exchange for peace and quiet under a lawful constitution.[35]

The civilizing effect of such a constitution lifts man from animality into the pristine world of human rationality. Kant's emphasis on war and antagonism is worth noting. Wars, strife, and separation of states are attempts on the part of Nature to make humans into the sort of rational and self-legislating creatures they were intended to be. Strife, wars, and antagonism have a purging effect. Through destruction, new political bodies are established and in turn annihilated, until the best civic constitution emerges, which creates a state that can legislate for and maintain itself automatically.[36] Individual violation of rights for Kant may be carried over to states. Kant's idea of a cosmopolitan condition is the last step of perfection necessary to the tacit code of civil and public right.

Kant assigns Nature a purposiveness that is its proper attribute, as conceived by rational persons. The purpose we attribute to Nature is that she makes moral beings out of natural beings, who are the raw material of history. The aim of history is to make humans perfect beings. The individualistic character that seems to be assigned thereby to history is counterbalanced by the fact that completion cannot be reached in the individual but only in the species. Nature endows humans with reason and enables them to attain that completion.[37]

The idea that Nature's purposiveness culminates in the development of higher moral maturity in humans is important in Kantian morality. Part of humankind's moral maturity is accomplished through the empirical contingencies humanity faces. Lessons are drawn from the evils visited upon humans because of their developed capacities. Kant writes:

> Purposeless savagery held back the development of the capacities of our race; but finally, through the evil into which it plunged mankind, it forced our race to renounce this condition and to enter into a civic order in which those capacities could be developed. The same is done by the barbaric freedom of established states. Through wasting the powers of the commonwealth in armaments to be used against each other, through devastation brought on by war, and even more by the necessity of holding themselves in constant readiness for war, they stunt the full development of human nature. But because of the evils which thus arise, our race is forced to find, above the (in itself healthy) opposition of states which is a consequence of their freedom, a law of equilibrium and a united power to give it effect. Thus it is forced to institute a cosmopolitan condition to secure the external safety of each state.[38]

Nature has as its end that self-legislating beings will voluntarily bring about peace. Nature guarantees a perpetual peace, but this peace as the end goal of nature, along with her other methodical arrangements, cannot be deduced from reasoning. It can only be supposed. The supposition is a prerequisite for the formation of any order.

This peace, however, which manifests itself as a sort of cosmopolitical order among nations, ought to, on the basis of Kant's ethics, also culminate in a kingdom of ends inhabited by self-legislating human beings who recognize their common identity as rational creatures. Ideally this constitutive feature should take precedence over the contingent factors that Kant deemed vital as conditions for the ethical training of persons. These factors are those purposive parts of Nature that work to make moral creatures of natural creatures.

In "What Is Enlightenment?" Kant makes it clear that enlightenment is a clarion call for individuals to display the courage needed to use their own rational resources without direction from another; it is a call for individuals to emerge out of immaturity. It appears to be a minimum prerequisite for the realization of an enlightened age, which in Kant's time still had not happened.

Kant displays optimism about individuals' ability to use their own understanding. In a free society human rationality will flourish. However, he advises us to bear in mind that because this flourishing of rationality will occur in degrees and at different times in different people, the public achievement of enlightenment must proceed slowly. Kant, following in the vein of Plato and Socrates—both of whom spurned revolution because it leads to despotism—warns that a reform in ways of thinking can never occur via revolution. Enlightenment and institutional changes will come slowly for most people

Kant's ethical cosmopolitanism emerges as an offshoot of the Enlightenment demand for, and cultivation of, reason. Rational creatures expressing the freedom they have set for themselves as reasonable beings—which is incidentally what makes them free and autonomous beings in Kant's framework—plausibly may reach a stage in their moral development where they no longer have to rely on the edicts, norms, values, and principles of the state to regulate their lives and their conduct with each other. As self-legislating rational beings who aspire to a kingdom of fair and just ends and whose will and reason are in accord, beings in whom the will chooses what reason recognizes for the good—that is, reason detached from inclinations—they are beyond the tutelage of the tribe.

All that I have described, therefore, as tribal fixations, which would include treating the ends of the community and the edicts and sentiments of the Natural Attitude as metaphysically serious and morally immutable, ought to be, on the basis of Kantian morality, irrelevant. That is, Kantian morality and metaphysics would eventually have to admit that the postulates of the Natural Attitude (postulates that Kant himself would admit are instrumental in the metamorphosis from animality to civility in natural beings) will become secondary and irrelevant in the moral consciousness of rational persons. Kant writes: "Men work themselves gradually out of barbarity if only intentional artifices are not made to hold them in it."[39] The Natural Attitude and the principles, moralities, and values subsumed under it may be classified as hypothetical imperatives. (An imperative is a command to a particular course of action.) Hypothetical imperatives are grounded in the inclinations and as such cannot be the basis for morality. Inclinations cannot be commanded or universalized. They are concerned with specific ends that are contingently or instrumentally determined, as opposed to categorical imperatives, which are the absolute moral law and the basis for all moral conduct. The categorical imperative's formal maxim: So act that you can will the maxim (principle) of your action to be a universal law binding upon the will of every rational person.

Kant's ethical cosmopolitanism is not as explicitly stated as is his vague theory of a cosmopolitan world order as delineated in *Perpetual Peace* and his "Idea of a Universal History." His ethical cosmopolitanism may be logically inferred from his moral philosophy. The universal laws of reason, which are binding on all persons, stand above any edicts of the nation, tribe, or community. When I say the laws of reason stands above such edicts, I mean they stand above them ethically, not politically. This important point can be explained by examining Kant's categorization of reason in two realms: the private and the public, with the imperative that obedience is to follow orders and commands when reason is applied in the private realm but is inapplicable in the public sphere. Scholars have the right to use their reason freely and are not bound by the legalities and strictures that bind others. They act as members of the world community or a "society" of world citizens by displaying their reason before the reading public. Those employed by, or participating in, a particular segment of society are not prevented from thinking and reasoning for themselves, but their reason is denied actual expression and is curtailed by a prima facie obligation to obey the law. Kant reminds us that many of the affairs conducted in the public interest require "a certain mechanism through which some members of the community must passively conduct themselves with an artificial unanimity, so that the government may direct them to public ends."[40]

There are problems with this distinction, but a discussion of them is outside the scope of this book. The point I wish to make, however, is that even when one is compelled to obey the law of the nation, it does not follow on Kant's account that one's moral consciousness is also regulated by the coercive legal power of the state. One's moral consciousness is self-regulated, or regulated by the power of one's own reason, which obeys universal moral law. Kant in this case seems like a radical cosmopolitan, especially when one considers his idea that moral freedom is an ethical problem whose solution is independent of political circumstances.

It is, therefore, conceivable that one could live in a tribalistic society under the leadership of a "benevolent" despot where one would be required to respect a law that stipulates that one cannot do business with persons of another race. One may find the law objectionable. In obeying the law, one can still refrain from having the law impinge on and pollute one's moral consciousness. Public obedience is not coterminous with moral sanction. The metaphysical stamp of moral objectivity comes from the dictates of universal reason rather than the societal sanction of those with political power. The distinction is crucial. Kant does not want to maintain that the hypothetical imperatives of the tribe could in any way impinge upon the sanctity of universal reason, which is guiding one's moral consciousness. Reinhold Aris writes: "Kant's legislature of reason is abstract and not confined within national frontiers."[41] In Kant's theoretical morality only the universal is real. The empirically grounded and individual facts are philosophically insignificant. The defining feature of Kant's ethical system, the categorical imperative, which states that one acts according to a maxim that can be adopted at the same time as a universal law, is granted by the autonomous will of the individual, which is a quality of the will by which the will gives law unto itself.

The law has to carry absolute necessity for it to be morally valid on the ground of obligation. The ground of obligation is found neither in so-called human nature nor in the circumstances of the world. Rather, it is located in the a priori, in the concepts of pure reason. For Kant principles based on the empirical and experiential may be termed practical rules but never moral laws. Moral philosophy has to be based on the part of reason that is pure. The individual is capable of the idea of a pure reason, but because of passions and inclinations the task is not easy. For an action to be morally good, it must not only conform to the moral law, it must also be done for the sake of the law, that is, performed as an end in itself.[42] Kantian morality does not permit moral laws to spring from the conclusions drawn from empirical and comparative analysis. This type of methodology would leave us with no absolutely certain way of knowing what is right. Through reason humans come up with principles by which to judge all actions. His metaphysics of morals is a regulator of the behaviors of all person regardless of contingent phenomena that may affect their lives. Reason, rather than being the slave of existential factors and passions, leads the class of moral actions embodied under the principle.

Kantian morality culminates in the idea of a kingdom of free, rational, and autonomous agents. All such persons are equal in humanity, and all are to be treated as ends in themselves regardless of where they may reside. If Kant the political thinker seems to problematize his ethical theory (as, for example, his idea that nature properly demarcates persons into different nations and national identities), then his high moral theory stands as the ultimate corrective to the necessities of empirical man in an empirical world. The demarcation is not a moral end for Kant; it is instead a realistic assessment of the social factors that will assist humans in their striving toward enlightenment.

Nussbaum argues that Kant inherited this idea of a kingdom of free rational beings equal in humanity from the Stoics, who emphasized reason rather than personhood and superficial descriptions of people's background and practical goals.[43]

Kant's ethical cosmopolitanism, therefore, has to be distinguished from his political cosmopolitanism. In his political cosmopolitanism he sketched a loosely conceived federation, a kind of international society of republican nation-states based on voluntary acceptance of the rule of law and mutual respect for one another's internal and external sovereignty. At the core of Kant's argument is his claim that

> world peace is possible only if states first become republican, since only in a political order in which the rights of individuals are guaranteed through the separation of powers, the rule of law, and representative government is it likely that the bellicose ambitions of monarchs will be sufficiently curbed. Moreover, only a republic in which citizens are free to deliberate and express their opinions about public policy—that is, one that conforms to what Kant calls the "transcendental principle of publicity"— will ensure the sort of internal or domestic conditions necessary for realizing international peace.[44]

Kant, however, is no political revolutionary, as his essay on enlightenment makes clear. Citizens have an obligation to obey the laws even when the laws conflict with their moral conscience. Nussbaum writes: "For both Kant and the Stoics, there is sometimes and in some ways a tendency to treat the moral imperative as displacing the political imperative, respect for dignity at times taking the place of rather than motivating changes in the external circumstances of human lives, given that for both the good will is invulnerable to disadvantages imposed by these circumstances."[45]

Kant's political cosmopolitanism seems to be motivated by empirical concerns. A cosmopolitical right is not just an exercise of fantasy; it "is the last step of perfection necessary to the tacit code of civil and public right."[46] But it is more than just empirical concerns. Kant has to make sure that his ethical theory is compatible with a theory of politics. Morality for Kant, above everything else, is a practical state of affairs. It is the sum of the absolute laws according to which we ought to act. It would be absurd, he argues, to grant the idea of duty all its authority and at the same time pretend that it is incapable of being fulfilled. This would kill the very idea of duty. Kant writes:

> Politics, inasmuch as it is a practical jurisprudence, cannot therefore be in contradiction to morality, considered as the theory of right (that is to say, there is no opposition between the theory and the practice); unless by morality were meant the sum of the rules of prudence, or the theory of the most proper means to accomplish the views of self-interest; i.e. except every idea of morality were entirely rejected.[47]

Kant's ethical cosmopolitanism, his notion of a kingdom of rational humans who affirm one another's dignity and humanity, is not dependent on his idea of a cosmopolitical order. To the extent that his ethical theory is not at all dependent on any metaphysical picture of the world as it stands, his inferred moral cosmopolitanism is a logical offshoot of the a priori principles found in pure reason, which grounds his morality. But there is also the sense that this ethical ideal is most likely realized within a cosmopolitical world order. There is the idea that on their own, most persons are simply incapable of realizing an ethical cosmopolitanism without elaborate social mechanisms such as hospitality, respect, rules governing monetary loans among nations, constitutional regulations regarding international relations, and policies toward foreigners and their admittance.

Kantian and Stoic affirmation of rational humanity is both hopeful and problematic. Enlightenment constructions of rationality, as is well known, have been problematic to the extent that they have been made to exclude groups who fall outside its delineations. The exploitation of constructs of reason and rationality seems more a problem of the moral ethos of those employing the concept for pernicious purposes and less a problem of the concepts themselves. The challenge for future ethical cosmopolitans, therefore, is not to give up notions of universal reason but rather to expand and modify such notions: to widen immensely the membership of the human community and to allow the voices of Others to play a crucial role in our refiguring of concepts of reason and rationality. It is true that we may never get away from the question "Whose reason?" But to the extent that inclusion rather than exclusion is a criterion of reassessing our suppositions about reason, the question becomes less ominous. Cosmopolitans cannot abandon reason for the simple reason that they are attempting to morally persuade others by rational means to share in their conception of the good. Cosmopolitans will have to continue explaining why their conception of cosmopolitanism as a moral ideal is a very good way of living in the world.

Cosmopolitans will need to continue (to the extent that they rely on moral suasion as a means to their goals) explaining to those whose behaviors they deem morally pernicious why they would be better off embracing the cosmopolitan ideal. The ultimate challenge, of course, is for any cosmopolitan to attempt to do this without recourse to reason and, beyond that, the very idea of an accessible and shared universal human reason.

NOTES

INTRODUCTION

1. See Arend Lijphart, *Democracy in Plural Societies* (New Haven: Yale University Press, 1977).

2. See Julia Kristeva, *Nations without Nationalism* (New York: Columbia University Press, 1993).

3. For an interesting discussion of the ethos of a cosmopolitan society, see Timothy C. Earle and George T. Cvetkovich, *Social Trust: Toward a Cosmopolitan Society* (Westport, Conn.: Praeger, 1995).

CHAPTER 1

1. Edward E. Sampson, "The Deconstruction of the Self," in *Texts of Identity*, ed. John Shotter and Kenneth J. Gergen (London: Sage, 1989), 13.

2. See, e.g., Frithjof Bergmann, "Freedom and the Self," in *Self and Identity*, ed. Daniel Kolak and Raymond Martin (New York: Macmillan, 1991), 409. Bergmann makes the point that we experience language this way as well. He writes: "The sentences we form, the words we overhear ourselves speak, seem awkward and inflexible. We are like a farmer writing. Our medium of thought is still impersonal and copied. Then starts the arduous and never quite successful process of moving this crust back. One opens cracks, experiments and rearranges and gradually bits take on a character that is more private, until through continuous alterations we slowly make what we are saying more nearly our own. Some great writers persist in this effort till even a single sentence out of context is recognizable as Kafka or as Brecht."

3. Alfred Schutz, *The Problem of Social Reality* (The Hague: Martinus Nijhoff, 1962), 13.

4 José Ortega y Gasset, *Man and Crisis* (New York: W. W. Norton, 1958), 97.

5. Ortega, *Man and Crisis*, 45. Emphasis mine.

6. Owen Flanagan, *Varieties of Moral Personality* (Cambridge: Harvard University Press, 1993).

7. Daniel Kolak and Raymond Martin, eds., introduction to part 3 of *Self and Identity* (New York: Macmillan, 1991), 343. Emphasis mine.

8. Jack Crittenden, *Beyond Individualism: Reconstructing the Liberal Self* (New York: Oxford University Press, 1992).

9. John Dewey, *Ethics* (Carbondale: Southern Illinois University Press, 1978), 340.

10. *The Philosophy of John Dewey*, ed. John McDermott (New York: Putnam, 1973; reprint, 2 vols. in 1, Chicago: University of Chicago Press, 1981), xxix.

11. Diana Meyers, *Self, Society, and Personal Choice* (New York: Columbia University Press, 1989), 90.

12. Jean-Jacques Rousseau, *Les Confessions* (1782), ed. P. Grosclaude (Paris, 1947), 33, quoted in Steven Lukes, *Individualism* (New York: Harper & Row, 1973), 67.

13. Robert Pollock, "Process and Experience," in *John Dewey: His Thought and Influence*, ed. John Blewett (New York: Fordham University Press, 1960), 173.

14. The importance of this will become more evident when I discuss the notion of the moral cosmopolitan personality.

15. *Philosophy of John Dewey*, 276.

16. *Philosophy of John* Dewey, 276.

17. Dewey, *Ethics*, 341.

18. Dewey, *Ethics*, 341.

19. Pollock, "Process and Experience," 173.

20. Pollock, "Process and Experience," 180.

21. Pollock, "Process and Experience," 181.

22. Crittenden, *Beyond Individualism*, 39–140.

23. Pollock, "Process and Experience," 181.

24. Charles Taylor, *Sources of the Self: The Making of Modern Identity* (Cambridge: Harvard University Press, 1989), 167.

25. Taylor, *Sources of the Self*, 170. Locke believed that this remaking or becoming should follow the law laid down by God in the form of Natural Law.

26. Crittenden argues in *Beyond Individualism* that this is his overall aim. He means by sociality that one's social ethos towards others need not be limited to one's immediate community and social environment. I should also add that while I am making liberal use of Taylor's insights, I am not endorsing his communitarianism at all.

27. *The Moral Writings of John Dewey*, ed. James Gouinlock (Amherst, Mass.: Prometheus Books, 1994), 98.

28. Michael Sandel, *Liberalism and the Limits of Justice* (New York: Cambridge University Press, 1982), 58.

29. Sandel, *Liberalism and Limits of Justice*, 65.

30. Sandel, *Liberalism and Limits of Justice*, 58.

31. Crittenden, *Beyond Individualism*, 3.

32. Crittenden, *Beyond Individualism*, 151.

33. Crittenden, *Beyond Individualism*, 162.

34. Crittenden, *Beyond Individualism*, 75.

35. Crittenden, *Beyond Individualism*, 76.

36. John Gray, "Political Power, Social Theory, and Essential Contestability," in *The Nature of Political Theory* (New York: Oxford University Press, 1983).

37. Crittenden, *Beyond Individualism*, 76.

38. Crittenden, *Beyond Individualism*, 76.

39. Marilyn Friedman, "Feminism and Modern Friendship: Dislocating the Community," in *Feminism and Political Theory*, ed. Cass R. Sunstein (Chicago: University of Chicago Press, 1990).

40. Crittenden, *Beyond Individualism*, 76

41. Crittenden, *Beyond Individualism*, 76.

42. Meyers, *Self, Society, and Personal Choice*, 48.

43. Meyers, *Self, Society, and Personal Choice*, 48.

44. Meyers, *Self, Society, and Personal Choice*, 49

45. Friedman, "Feminism and Modern Friendship."

46. Calvin Schrag, *The Resources of Rationality* (Indianapolis: Indiana University Press, 1992), chap. 3.

47. Friedman, "Feminism and Modern Friendship," 151.

48. Friedman, "Feminism and Modern Friendship," 152.

CHAPTER 2

1. Walter Kohan, "The Origin, Nature, and Aim of Philosophy in Relation to Philosophy for Children," *Thinking* 12, no. 2 (1995): 28.

2. Leonard Harris, "Rendering the Text," in *The Philosophy of Alain Locke: Harlem Renaissance and Beyond*, ed. Leonard Harris (Philadelphia: Temple University Press, 1989), 10.

3. Jean-Paul Sartre, *Existentialism and Human Emotions* (New York: Carol Publishing, 1993), 15.

4. Sartre, *Existentialism and Human Emotions*, 15.

5. Joseph S. Catalano, *A Commentary on Jean-Paul Sartre's "Being and Nothingness,"* (New York: Harper & Row, 1974), 10.

6. Sartre, *Existentialism and Human Emotions*, 16.

7. José Ortega y Gasset, *History as a System and Other Essays toward a Philosophy of History* (New York: W. W. Norton, 1962), 111.

8. Ortega, *History as System*, 112.

9. See Miguel de Unamuno, *The Tragic Sense of Life* (New York: Dover, 1954); see also Paul Ilie, *Unamuno: An Existentialist View of the Self* (Madison: University of Wisconsin Press, 1967).

10. Ilie, *Unamuno*, 99.

11. Ilie, *Unamuno*, 99.

12. Ilie, *Unamuno*, 100.

13. Although Sartre argues against a human nature, he recognizes the existence of a human condition. That is, the human as a creature living in the world faces, along with other human beings like herself, certain conditions, namely, freedom, responsibility, choice, and the necessity of living and being mortal in the world, working in the world, and being in the midst of other people. These limits of human existence are "neither subjective nor objective, or rather, they have an objective and a subjective side. Objective because they are to be found everywhere and are recognizable everywhere; subjective because they are lived and are nothing if man does not live them, that is, freely determine his existence with reference to them" Sartre, *Existentialism and Human Emotions*, 38.

14. Catalano, *Commentary on "Being and Nothingness,"* 9.

15. Some degree of becoming is possible. A commitment to becoming is precisely what

makes robust self-creation possible. Becoming is possible even under the most constraining and delimiting of paradigms to the extent that one can go from one coordinate point of the paradigm to the next and not betray the substantive nature of who one really is.

16. Edward Casey, "Man, Self, and Truth," *Monist* 55, no. 2 (April 1971): 230.

17. Casey, "Man, Self, and Truth," 228. Casey presents an interesting outline of the ways in which we might go beyond the single-essence theory and points to ways in which a plurality of essences or of traits might make more sense than fixation upon one essential trait possessed by all humans.

18. William McBride, *Sartre's Political Theory* (Indianapolis: Indiana University Press, 1991).

19. Sartre, *Existentialism and Human Emotions*, 16.

20. Naomi Zack, *Thinking about Race* (Belmont, Calif.: Wadsworth, 1998).

21. Ortega, *History as System*, 133.

22. Unamuno, *Tragic Sense of Life*, 45.

23. Jean-Paul Sartre, *Being and Nothingness: A Phenomenological Essay on Ontology*, trans. Hazel Barnes (New York: Washington Press, 1956).

24. Sartre, *Being and Nothingness*, 171.

25. José Ortega y Gasset, "Man Has No Nature," in *Existentialism from Dostoevsky to Sartre*, ed. Walter Kaufmann (New York: New American Library, 1975), 155.

26. David Cooper, *Existentialism* (Oxford: Blackwell,1990), 152.

27. Cooper, *Existentialism*, 152.

28. Cooper, *Existentialism*, 157.

29. Ilie, *Unamuno*, 106.

30. Paul Schmidt, *Rebelling, Loving, and Liberation: A Metaphysics of the Concrete* (Albuquerque, N.M.: Hummingbird Press, 1971), 106.

31. Alfred Schutz, *The Problem of Social Reality* (The Hague: Martinus Nijhoff, 1962), 209–10.

32. Sartre, *Being and Nothingness*, 640.

33. Sartre, *Existentialism and Human Emotions*, 23.

34. Sartre, *Existentialism and Human Emotions*.

35. Sartre, *Existentialism and Human Emotions*, 32.

36. Sartre, *Existentialism and Human Emotions*, 32.

37. Sartre, *Being and Nothingness*, 559.

38. Cooper, *Existentialism*, 152.

39. Wade Baskin, *Jean-Paul Sartre: To Freedom Condemned—A Guide to His Philosophy* (New York: Philosophical Library, 1960), 22.

40. Ortega, *History as System*, 112.

41. In view of reports that scientists might in the future be able to locate the aging gene and arrest its development, I wonder with what assurance we can assert that aging is a brute fact of existence. It seems that at least we can assert this with some degree of certainty as it relates to our lives.

42. Cooper, *Existentialism*, 76.

43. Sartre, *Being and Nothingness*, 24.

44. William McBride, "Jean-Paul Sartre: Man, Freedom, and Praxis," in *Existential Philosophers: Kierkegaard to Merleau-Ponty*, ed. George Alfred Schrader Jr. (New York: McGraw, 1967), 270.

45. Sartre, *Being and Nothingness*, 265.

46. Sartre, *Being and Nothingness*, 127.

47. David L. Norton, *Personal Destinies: A Philosophy of Ethical Individualism* (Princeton, N.J.: Princeton University Press, 1976), 114.

48. Sartre, *Being and Nothingness*, 567.

49. Sartre, *Being and Nothingness*.

50. Sartre, *Being and Nothingness*, 616.

51. Sartre, *Being and Nothingness*, 618.

52. Sartre, *Being and Nothingness*, 638.

53. Sartre, *Being and Nothingness*, 622.

54. Sartre, *Being and Nothingness*, 622.

55. Emphasis mine.

56. Sartre, *Existentialism and Human Emotions*, 52.

57. Sartre, *Being and Nothingness*, 572. Emphasis mine.

58. Sartre, *Being and Nothingness*, 327.

59. Sartre, *Being and Nothingness*, 327.

60. Sartre paraphrased by McBride in "Man, Freedom, and Praxis," 275.

61. Catalano, *Commentary on "Being and Nothingness,"* 162.

62. George Stack, *Sartre's Philosophy of Social Existence* (St. Louis, Mo.: Warren H. Green, 1977), 31.

63. Stack, *Sartre's Philosophy of Social Existence*, 31.

64. Stack, *Sartre's Philosophy of Social Existence*, 32.

65. Sartre, *Being and Nothingness*, 666–67.

66. McBride, *Sartre's Political Theory*, 8.

67. Sartre, *Being and Nothingness*, 568.

68. I will return to these examples in the section dealing with ontological rebellion. I mention them here as a way of philosophically setting the stage for what is to come.

69. Gabriel Marcel, *The Mystery of Being*, vol. 2, *Faith and Reality* (Chicago: Henry Regnery, 1951), v.

70. Marcel, *Mystery of Being*, 40.

71. Marcel, *Mystery of Being*, 40.

72. Marcel, *Mystery of Being*, 137.

73. Patricia Sanborn, "Gabriel Marcel's Conception of the Realized Self: A Critical Exploration," *Journal of Existentialism* 8 (Winter 1967–1968): 134.

74. Sanborn, "Marcel's Conception of the Realized Self," 137.

75. Sanborn, "Marcel's Conception of the Realized Self."

76. Marcel, *Mystery of Being*, 164.

77. Unamuno, *Tragic Sense of Life*, 38.

78. Unamuno, *Tragic Sense of Life*, 110.

79. Unamuno, *Tragic Sense of Life*, 57.

80. Unamuno, *Tragic Sense of Life*, 111.

81. From a section of Unamuno's novella *Como se hace una novela*, in *Miguel de Unamuno: The Contrary Self*, by Frances Wyers (London: Tamesis Books, 1976), 38.

82. Wyers, *Contrary Self*, 38.

83. Wyers, *Contrary Self*, 38–39.

84. Wyers, *Contrary Self*, 50.

85. For an interesting discussion of this, see Daniel J. Meckel and Robert L. Moore, eds., *Self and Liberation: The Jung/Buddhism Dialogue* (New York: Paulist Press, 1992). Although I am reluctant to make trivial comparisons between the self presented in these two schools of thought and the philosophy of existentialism, I am intrigued by the varied conceptions of freedom within Buddhist thought in conjunction with a self that seeks liberation from many of the problematic aspects of the Natural Attitude.

86. José Ortega y Gasset, *Man and Crisis* (New York: W. W. Norton, 1958).

87. Ortega, *Man and Crisis*, 93.

88. I recall a beautiful phrase whose source eludes me: "One's spiritual metabolism needs a personalized diet."

89. Sartre, *Being and Nothingness*, 135.

90. Sartre, *Being and Nothingness*, 147.

91. Sartre, *Being and Nothingness*, 153.

92. Sartre, *Being and Nothingness*, 796.

93. See also Sartre's *Anti-Semite and Jew* (trans. George J. Becker [New York: Schoken Books, 1965]) for his portrayal of the caricatured gestures of the inauthentic Jew.

94. Cooper, *Existentialism*, 185.

95. Cooper, *Existentialism*.

96. Schmidt, *Rebelling, Loving, and Liberation*, 101.

97. Leonardo Buff, *The Path to Hope: Fragments from a Theologian's Journey* (Maryknoll, N.Y.: Orbis Books, 1993), 76.

98. Cooper, *Existentialism*, 68.

99. Schmidt, *Rebelling, Loving, and Liberation*, 1.

100. Schmidt, *Rebelling, Loving, and Liberation*.

101. Schmidt, *Rebelling, Loving, and Liberation*, 11.

102. Schmidt, *Rebelling, Loving, and Liberation*, 17.

103. Schmidt, *Rebelling, Loving, and Liberation*, 48

104. Schmidt, *Rebelling, Loving, and Liberation*, 50.

105. Schmidt, *Rebelling, Loving, and Liberation*, 50.

106. Schmidt, *Rebelling, Loving, and Liberation*, 58.

107. Schmidt, *Rebelling, Loving, and Liberation*, 108.

108. Schmidt, *Rebelling, Loving, and Liberation*, 109.

109. Schmidt, *Rebelling, Loving, and Liberation*, 111–12.

110. Schmidt, *Rebelling, Loving, and Liberation*, 671.

111. Emilio Marinetti quoted in Stewart Ewen, *All Consuming Images: The Politics of Style in Contemporary Culture* (New York: Basic Books, 1988), 18.

112. Friedrich Nietzsche, *Untimely Meditations (1873–1876)*, trans. R. J. Hollingdale (Cambridge: Cambridge University Press, 1983), 62.

113. Sartre, *Being and Nothingness*, 671.

114. Sartre, *Being and Nothingness*, 671.

115. Sartre, *Being and Nothingness*, 677.

116. Charles Mills, *The Racial Contract* (Ithaca, N.Y.: Cornell University Press, 1997), 19.

117. Naomi Zack, "Race, Life, Death, Tragedy, and Good Faith," in *Existence in Black*, ed. Lewis Gordon (New York: Routledge, 1997).

118. Zack, "Race, Life, Death," 99.

119. Zack, "Race, Life, Death," 106–7.

120. Zack, "Race, Life, Death," 106, 107.

121. Zack, "Race, Life, Death," 102.

122. Zack, "Race, Life, Death," 104.

123. Zack, "Race, Life, Death," 105.

124. Zack, "Race, Life, Death," 101.

125. Zack, "Race, Life, Death," 102–3.

126. Zack, "Race, Life, Death," 103.

127. Zack, "Race, Life, Death," 103.

128. Judi Krishnamurti is one Indian philosopher who has repeatedly tried to capture a metaphysics of the concrete and to articulate the ontological rebellion that is vital for the possession of any meaningful sense of freedom. He writes: "What produces order is inquiry into freedom—not intellectual inquiry, but doing the actual work of breaking down our conditioning, our limiting prejudices, our narrow ideas, breaking down the whole psychological structure of society, of which we are a part. Unless you break through all that, there is no freedom, and therefore there is no order" *On Freedom* (New York: HarperSanFrancisco, 1991), 98–99. He writes further: "So one has to find out if there is a discipline that is not conformity, because conformity destroys freedom, it never brings freedom into being. Look at the organized religions throughout the world, the political parties. It is obvious that conformity destroys freedom. . . . The discipline of conformity, which is created by the fear of society and is part of the psychological structure of society, is immoral and disorderly, and we are caught in it" (100).

129. See Naomi Zack's *Race and Mixed Race* (Philadelphia: Temple University Press, 1993); see also Naomi Zack, "Life after Race," in *American Mixed Race: The Culture of Microdiversity,* ed. Naomi Zack (Lanham, Md.: Rowman & Littlefield, 1995).

130. Zack, *American Mixed Race,* 298.

131. David Hollinger, "Post Ethnic America," *Contention* 2, no. 1 (Fall 1992): 87

132. Hollinger here refers to Mary C. Waters, *Ethnic Options: Choosing Identities in America* (Berkeley and Los Angeles: University of California Press, 1990), 147. The term *symbolic ethnicity* used by Waters was coined by Herbert Gans. See his "Symbolic Ethnicity in America," *Ethnic and Racial Studies* 2 (1979): 1–20.

133. Hollinger, "Post Ethnic America," 87.

134. Hollinger, "Post Ethnic America," 87. Hollinger here relies on Waters, *Ethnic Options.* I am paraphrasing his assessment of Waters.

CHAPTER 3

1. Indeed, think of the ways in which our creative imagination operates in the classroom as teachers, as parents in the care of our children who come to us when faced with crises, and the myriad ways in which we are called upon to think on the spot when faced with life's many challenges.

2. Karen Hanson, *The Self Imagined: Philosophical Reflections on the Social Character of Psyche* (New York: Routledge, 1986), 74.

3. Anthony Appiah, "Cosmopolitan Patriots," *Critical Inquiry* 23, no. 3 (Spring 1997).

4. Richard Shusterman, *Practicing Philosophy: Pragmatism and the Philosophical Life* (New York: Routledge, 1997), 37.

5. Shusterman, *Practicing Philosophy*.

6. Benjamin Llamzon, *The Self Beyond: Toward Life's Meaning* (Chicago: Loyola University Press, 1973).

7. Llamzon, *The Self Beyond*, 27.

8. Llamzon, *The Self Beyond*, 34.

9. Elliot Deutsch, *Creative Being: The Crafting of Person and World* (Honolulu: University of Hawaii Press, 1992).

10. Shusterman, *Practicing Philosophy*, 182.

11. Shusterman, *Practicing Philosophy*, 184.

12. Paul Anthony Kerby, *On Narrative* (Bloomington: Indiana University Press, 1991), 40.

13. Kerby, *On Narrative*, 52.

14. Charles Taylor, *Sources of the Self: The Making of Modern Identity* (Cambridge: Harvard University Press, 1989), 47.

15. Taylor, *Sources of the Self*, 48.

16. Freud has an interesting discussion of the notion of group mind. See Sigmund Freud, *Group Psychology and the Analysis of the Ego* (New York: W. W. Norton, 1959), esp. 63.

17. Alasdair MacIntyre, *After Virtue* (Notre Dame, Ind.: University of Notre Dame Press, 1984), 211. See also Barbara Hardy, "Towards a Poetics of Fiction: An Approach through Narrative," *Novel* 2 (1968): 5–14.

18. MacIntyre, *After Virtue*, 215.

19. MacIntyre, *After Virtue*, 217.

20. MacIntyre, *After Virtue*, 218.

21. MacIntyre, *After Virtue*, 219.

22. Mark Freeman, *Rewriting the Self: History, Memory, and Narrative* (New York: Routledge, 1993), 5.

23. Freeman, *Rewriting the Self*, 19.

24. Freeman, *Rewriting the Self*, 21.

25. Freeman, *Rewriting the Self*, 23

26. Freeman, *Rewriting the Self*, 30.

27. *The Confessions of St. Augustine*, bk. 8, chap. 5, trans. Rex Warner (New York: Penguin, 1963), 168.

28. Freeman, *Rewriting the Self*, 38. See also Paul Ricoeur, *Hermeneutics and the Human Societies* (Cambridge: Cambridge University Press, 1981).

29. *Confessions of Augustine*, bk. 8, chap. 12, 182.

30. Paul Ricoeur, *Oneself as Another* (Chicago: University of Chicago Press, 1992), 147–48.

31. Aldo Tassi, "Person as the Mask of Being," *Philosophy Today* (Summer 1993): 201.

32. Tassi, "Person as Mask of Being," 201.

33. Tassi, "Person as Mask of Being," 202.

34. Deutsch, *Creative Being*, 24.

35. Tassi, "Person as Mask of Being," 202.

36. Tassi, "Person as Mask of Being," 203.

CHAPTER 4

1. David Hollinger, "Post Ethnic America," *Contention* 2, no. 1 (Fall 1992): 83.

2. Timothy C. Earle and George T. Cvetkovich, *Toward a Cosmopolitan Society* (Westport, Conn.: Praeger, 1995), 102. Emphasis mine.

3. Malcolm Gladwell, "Black like Them," *New Yorker,* 26 April–5 May 1996, 77–78

4. Judi Krishnamurti, *Freedom from the Known* (New York: HarperSanFrancisco, 1969), 77.

5. Cornel West, "I'm Ofay, You're Ofay: A Conversation with Noel Ignatiev and William 'Upski' Wimsatt," *Transition* 7, no. 1 (The White Issue): 179.

6. Naomi Zack, *Thinking about Race* (Belmont, Calif.: Wadsworth, 1998), 61.

7. See Charles Mills, *The Racial Contract* (Ithaca, N.Y.: Cornell University Press, 1997).

8. Carl Jung, *Analytic Theory and Practice* (New York: Pantheon Books, 1986), 50–51.

9. Julia Kristeva, *Strangers to Ourselves* (New York: Columbia University Press, 1991), 12.

10. Kristeva, *Strangers to Ourselves,* 29.

11. Kristeva, *Strangers to Ourselves,* 29.

12. David Bromwich, "Culturalism: The Death of Euthanasia," *Dissent* (Winter 1995): 98.

13. Bromwich, "Culturalism," 95.

14. Bromwich, "Culturalism," 102.

15. See, e.g., Judith Lichtenberg's article, "How Liberal Can Nationalism Be?" *Philosophical Forum* 27, no. 1–2 (Fall–Winter 1996): 63.

16. Jeremy Waldron, "Multiculturalism and Melange," in *Public Education in a Multicultural Society: Policy, Theory, Critique,* ed. Robert Fullinwider (Cambridge: Cambridge University Press, 1996), 95.

17. Wilfrid Desan, *Let the Future Come* (Washington, D.C: Georgetown University Press, 1987), 143.

18. Azizah Al-Hibri, "Legal Reform Reviving Human Rights in the Muslim World," *Harvard International* 20, no. 3 (Summer 1998): 50.

19. Kristeva, *Strangers to Ourselves,* 16.

20. Kristeva, *Strangers to Ourselves,* 181.

21. Kristeva, *Strangers to Ourselves,* 182.

22. Kristeva, *Strangers to Ourselves,* 191.

23. Kristeva, *Strangers to Ourselves,* 192.

24. Mark Freeman, *Rewriting the Self: History, Memory, and Narrative* (New York: Routledge, 1993), 45.

CHAPTER 5

1. Anne Colby and William Damon, "The Uniting of Self and Morality in the Development of Extraordinary Moral Commitment," in *The Moral Self,* ed. Gil G. Noam and Thomas E. Wren (Cambridge: MIT Press, 1993), 152.

2. The child does not experience this realization in any robust conceptual or cognitive manner; it is more like a preconceptual awareness.

3. Frederick Copleston, *A History of Philosophy* (New York: Doubleday, 1994), 349.

4. Karen Armstrong, *In the Beginning: A New Interpretation of Genesis* (New York: Knopf, 1996), 55.

5. Armstrong, *In the Beginning*, 56.

6. Leonard Harris, "Alain Locke: Community and Citizenship," *Modern Schoolman* 74 (May 1997): 337.

7. Anthony Appiah, "Cosmopolitan Patriots," *Critical Inquiry* 23, no. 3 (Spring 1997): 633.

8. Appiah, "Cosmopolitan Patriots," 635.

9. Martha Nussbaum with respondents, *For Love of Country: Debating the Limits of Patriotism*, ed. Joshua Cohen (Boston: Beacon Press, 1996), 15.

10. Martha Nussbaum, *Cultivating Humanity* (Cambridge: Harvard University Press, 1997), 9.

11. Nussbaum, "Patriotism and Cosmopolitanism," in *For Love of Country*, 9.

12. Nussbaum, *Cultivating Humanity*, 10.

13. Nussbaum, *Cultivating Humanity*, 11.

14. Hilary Putnam, "Must We Choose between Patriotism and Universal Reason?" in *For Love of Country*, 95–96.

15. Robert Pinsky, "Eros against Esperanto," in *For Love of Country*, 89.

16. Pinsky, "Eros against Esperanto," 89.

17. Leo Marx, "Neglecting History," *Boston Review*, October/November 1994, 19.

18. Marx, "Neglecting History," 19.

19. Benjamin Barber, "Constitutional Faith," in *For Love of Country*, 32.

20. Charles Mills, *The Racial Contract* (Ithaca, N.Y.: Cornell University Press, 1997), 19.

CHAPTER 6

1. John Rawls, *Political Liberalism* (New York: Columbia University Press, 1993), 140.

2. Rawls, *Political Liberalism*, xxvii.

3. Rawls, *Political Liberalism*, 81.

4. Rawls, *Political Liberalism*, 13.

5. John Stuart Mill, *On Liberty and Utilitarianism* (New York: Bantam Books, 1993), 105.

6. Mill, *On Liberty and Utilitarianism*, 106.

7. John Danley, "Community and the Corporation in Contemporary Communitarianism," in "1998 Proceedings of the Ninth Annual Conference, International Association of Business and Society," ed. J. Carlton and K. Rahbein, 371–76.

8. Derek Phillips, *Looking Backward: A Critical Appraisal of Communitarian Thought* (Princeton, N.J.: Princeton University Press, 1993), 14. Phillips comes to this definition via a distillation of the works of Robert Bellah, Michael Sandel, Charles Taylor, and Alasdair MacIntyre.

9. Charles Taylor, *Hegel and Modern Society* (Cambridge: Cambridge University Press, 1979), 157–59.

10. Will Kymlicka, *Liberalism, Community, and Culture* (New York: Clarendon Press, 1989), 50.

11. Jeremy Waldron, "The Cosmopolitan Alternative," in *The Rights of Minority Cultures*, ed. Will Kymlicka (New York: Oxford University Press, 1995), 113.

12. This is a point emphasized by Danley in "Community and the Corporation in Contemporary Communitarianism."

13. Waldron, "The Cosmopolitan Alternative," 105.

14. Jean-Paul Sartre and Benny Levy, *Hope Now: The 1980 Interviews*, trans. Adrian Van Den Hoven (Chicago: University of Chicago Press, 1996), 69.

15. Kymlicka, *Liberalism, Community, and Culture*, 84.

16. Kymlicka, *Liberalism, Community, and Culture*, 86.

APPENDIX

1. Derek Heater, *World Citizenship and Government: Cosmopolitan Ideas in the History of Western Political Thought* (New York: St. Martin's, 1996), 8.

2. T. J. Schlereth, *The Cosmopolitan Ideal in Enlightenment Thought: Its Form and Function in the Ideas of Franklin, Hume, and Voltaire, 1694–1790* (Notre Dame, Ind.: University of Notre Dame Press, 1977), xvii.

3. Martha Nussbaum, "Kant and Cosmopolitanism," in *Perpetual Peace: Essays on Kant's Cosmopolitan Ideal*, ed. James Bohman and Matthias Lutz-Bachmann (Cambridge: MIT Press, 1997), 29–30.

4. Heater, *World Citizenship*, x–xi.

5. Heater, *World Citizenship*, 5.

6. Heater, *World Citizenship*, 5.

7. Heraclitus, fr. 114, quoted in H. C. Baldry, *The Unity of Mankind in Greek Thought* (Cambridge: Cambridge University Press, 1965), 26–27.

8. Sophocles, *The Thebian Plays*, trans. E. F. Watling (Harmondsworth, England: Penguin, 1947), 138.

9. Heater, *World Citizenship*, 6.

10. Heater, *World Citizenship*, 13. Heater here is relying on the text of Plutarch, "On the Virtue of Alexander," in *Moralia*, vol. 4, trans. F. C. Babbitt (London: Heinemann, 1957).

11. Heater, *World Citizenship*, 15.

12. Cicero, *De Officiis*, trans. W. Miller (London: Heinemann, 1956), 1: 50.

13. Quoted in Heater, *World Citizenship*, 18. Heater is here relying on Seneca, *Moral Essays*, vol. 7, trans. J. W. Basore (London: Heinemann, 1958), 20.5;. and Seneca, *Epistulae Morales*, vol. 1, trans. R. M. Gummere (London: Heinemann, 1961), 18.4.

14. Seneca quoted in Heater, *World Citizenship*, 18.

15. Heater, *World Citizenship*, 18. Heater is here relying on Seneca, "On the Tranquility of Mind," 4.4.

16. Schlereth, *Cosmopolitan Ideal*.

17. Nussbaum, "Kant and Cosmopolitanism," 31.

18. Heater, *World Citizenship*, 19.

19. Marcus Aurelius Antoninus, *The Communing with Himself*, trans. C. R. Haines (London: Heinemann, 1961), 7.9.

20. Nussbaum, "Kant and Cosmopolitanism," 31.

21. Heater, *World Citizenship*, 20.

22. Heater, *World Citizenship*, 20.

23. Nussbaum, "Kant and Cosmopolitanism," 20.

24. Schlereth, *Cosmopolitan Ideal*, xii–xiii.

25. Schlereth, *Cosmopolitan Ideal*, xii–xiii.

26. David Hume, "The Dignity or Meanness of Human Nature," in *Essays: Moral, Political, Literary*, ed. T. H. Green and T. H. Grosse (London: Longmans, 1875) 1:152.

27. Immanuel Kant, *Kant Selections*, ed. Lewis White Beck (New York: Macmillan, 1988), 415.

28. *Kant Selections*, 416.

29. *Kant Selections*, 416.

30. *Kant Selections*.

31. Hardy E. Jones, *Kant's Principle of Personality* (Madison: University of Wisconsin Press, 1971), 9.

32. *Kant Selections*, 416.

33. *Kant Selections*, 418.

34. *Kant Selections,* 419.

35. *Kant Selections*, 420.

36. *Kant Selections,* 421.

37. Reinhold Aris, *History of Political Thought in Germany from 1789–1850* (London: Allen & Unwin, 1936), 76.

38. *Kant Selections*, 421.

39. *Kant Selections*, 466.

40. Kant, "What Is Enlightenment?" in *Kant Selections*, 463.

41. Aris, *Political Thought in Germany*, 71.

42. *Kant Selections*, 263.

43. Nussbaum, "Kant and Cosmopolitanism," 36.

44. Kenneth Baynes, "Communitarian and Cosmopolitan Challenges to Kant's Conception of World Peace," in *Perpetual Peace: Essays on Kant's Cosmopolitan Ideal*, ed. James Bohman and Matthias Lutz-Bachmann (Cambridge: MIT Press, 1997), 220.

45. Nussbaum, "Kant and Cosmopolitanism," 39.

46. Immanuel Kant, *Perpetual Peace* (New York: Columbia University Press, 1936), 41.

47. Kant, *Perpetual Peace*, 41.

BIBLIOGRAPHY

Al-Hibri, Azizah. "Reviving Human Rights in the Muslim World." *Harvard International* 20, no. 3 (Summer 1998): 50–53.

Antoninus, Marcus Aurelius. *The Communing with Himself,* 7. Translated by C. R. Haines. London: Heinemann, 1961.

Appiah, Anthony. "Cosmopolitan Patriots." *Critical Inquiry* 23, no. 3 (Spring 1997): 617–39.

Aris, Reinhold, *History of Political Thought in Germany from 1789–1850.* London: Allen & Unwin, 1936.

Armstrong, Karen. *In the Beginning: A New Interpretation of Genesis.* New York: Knopf, 1996.

Augustine. *The Confessions of St. Augustine.* Translated by Rex Warner. New York: Penguin, 1963.

Baldry, H. C. *The Unity of Mankind in Greek Thought.* Cambridge: Cambridge University Press, 1965.

Barber, Benjamin. "Constitutional Faith." In *For Love of Country: Debating the Limits of Patriotism,* by Martha Nussbaum with respondents, edited by Joshua Cohen. Boston: Beacon Press, 1996.

Baskin, Wade. *Jean-Paul Sartre: To Freedom Condemned—A Guide to His Philosophy.* New York: Philosophical Library, 1960.

Baynes, Kenneth. "Communitarian and Cosmopolitan Challenges to Kant's Conception of World Peace." In *Perpetual Peace: Essays on Kant's Cosmopolitan Ideal,* edited by James Bohman and Matthias Lutz-Bachmann. Cambridge: MIT Press, 1997.

Bergmann, Frithjof. "Freedom and the Self." In *Self and Identity,* edited by Daniel Kolak and Raymond Martin. New York: Macmillan, 1991.

Boss, Judith. *Ethics for Life: An Interdisciplinary and Multicultural Introduction.* Mountain View, Calif.: Mayfield, 1988.

Bromwich, David. "Culturalism: The Death of Euthanasia." *Dissent* (Winter 1995): 89–106.

Buff, Leonardo. *The Path to Hope: Fragments from a Theologian's Journey.* Translated by Phillip Berryman. Maryknoll, N.Y.: Orbis Books, 1993.

Casey, Edward. "Man, Self, and Truth." *Monist* (April 1971): 218–54.

Catalano, S. Joseph. *A Commentary on Jean-Paul Sartre's "Being and Nothingness."* New York: Harper & Row, 1974.

Cicero. *De Officiis.* Vol. 1. Translated by W. Miller. London: Heinemann, 1956.

Colby, Anne, and William Damon. "The Uniting of Self and Morality in the Development of Extraordinary Moral Commitment." In *The Moral Self,* edited by Gil G. Noam and Thomas E. Wren. Cambridge: MIT Press, 1993.

Collins, James. *The Existentialist.* Chicago: Henry Regnery, 1968.

Cooper, David. *Existentialism.* Oxford: Blackwell, 1990.

Copleston, Frederick. *A History of Philosophy.* New York: Doubleday, 1994.

Crittenden, Jack. *Beyond Individualism: Reconstituting the Liberal Self.* New York: Oxford University Press, 1992.

Danley, John. "Community and the Corporation in Contemporary Communitarianism." In "1998 Proceedings of the Ninth Annual Conference International Association of Business and Society," edited by J. Carlton and K. Rahbein, 371–76.

Desan, Wilfrid. *Let the Future Come.* Washington, D.C.: Georgetown University Press, 1987.

Deutsch, Elliot. *Creative Being: The Crafting of Person and World.* Honolulu: University of Hawaii Press, 1992.

Dewey, John. *Ethics.* Vol. 5 of *The Middle Works of John Dewey, 1899–1924.* Edited by Jo Ann Boydston. Carbondale: Southern Illinois University Press, 1978.

————. *The Moral Writings of John Dewey.* Edited by James Gouinlock. Amherst, Mass.: Prometheus Books, 1994.

————. *The Philosophy of John Dewey.* Edited by John McDermott. New York: Putnam, 1973. Reprint (2 vols. in 1), Chicago: University of Chicago Press, 1981.

Earle, Timothy C., and George T. Cvetkovich. *Social Trust: Toward a Cosmopolitan Society.* Westport, Conn.: Praeger, 1995.

Ewen, Stewart. *All Consuming Images: The Politics of Style in Contemporary Culture.* New York: Basic Books, 1988.

Flanagan, Owen. *Varieties of Moral Personality.* Cambridge: Harvard University Press, 1993.

Freeman, Mark. *Rewriting the Self: History, Memory, and Narrative.* New York: Routledge, 1993.

Freud, Sigmund. *Civilization and Its Discontents.* 1961; reprint, New York: W. W. Norton, 1989.

————. *Group Psychology and the Analysis of the Ego.* New York: W. W. Norton, 1959.

Friedman, Marilyn. "Feminism and Modern Friendship: Dislocating the Community." In *Feminism and Political Theory,* edited by Cass R. Sunstein. Chicago: University of Chicago Press, 1990.

Fullinwider, Robert K., ed. *Public Education in a Multicultural Society: Policy, Theory, Critique.* Cambridge: Cambridge University Press, 1996.

Gans, Herbert. "Symbolic Ethnicity in America." *Ethnic and Racial Studies* 2 (1979): 1–20.

Gauthier, David. "The Liberal Individual." In *Communitarianism and Individualism,* edited by Shlomo Avineria and Avner de-Shalit. Oxford: Oxford University Press, 1992.

Gladwell, Malcolm. "Black like Them." *New Yorker,* 26 April–5 May 1996, 77–78.

Gray, John. "Political Power, Social Theory, and Essential Contestability." In *The Nature of Political Theory,* edited by D. Miller and L. Siendentop. New York: Oxford University Press, 1983.

Hanson, Karen. *The Self Imagined: Philosophical Reflections on the Social Character of Psyche.* New York: Routledge, 1986.

Harris, Leonard. "Alain Locke: Community and Citizenship." *Modern Schoolman* 74 (May 1997): 337–46.

————, ed. *The Philosophy of Alain Locke: Harlem Renaissance and Beyond.* Philadelphia: Temple University Press, 1989.

Heater, Derek. *World Citizenship and Government: Cosmopolitan Ideas in the History of Western Political Thought.* New York: St. Martin's, 1996.

Hiley, David R., James F. Bohman, and Richard Shusterman, eds. *The Dialogical Self: The Interpretive Turn—Philosophy, Science, Culture.* Ithaca, N.Y.: Cornell University Press, 1991.

Hollinger, David. "Post Ethnic America." *Contention* 2, no. 1 (Fall 1992): 79–95.

Hume, David. "The Dignity or Meanness of Human Nature." In *Essays: Moral, Political, Literary.* Edited by. T. H. Green and T. H. Grosse London: Longmans, 1875.

Husserl, Edmund. *Phenomenology and the Crisis of Philosophy.* Translated by Quentin Lauer. New York: Harper & Row, 1965.

Ilie, Paul. *Unamuno: An Existentialist View of the Self.* Madison: University of Wisconsin Press, 1967.

Jones, Hardy E. *Kant's Principle of Personality.* Madison: University of Wisconsin Press, 1971.

Jung, Carl. *Analytic Theory and Practice.* New York: Pantheon Books, 1986.

Kant, Immanuel. *Perpetual Peace.* New York: Columbia University Press, 1936.

———. *Kant Selections.* Edited by Lewis White Beck. New York: Macmillan, 1988.

Kerby, Paul Anthony. *On Narrative.* Bloomington: Indiana University Press, 1991.

Kohan, Walter. "The Origin, Nature, and Aim of Philosophy in Relation to Philosophy for Children." *Thinking* 12, no. 2 (1995): 25–30.

Krishnamurti, Judi. *Freedom from the Known.* New York: HarperSanFrancisco, 1969.

———. *On Freedom.* New York: HarperSanFrancisco, 1991.

Kristeva, Julia. *Nations without Nationalism.* New York: Columbia University Press, 1993.

———. *Strangers to Ourselves.* New York: Columbia University Press, 1991.

Kymlicka, Will. *Liberalism, Community, and Culture.* New York: Clarendon Press, 1989.

Lichtenberg, Judith. "How Liberal Can Nationalism Be?" *Philosophical Forum* 27, no. 1–2 (Fall–Winter 1996): 53–72.

Lijphart, Arend. *Democracy in Plural Societies.* New Haven: Yale University Press, 1977.

Llamzon, Benjamin. *The Self Beyond: Toward Life's Meaning.* Chicago: Loyola University Press, 1973.

Lukes, Steven. *Individualism.* New York: Harper & Row, 1973.

MacIntyre, Alasdair. *After Virtue.* Notre Dame, Ind.: Notre Dame University Press, 1984.

Marcel, Gabriel. *The Mystery of Being.* Vol. 2, *Faith and Reality.* Chicago: Henry Regnery, 1951.

Marx, Leo. "Neglecting History." *Boston Review* (October/November 1994): 19.

McBride, William L. "Jean-Paul Sartre: Man, Freedom, and Praxis." In *Existential Philosophers: Kierkegaard to Merleau-Ponty,* edited by George Alfred Schrader Jr. New York: McGraw, 1967.

———. *Sartre's Political Theory.* Indianapolis: Indiana University Press, 1991.

Meckel, Daniel J., and Robert L. Moore, eds. *Self and Liberation: The Jung/Buddhism Dialogue.* New York: Paulist Press, 1992.

———. *Sartre's Political Theory.* Indianapolis: Indiana University Press, 1991.

Meyers, Diana. *Self, Society, and Personal Choice.* New York: Columbia University Press, 1989.

Mill, John Stuart. *On Liberty and Utilitarianism.* New York: Bantam Books, 1993.

Mills, Charles. *The Racial Contract.* Ithaca, N.Y.: Cornell University Press, 1997.

Mumford, Lewis. *Transformations of Man.* Gloucester, Mass.: Peter Smith, 1978.

Nietzsche, Friedrich. "On Truth and Lies in an Extra-Moral Sense." In *The Portable Nietzsche,* edited by Walter Kaufmann. New York: Penguin Books, 1954.

———.*Untimely Meditations (1873–1876).* Translated by R. J. Hollingdale. Cambridge: Cambridge University Press, 1983.

Norton, David L. *Personal Destinies: A Philosophy of Ethical Individualism.* Princeton, N.J.: Princeton University Press, 1976.

Nussbaum, Martha. "Kant and Cosmopolitanism." In *Perpetual Peace: Essays on Kant's Cosmopolitan Ideal,* edited by James Bohman and Matthias Lutz-Bachmann. Cambridge: MIT Press, 1997.

———. *Cultivating Humanity.* Cambridge: Harvard University Press, 1997.

Nussbaum, Martha, with respondents. *For Love of Country: Debating the Limits of Patriotism,* edited by Joshua Cohen. Boston: Beacon Press, 1996.

O'Malley, John. *The Fellowship of Being: An Essay on the Concept of Person in the Philosophy of Gabriel Marcel.* The Hague: Martinus Nijhoff, 1996.

Ortega y Gasset, José. *Man and Crisis.* New York: W. W. Norton, 1958.

———. *History as a System and Other Essays toward a Philosophy of History.* New York: W. W. Norton, 1962.

———. "Man Has No Nature." In *Existentialism from Dostoevsky to Sartre,* edited by Walter Kaufmann. New York: New American Library, 1975.

Phillips, Derek. *Looking Backward: A Critical Appraisal of Communitarian Thought.* Princeton, N.J.: Princeton University Press, 1993.

Pinsky, Robert. "Eros against Esperanto." In *For Love of Country: Debating the Limits of Patriotism,* by Martha Nussbaum with respondents, edited by Joshua Cohen. Boston: Beacon Press, 1996.

Pollock, Robert. "Process and Experience." In *John Dewey: His Thought and Influence,* edited by John Blewett. New York: Fordham University Press, 1960.

Putnam, Hilary. "Must We Choose between Patriotism and Universal Reason?" In *For Love of Country: Debating the Limits of Patriotism,* by Martha Nussbaum with respondents, edited by Joshua Cohen. Boston: Beacon Press, 1996.

Rawls, John. *A Theory of Justice.* Cambridge: Harvard University Press, Belknap Press, 1971.

———. *Political Liberalism.* New York: Columbia University Press, 1993.

Ricoeur, Paul. *Oneself as Another.* Chicago: University of Chicago Press, 1992.

———. *Hermeneutics and the Human Societies.* Cambridge: Cambridge University Press, 1981.

Sampson, Edward E. "The Deconstruction of the Self." In *Texts of Identity,* edited by John Shotter and Kenneth J. Gergen. London: Sage Publications, 1989.

Sanborn, Patricia. "Gabriel Marcel's Conception of the Realized Self: A Critical Exploration." *Journal of Existentialism* 8 (Winter 1967–1968): 133–59.

Sandel, Michael. *Liberalism and the Limits of Justice.* New York: Cambridge University Press, 1982.

Sartre, Jean-Paul. *Anti-Semite and Jew.* Translated by George J. Becker. New York: Schoken Books, 1965.

———. *Being and Nothingness: A Phenomenological Essay on Ontology.* Translated by Hazel Barnes. New York: Washington Press, 1956.

———. *Existentialism and Human Emotions.* New York: Carol Publishing, 1993.

Sartre, Jean-Paul, and Benny Levy. *Hope Now: The 1980 Interviews.* Translated by Adrian Van Den Hoven. Chicago: University of Chicago Press, 1996.

Schlereth, T. J. *The Cosmopolitan Ideal in Enlightenment Thought: Its Form and Function in the Ideas of Franklin, Hume, and Voltaire, 1694–1790.* Notre Dame, Ind.: University of Notre Dame Press, 1977.

Schmidt, Paul. *Rebelling, Loving, and Liberation: A Metaphysics of the Concrete.* Albuquerque, N.M.: Hummingbird Press, 1971.

Schrag, Calvin O. *The Resources of Rationality.* Indianapolis: Indiana University Press, 1992.

Schutz, Alfred. *The Problem of Social Reality.* Edited by Maurice Natanson. The Hague: Martinus Nijhoff, 1962.

Seneca. *Epistulae Morales.* Vol. 1. Translated by R. M. Gummere. London: Heinemann, 1961.

———. *Seneca: Moral Essays.* Translated by J. W. Basore. London: Heinemann, 1958.

Shusterman, Richard. *Practicing Philosophy: Pragmatism and the Philosophical Life.* New York: Routledge, 1997.

Sophocles. *The Thebian Plays.* Translated by E. F. Watling. Harmondsworth, England: Penguin, 1947.

Stack, George. *Sartre's Philosophy of Social Existence.* St. Louis, Mo.: Warren H. Green, 1977.

Tassi, Aldo. "Person as the Mask of Being." *Philosophy Today* (Summer 1993): 201–10.

Taylor, Charles. *Sources of the Self: The Making of Modern Identity.* Cambridge. Harvard University Press, 1989.

———. *Hegel and Modern Society* .Cambridge: Cambridge University Press, 1979.

Tillich, Paul. *The Courage to Be.* New Haven: Yale University Press, 1982.

Unamuno, Miguel de. *Tragic Sense of Life.* New York: Macmillan, 1921. Reprint, New York: Dover, 1954.

Waldron, Jeremy. "Multiculturalism and Melange." In *Public Education in a Multicultural Society: Policy, Theory, Critique,* edited by Robert Fullinwider. Cambridge: Cambridge University Press, 1996.

———. "The Cosmopolitan Alternative." In *The Rights of Minority Cultures,* edited by Will Kymlicka. New York: Oxford University Press, 1995.

Waters, Mary C. *Ethnic Options: Choosing Identities in America.* Berkeley and Los Angeles: University of California Press, 1990.

West, Cornel. "I'm Ofay, You're Ofay: A Conversation with Noel Ignatiev and William 'Upski' Wimsatt." *Transition* 7, no. 1 (The White Issue): 176–98.

Wyers, Frances. *Miguel de Unamuno: The Contrary Self.* London: Tamesis Books, 1976.

Zack, Naomi. *Race and Mixed Race.* Philadelphia: Temple University Press, 1993.

———. *Thinking about Race.* Belmont, Calif.: Wadsworth, 1998.

———. "Race, Life, Death, Tragedy, and Good Faith." In *Existence in Black,* edited by Lewis Gordon. New York: Routledge, 1997.

———, ed. *American Mixed Race: The Culture of Microdiversity.* Lanham, Md.: Rowman & Littlefield, 1995.

INDEX

ABOUT THE AUTHOR

Jason D. Hill is assistant professor in the Department of Philosophical Studies at Southern Illinois University at Edwardsville and a postdoctoral fellow in the Society for the Humanities at Cornell University. He is currently writing a book on cosmopolitan justice and human rights.